# The Other Black Church

# The Other Black Church

## Alternative Christian Movements and the Struggle for Black Freedom

Joseph L. Tucker Edmonds

LEXINGTON BOOKS/FORTRESS ACADEMIC
*Lanham • Boulder • New York • London*

Published by Lexington Books/Fortress Academic
Lexington Books is an imprint of The Rowman & Littlefield Publishing Group, Inc.
4501 Forbes Boulevard, Suite 200, Lanham, Maryland 20706
www.rowman.com

6 Tinworth Street, London SE11 5AL, United Kingdom

Copyright © 2021 The Rowman & Littlefield Publishing Group, Inc.

*All rights reserved.* No part of this book may be reproduced in any form or by any electronic or mechanical means, including information storage and retrieval systems, without written permission from the publisher, except by a reviewer who may quote passages in a review.

British Library Cataloguing in Publication Information Available

**Library of Congress Control Number: 2020946997**

ISBN: 978-1-9787-0480-0 (cloth)
ISBN: 978-1-9787-0482-4 (pbk)
ISBN: 978-1-9787-0481-7 (electronic)

# Contents

| | |
|---|---:|
| Introduction | 1 |
| 1 The Canonical Black Body | 23 |
| 2 Bound No More: Charles Mason, Black Scriptures, and the Working-Class Body | 45 |
| 3 Deracinated Democracy and the Black Divine | 79 |
| 4 The Whole Body: Alternative Christian Economic Self-Determination and the Black Madonna | 101 |
| 5 Toward Embodied Freedom: Crisis and Collaborations on the Margins of the Black Church Tradition | 143 |
| Bibliography | 161 |
| Index | 175 |
| About the Author | 185 |

# Introduction

As the diverse communities and organizations of Black and brown youth in the United States, most often described as the Black Lives Matter (BLM) Movement in the popular press, were organizing in response to the onslaught of police violence on Black bodies and the deaths of Michael Brown, Freddie Gray, Sandra Bland and George Floyd, one of the early leaders of the movement, Patrisse Cullors, made the following claim:

> I mean, to be honest with you, so many of us in the Black Lives Matter Movement have either been pushed out of the church because many of us are queer and out, many of us—the church has become very patriarchal for us as women and so that's not necessarily where we have found our solace.[1]

Cullors was part of a growing chorus of critics of, and challenges to, the cultural hegemony of the Black church and Black church leadership as the only or singular model of resistance. The BLM Movement and other young activists were highlighting not only the democratic and universal accessibility of recent movements, but she was demarcating a rupture or break from the Black church tradition, its hierarchical model, its "narrative of civility," and its dependence on male, heterosexual leadership. This activist was simultaneously questioning the Black public's dependence on and default to the language and logics of the Black church tradition as well as the inability to see the erasure of these other sites of resistance. Another BLM Movement activist, DeRay Mckesson, continued,

> [There] was no organizing committee, no charismatic leader, no church group or school club that led us in the streets . . . It is powerful to remember that the

movement began as everyday people came out of their homes and refused to be silenced by the police.[2]

These young activists were not alone in their concern with the outsized role the Black church, specifically leaders from mainline Christian organizations, had on the organization and tone of the Black public and the various mechanisms of resistance. From Eddie Glaude's provocative pronouncement in 2010, "That the Black Church Is Dead," to a variety of twenty-first century organizations calling for a more expansive engagement with humanist organizations and religious movements outside of the Judeo-Christian tradition, there is and was evidence of a shift in the Black public sphere and its relationship to the Black Christian tradition.[3] While a number of theorists have written about the Black church's demise or irrelevance, that narrative is too hasty and reductive. There are activists and movements like the Rev. William Barber and his reinvigoration of the Poor People's Campaign, Yvette Flounder and her creation of affirming ministries and institutions to the Black LGBTQ community, and the faith-based People Improving Communities through Organizing (PICO) and other interfaith movements that have galvanized the disparate factions of the Black public to both challenge the idea of one dominant Black church and re-suture a vision for Black Christianity and engage the current political landscape.[4] Additionally, there are a number of cultural theorists and historians who suggest that the Black church remains a compelling symbol and contested space for the Black public.[5] In conversation with all of these interventions, this book argues that the Black church is not dead or irrelevant, but that it has been primarily imagined and often theorized as an ideologically narrow, normatively bound, and politically cautious set of organizations and leaders, especially when dealing with marginal populations. This limited version of the church is usually defined by focusing on a narrow subset of organizations and denominations that have historic charters and institutional structures which adhere to normative readings of the Biblical text. The broad Black church tradition, however, is not limited to these historic organizations or particular Biblical reading strategies, but it can be defined as the larger constellation of Black sacred spaces, both physical and philosophical, developed for the purposes of narrating Black subjectivity and attempting to restore the broken spirits, bodies, and lives of African Americans. In this latter case, the Black church includes the Black Lives Matter Movement, and the BLM Movement's critique is not of the broad Black church tradition but rather certain factions or models that have dominated the Black church tradition throughout the modern era. Thus, the BLM Movement and others' dismissal of the Black church was actually a call to reconsider the power (real or perceived) of certain dominant factions of the Black church as well as a necessary invitation to return to other, less engaged aspects of the Black sacred sphere.

In addition to narrating the declining significance of the Black church, the popular press read these debates between the Black church and contemporary activist movements as the fissure between a new humanist tradition that eschewed the doctrinal statements or ecclesial concerns of traditional African American communities and the more normative Black church.[6] However, this book argues that sacrality is deeply important to both of these groups, specifically the sacrality and protection of the Black body. Patrisse Cullors also argued that a deep suspicion of traditional religious models

> hasn't stopped us from being deeply spiritual in this work. And I think, for us, that looks like healing justice work, the role of healing justice, which is a term that was created probably about seven or eight years ago and was really looking at how, as organizers, but also as people that are marginalized that are impacted by racism and patriarchy, that are impacted by white supremacy, how do we show up in this work as our whole selves?[7]

There, moreover, was not a negation of the religious or the sacred in the BLM Movement, but there was a demand for reconstituting and reconsidering of the Black sacred and allowing a broader range of groups to have a voice and role in this sacred sphere. The BLM Movement leaders' evocation of Black theologians, womanist scholars, and other sacred traditions spoke to their faith in or at least deep respect for religious resources, languages, and symbols that have and could animate the Black public, specifically young African Americans. Thus, they were looking for an alternative tradition or alternative genealogy of the Black sacred that would align with their values, norms, and concerns. This alternative tradition is none other than the history of the "other Black churches," the movements that include the African spirituality of the enslaved church and the radical Christian, Christian-adjacent, and Afro-centric communities that embraced emerging canons and theologies associated with the broad Black Christian tradition beginning in the seventeenth century. Thus, the BLM Movement was articulating a deep connection to this broad tradition by attending to the Black body, engaging numerous institutions within the Black sacred sphere and affirming the presence of diverse Black lives, specifically the lives of those on the margins of gender, sexuality, and class.

Therefore, this book does not spend time looking at the prognostications of the Black church and its demise, but it examines the many institutions, practices, and prophetic figures that are in relationship with the idea of the dominant Black church, use language and ideas associated with the Black church, or are associated with the Black church and institutions/organizations connected to the Black sacred sphere. These adjacent institutions are sometimes understood as other, fugitive, or alternative, but they all share a provenance with the cultural and liturgical traditions of normative Black Christian traditions and the dominant Black culture. The long history of the Black church and its relationship to the many and diverse aspects of the Black public should not be ignored, invalidated, or flattened by these critiques or concerns. Rather, these critiques function as an invitation to revisit the shape and impact of the Black Christian tradition. The way that the Black church has functioned as a physical as well as philosophical space for Black thought and Black organizing is critical to this analysis and is highlighted when movements like BLM today and the alternative movements of yesteryear return to the church's iconography, practices, and even its discursive strategy in the public domain. These movements, including BLM, are deeply indebted to and conscious of Black Christianities and the legacy of the broad Black church tradition.

As this book suggests, the Black church has at times been defined or organized around a rejection of outlying or marginal Christian communities or what Kelly Brown Douglas describes as a "narrative of civility."[8] This distinction between the mainline and marginal communities has often placed the dominant Black church as the protector of the Black middle class or those desiring middle-class identity, their interests, and their eventual integration into certain segments of imperialist and colonialist societies. This division often represented a deep debate or set of debates within the Black public sphere around Black sacrality and Black liberation. Therefore, when we address the debate between the Black church and other movements, what is being highlighted is the variety of opinions not simply on theology and distinct codes of respectability, but what it means to be Black and free in any particular moment. The Black church or its dominant representatives have never had a monopoly on the terms "Black," "church," or "freedom," and these new movements and alternative Christianities highlight the different expressions of those terms. Furthermore, the church has never been made up of just one particular set of interests or community. There is the broad Black church tradition and its struggle for recognition among new and marginal populations is what separates it from the normative Black church tradition. Historically, the broad Black church tradition made space for women, new scriptural readings, and even new constructions of class and cultural identity, and today, the BLM Movement and its attention to gender, class, and sexuality are a part of that trajectory. The BLM Movement in this sense finds a deep resonance with this broader Black church tradition. It is this broader Black church tradition (or the Black sacred sphere) and variety of practices within those traditions that this book endeavors to unravel.

In many ways, the history of the broader, more inclusive Black church tradition is necessary for engaging contemporary movements. The broader tradition provides the tool and resources for thinking about the diverse responses to African American suffering and degradation and the status of the sacred and psychic well-being of its multiple populations. The Black church tradition, in the modern moment, is everywhere, and there is a response to the demonized Black body and there are attempts to valorize that body. The BLM Movement and its relationship to sacrality is an example of how the category of the "other Black church" or this broad Black church tradition opens up new approaches to the Black body, resistance to the colonial nation-state, and new visions for a more inclusive democratic future. This book is a return to the first half of the twentieth century, when the Black church or the concept of the Black church was also being recreated, reconfigured, or critiqued by elements of the Black public. Furthermore, it explores how alternative movements, then, through their invocation of the Black body and critique of the exclusive practices of United States-based democracy, reignited a debate on the importance and role of the sacred in the Black public sphere.

## CULTURAL REVOLUTION AND THE BROAD CHRISTIAN TRADITION

While the twentieth century was deeply impacted by a number of revolutionary impulses within the Black public sphere, from the demands for full and equal participation emerging from the Niagara conference to the cultural reformation evidenced by the literary and artistic explosion of the Harlem Renaissance, there was an equally important, albeit less theorized, cultural irruption in the domain of the sacred. This was the entrance of alternative Christian movements into the center of the Black public sphere. These movements were not wayward or irrelevant to the Black public sphere, but they were articulating a new way of being Black, religious, and citizen in the twentieth century. From Father Divine's public debate with Marcus Garvey, Charles Mason's demand for conscientious objection and full democratic participation, and Albert Cleage's creation of Shrines throughout the country, these alternative Christian movements and their leaders were at the center of the public discourse and are a critically important part of a new language, disciplines, and ideas that transformed the trajectory of Black freedom at the beginning of the twentieth century.

*The Other Black Church* explores alternative Christian movements in the twentieth century and their relationship to African Americans' struggle for freedom and the ways that these movements altered the discussion on citizenship, reframed the possibility of democracy, and reinserted Black bodies and visions for these bodies into the broader discourse.[9] This book looks at these alternative movements through three particular lenses: the development and deployment of canons on the Black sacred body, the limits of the state and resistance to the state apparatus, and the emergence of new models of economic empowerment and protest. In conversation with previous works that have explored religious movements within the Black public sphere, this work will engage these alternative Christian movements as critical to African American culture and life. Particularly, I will address the relationship between these alternative Christian projects and African Americans' demand for full citizenship and active participation in the construction of alternative visions for democracy. Over the course of this text, I will argue that alternative Christian movements and their facility and flexibility with Christian scripture alongside their canonization of certain symbols, texts, and even disciplines were central to African Americans' development of political movements, theological language, and economic projects challenging the status quo. Furthermore, they helped to reposition African Americans and the historically demarcated "Black Church" as fully vested state and transnational actors. These "other" Black churches within the broad tradition and their canons not only brought variety to the Black sacred sphere, but they challenged what was seen as normative and effective Black institutions and interventions. Mainstream Black Christian movements and their primary focus on respectability, integration, and the economic status quo have often overshadowed alternative Christianities. However, this text outlines how a more complete portrayal of Black Christianities, specifically alternative Christianities, will provide insight into the nature of African American resistance and the relationship between Black religion, the body, resistance, and the creation of alternatives to the state and the project of democracy.

Most importantly, this book will provide an extended look at alternative Christianities, their creative re-imagining, and the creation of canonical texts, and it will discuss the connection between their evolution and the rise of different visions for African American political resistance and economic empowerment in the twentieth century. It highlights how these movements were in conversation with each other, the broader Black sacred public, and the emerging discipline of Black theology. As a result, this book is not simply a historical encounter with these movements and their role in theorizing democracy and alternatives to it, but it is also an encounter with the development of Black theology and new racial theories in the twentieth century. This book straddles the fields of African American religion, critical theory, Black theology, and political theory, and it is particularly important as it explores the shape and trajectory of African American resistance and its relationship to alternative political and religious communities.

This book will look at the history of these movements and their relationship to a national and transnational discourse on re-imagining the Black body as well as their relationship to the development of what I will call modern Black theological thought, and what has historically been labeled and theorized as the Black church. While the book will both problematize and extend the category of the Black church, it is primarily in conversation with Kelly Brown Douglas, Curtis Evans, and Sylvester Johnson who identify the distinctive and evolving shape of the relationship between African Americans and the project of religion.[10] Brown Douglas in *Black Bodies and the Black Church* defines the Black church and argues that the "Blackness" of that church "depends upon its morally active commitment to advance the life, freedom, and dignity of all Black bodies."[11] This book will look at how this sacralization, maintenance, and protection of Black bodies was negotiated between a broad array of Christian and Christian-adjacent projects, especially those that will be considered alternative in this book. Nevertheless, the "other" movements studied in this text are essential for the ways in which they shaped a particular discourse on the formation, circulation, and protection of these bodies and helped to invigorate a larger discussion on the liberation of these bodies.

## THE ROLE OF ALTERNATIVE CHRISTIAN MOVEMENTS IN THE BLACK PUBLIC SPHERE

Historically, Christian movements that were outside of the purview of mainstream denominations or hierarchical control were viewed as suspect. From the earliest religious gatherings among the enslaved African populations to the alternative movements outlined in this book, they have been either considered nonreligious or seditious in some form. In the 1831 Statute of the State of North Carolina, the religious gatherings of enslaved African Americans were explicitly seen as illegal and heavily surveilled by the state.

> It shall not be lawful under any pretence for any slave, or free person of colour to preach or exhort in public or in any manner to officiate as a preacher or teacher in any prayer meeting, or other association for worship where slaves of different families are collected together; and if any free person of colour shall be thereof duly convicted on indictment before any court having jurisdiction thereof, he shall, for each offence, receive, not exceeding thirty-nine lashes on his bare back; and where any slave shall be guilty of a violation of this act, he shall, on conviction before a single magistrate, receive not exceeding thirty-nine lashes on his bare back.[12]

Similarly, the early independent African American denominations were seen as troubling to the mainstream based on the philosophical and theological claims that were at the center of their movements.[13] These early "alternative" religious movements, those that operated outside of white control and the logics of empire, were initially described as African-derived or as cultural movements that masqueraded as religion and were often seen as anti-Christian, anti-American, or distorting the Judeo-Christian tradition.[14] By naming them non-Christian and un-American, the organization adherents were primarily excluded from debates on their viability for, and eventual, participation in modern culture and governance. In addition to suspicion and surveillance of explicitly identified alternative religious movements, there was a similar surveillance or concern around the rise of African American social movements in the eighteenth and nineteenth centuries which either functioned as alternatives to traditional Christian communities or were designed to address or signify on the Christian commitments of the Black public. The rise of the freemasons, the order of the Black knights, the social club movements, and even Black fraternal and sorority organizations were often understood and imagined as adjacent to or dependent on a particular of reading of African American Christianity and critical to addressing key issues in the Black public sphere.[15] These social and cultural movements have either been described as alternative and outside of normative Christianity or seen as a part of the normative Black Christian tradition or Black public sphere. Again, the designation of some or many of the organizations as an alternative formation, cultural or religious, has historically been a mechanism to deny or limit their voices. Often these alternative movements were too connected to African institutions and rituals, too attentive to marginal populations like women or the working class, or were not aligned closely enough with the Christian imperial religion. Alternatively the alternative movements were regarded as deficient or deviant, and this designation often limited their impact and overall connection with the majority of the Black public sphere. When Curtis Evans highlights the burden of African American religion, he is highlighting the fact that their relationship to the sacred sphere either positions them as religious and outside of the realm of reason and rationality or religion as their primary or only mechanism to participate in the public sphere. Either way, he argues, it places a unique burden on African American religion and its role in the public sphere.[16] This burden or the focus on religion as the primary way of engaging in the public sphere also meant that religion, often Christianity, needed to have the flexibility or ability to do a wide set of tasks for the Black body politic while being legible and legitimate to a broader Christian public. By locating certain Christian communities or organizations outside of Christianity and the "Black Church," this meant that their interventions or innovations around citizenship and resistance were often elided, erased, or undervalued. However, by knitting these alternative movements back into the Black sacred sphere and naming them as critical to the formation known as the Black church tradition, we are able to more clearly see their impact on the multiple and interpolated trajectories of Black freedom in the twentieth century.

Many of these alternative religious movements have not been fully engaged in any full-length treatises, and they have not been fully theorized by Black theologians. This book will argue that the Church of God in Christ movement under Charles Mason, the Father Divine Movement primarily located in North America, and the Shrine of the Black Madonna provide competing visions of Christianity and democratic participation that not only need to be reread from the perspective of their alternative construction of Christianity, but from a renewed interest in the variety and dissonance of Black religious projects that are attempting to transform what constitutes Black religion, the Black church tradition, and participation in modern democracy simultaneously. These movements highlight the import of religion, specifically alternative religions, in the Black public sphere and the ways in which alternative religions were not a break with modernity or a rejection of democracy but a critical and theological re-presentation of a competing or alternative vision of them. These movements' intersections and conversations with Black radical communities, practices of engaging and exploring theological and political questions across denominational, national, and class lines, and their appropriation and articulation of religious discourse outside of normative Christianity point to sets of discourses that have not been fully engaged in traditional theological scholarship or as central to the understanding of the Black Christian tradition.

While traditional theological scholarship as well as critical and political theory have recently begun to address alternative Christianities, I am arguing that these movements need to be engaged as central to Black religion and the Black public sphere.[17] In particular, by using the resources of political and cultural theory in conversation with alternative Christianities, we are better able to see their role in producing a critique of the modern project in the twentieth century and a competing vision of Black citizenship. Theorizing Black religion and Africana Christianities within the frame of competing modernities and in conversation with the construction of diverse and interconnected subjectivities challenges our hasty categorizations of alternative Black religions as fanatical, nontheological, and anti-modern. The diverse and diffuse nature of these alternative Christianities affords us the opportunity to rethink the role of the prophetic leader, the nation, the Black body, and the Black body politic as in conversation with, rather than a repetition or refusal of, Western modernity and democracy.[18] Therefore, these movements in the United States present a picture of Black religion that is connected to the production of sacred communities that are linked less to a formalized polity or a set of sacred practices and codes and more to a politics and strategy to resist state control and surveillance. This study of these prophets, their communities, and their formation of canons is a study of democracy and the production of networks, disciplines, and institutions developed and designed to provide alternatives to Black suffering and exclusion in the twentieth century.

## ALTERNATIVE MOVEMENTS AND THE OTHER BLACK CHURCH

These movements, all inaugurated during the first half of the twentieth century, recognized that church communities and texts constrained by the polity of Euro-American tradition, and the politics of Western imperialism were often antithetical to the logic of Black flourishing and Black bodies surviving as modern subjects. Thus, these alternative movements can be considered the "other Black church" because they created new canons and innovated as Christian-derived traditions that challenged and transformed the nation-state (and democracy) and introduced models in a prophetic, progressive transnational discourse on Black citizenship and economic development. This book does not argue that canon formation is a new phenomenon, but it suggests that by the end of the nineteenth century and the beginning of the twentieth that African American Christians began to take on the practice of canon formation or what Henry Bogues calls "creating complex prophetic redemptive traditions" as central to the Afro-diasporic religious impulse.[19] Thus, one of the key narrative themes of these movements is not simply a re-reading of the normative canonical texts, the Bible, or denominational tradition/polity, but the production of a canon, a set texts, figures, and politics, that engage the crisis of Africana people, their bodies, and their participation in the body politic at home and abroad. As a result, these movements are involved in the creation of traditions that challenge and engage the concept of normative scriptures, the role of Black identity and racialization, and the inherent economic and political inequality of settler-based democracy.

These movements present a vibrant picture of the heavily contested nature of Black Christianity at the beginning of the twentieth century (as well as Black religion more broadly) and the ways that discourses on citizenship and economic development[20] are being imagined and reformulated through the process of canon formation taking place alongside the cultural, political, and economic revolutions of the twentieth century. Overall, this book is a historical, critical encounter with these movements and brings them in conversation with a number of scholars of the Black sacred sphere including emilie townes' engagement of alterity, canonization, and Christianities; Brent Hayes Edwards' notion of the "practices of diaspora;" and Vincent Wimbush's theorization of scripture. This text does not focus on the genesis of these movements, but it focuses on the ways in which the founders, their institutional communication organs (e.g., newspapers, press releases, and national and international conferences), and the adherents communicated to a wider Black public, impacted Black mainstream institutions, and shaped the narrative of Black progress and freedom from the margins of the Black community.

## WHY THE OTHER BLACK CHURCH

This book will examine how the majority of the Black sacred tradition is still deeply invested in the construction and maintenance of the idea of the Black church. Like other studies that have examined the long civil rights movement or the many facets of the Black feminist movement, they have identified that there are some categories, constructions, or organizing principles that are hard to disrupt.[21] The normative category of gender, the beguiling category of rights/equality within a democratic framework, and the central role of the Christian church within the Black public sphere are difficult to decenter. Moreover, the category of the "church" is upheld by both community members/adherents as well as theorists of the Black cultural and political life. This book at once asks how did the Black public develop and maintain a seemingly singular relationship with the category of the "Black church" and why have disciplines like Black theology and Black religious studies upheld the central role and the narrow definition of what has become known as the "Black church," even while acknowledging ways that it has been disrupted and reconfigured by movements outside of the normative tradition. In this text, movements that are revising and challenging the entrenched definitions of Black, church, and the larger Black Christian tradition are examined. While these other movements have a great degree of continuity with the normative Black church, it is often in their appending of new texts or attending to new demographics that they extend and broaden the Black church tradition (or the broad Christian tradition). As a result of the shared semantic and demographic space, the idea of the "other" in this description of these movements may often feel too strong a descriptor because the leaders and figures of the alternative movements also played a key role in the maintenance and long-term viability of the Black church or normative Black sacred sphere. They are in conversation with Black churches and normative leaders, use traditional symbols and texts, and intermittently see themselves as a part of that disciplinary and institutional structure of Black ecclesiology and theology. Additionally, many theorists have argued that Black religious life has historically been organized around a shifting number of institutions that have used church as a shorthand rather than demonstrative of any ideological and theological claim.

The category of the church, in this regard, is just a placeholder for the spiritual strivings of a group and that marginal groups and organizations have always played a constitutive role in the creation and maintenance of the broader Black church and its traditions. These other movements are not outside of the tradition, but they introduce new models for engaging the public and in doing so, disrupt the public and the untenable and inaccurate presentation of a singular or unified vision. Thus, the other is not a disruption of an already broad and diverse Christian tradition, but rather it speaks to the multiple and competing voices within the Black public and Black sacred sphere.

Alternately, some may argue that the "other" or the designation of these movements as alternative is too weak in that it undermines the ways that these movements and churches are initially, and some throughout the history of their organizations, trying to displace the notion of a Black church and particularly identify its limitations and deficits. The "other Black church," in this case, may be no Black church at all except for its dogged attention to Black liberation and the Black body or for its attention to the community of people who were attracted to both. Thus "church" in this regard is not synonymous with Christianity, but it often signals the formation of communities of people who gather to engage and decipher the sacred and the sacred's relationship to communities of belonging.[22] Church or the Black church has often been conflated with Christian movements, and this book attends to the ways that church was and is a far more comprehensive and complicated term for the Black public. Furthermore, there are real discontinuities between the Black church and these other institutions. In particular, one may argue that their disregard for normative scriptures or the appending of new texts or ideas means that these movements are no longer Christian and thus not a part of the Black church tradition. Additionally, there are instances when there have been radical breaks or ruptures from the Black public or what has been called Afro-American Christianity and that by calling it other there is an implied similarity or shared enterprise that does not exist. While the nature of the otherness of these movements is heavily contested, what connects these movements with Blackness and the idea of the church is what I will address to close out the introduction.

## THE BLACKNESS OF THE BLACK CHURCH

These movements are the "Black church" in so much that the church is a contested space and an idea that is animated by issues around Black belonging and flourishing. In line with thinkers from Albert Raboteau on slave religion to Kelly Brown Douglas on the topic of the Black sexuality, the Black church specifies a particular interest in the spirituality of Black communities. The

Black church is less a signifier of a shared theological commitment, and more broadly it is a type of institution that engages a broad section of the African American public and provides a space for their grievances, both psychic and physical, to be addressed. Furthermore, it is a space where Black bodies have convened to do this type of work. So the Black church is as much a symbol of public spaces or discursive possibilities to address the questions of Black flourishing and viability as it is an instance of any set of Christian commitments.[23] Nevertheless, I use the historical category of the Black church to both introduce this broader phenomenon of Africana interactions with the sacred as well as to denote a historically contextualized set of ideas and commitments. Throughout the text, you will note that I will move from the Black church, as a historical and theological marker, to the notion of the Black sacred sphere that includes the Black church, the broad Christian tradition, and other Black religious formations. The Black church, however, has been known for its Christian commitments, its privileging of the Biblical text, its connection to the project of empire, and its prioritization of a certain set of racial and cultural practices of respectability. The other Black church or the other movements within the Black sacred sphere highlight the importance of the sacred and the role that spirituality has played in African and African American life without necessarily privileging the Bible, the Western political tradition, or Western Christian institutions. The argument here suggests that the trajectory for religious African Americans does not have to be Christianity, the Biblical text, or the adoption of certain social codes and standards. In many regards, these other churches were distinguished by their rejection of normative Christianity as well as certain notions of respectability, race, and even citizenship. The church, therefore, can be radical or fugitive when it is willing to discard much of what had been understood as canonical or normative for Christianity, Black communities, and Black religious formation.[24] These movements represent an explicit rejection of the norm and opt for what Eddie Glaude and Fred Moten call a "fugitive discourse" on Christianity, empire, and democracy.[25] These reconfigurations were an attempt to not only escape the limitations of Christianity, but they are meditations on the limitations of and erasures caused by the modern system more broadly. Nevertheless, the designation of church recognizes the desire or need to be tethered to this long tradition of signifying on and around Blackness and Black Christianity.[26] These significations, however, were a means to create something different and expansive for the purpose of restoring the Black body and the Black body politic and not for the maintenance or privileging of one form of Christianity or one singular definition of Blackness.

Moreover, if the category of the "other" and church is fraught, so too is the category of Black. While all of these movements highlight a relationship to African Americans and in most cases Black adherents representing the majority of the communities, it is also clear that Black racial identity and its centrality were as much a contested idea as it provided an effective means to denote group coherence or shared political affinity. In actuality, this narrative will introduce Blackness, Christianity, and resistance as much less stable or controllable variables. Blackness was neither a biological or cultural given for many of these movements, rather the role of Blackness was being negotiated and debated within these spaces. From Black as a cultural category that knitted together practices and traditions among a wide variety of groups to Blackness as a political category used by an aggrieved party, Blackness functioned in a number of roles. While Blackness as cultural or political operated as the dominant means for expressing Black racial identity, there were other constructions that challenged these normative configurations. Particularly, we will address the emergence of African-centered models of resistance, Black Christian nationalism, new models of ethno-religious citizenship, and an early form of post-racialism within these religious communities and the way these ideas transformed the Black public. Therefore, this text looks at the other constructions of Blackness and the ways in which Blackness was being utilized and deployed by different communities. Many of these organizations were asking "for whom was blackness being deployed and how did it protect them and enable them to flourish?" In a way similar to the studies that looked at working class and radical factions of the long civil rights movement, this study gives sustained attention to the other Blacks, specifically those fugitive Blacks who used religion and the sacred to innervate the public sphere and to introduce their particular trajectory and engagement with or disruption of the Black racial identity.[27]

These other "Blacks," including the movements studied here as well as groups that operated on the fringe of the Black public sphere, were part of the movements that were transforming the discussion of Blackness, Black religion, and ultimately the relationship of certain bodies to democracy. The argument is that these "other Blacks" and these "other churches" added to a robust and variegated Black public. Furthermore, this project addresses the impact of these movements' particular and often peculiar canonizing of the Black body, reconfiguring of democracy and democratic institutions, and envisioning of economic self-determination and sustainability on the public sphere.[28] This turn to the margins is not just the engagement of the populations traditionally associated with the margins of the Black public, but more importantly it helps us address the way that projects from the margin shifted democracy and the African American's relationship to it. This model of studying the margins is a means to engage the institutions and figures that were shaping responses and alternatives to the failure of democracy and normative Christianity rather than only attending to the normative group and its interventions.

On these margins of the Black public/Black sacred, there is a dogged attention to the Black body and the Black body's relationship to Black religion, especially alternative religions. While there has been considerable attention given to the body in the study of African American religion, this focus on the canonization of the Black body and the privileging of texts, systems, images, and ideas to support that canonization is critical.[29] This genealogy of the sacred Black body opens new vistas for thinking about the middle of the twentieth century and highlights movements and models that have creatively resisted and reconfigured democracy. This is a story of how their focus on the body and the reconfiguration of democracy mandated that the Black sacred public create institutions, practices, and even disciplinary formations able to and interested in engaging new forms of liberation and belonging. Alternative Christianities or the broad Christian tradition offer additional tools to look at the multiple and nuanced ways that African American communities interfaced with and offered new models of belonging and participation, especially within the borders of settler-based democracy, in the twentieth century United States. The variety of their interventions highlights not only diversity but how the context of their engagements spoke to a fractured Black public and its long struggle for various forms of Black freedom and self-determination.

The book is organized into six chapters. The introduction outlines the history of alternative Christian traditions in the Black public sphere and their role in disrupting and structuring the Black public. Furthermore the introduction defines the category of the "other Black church," denotes its significance and role within the broad Black church tradition, and its impact on shaping Black religion, the Black public sphere, and the vision for Black futures.[30] Particularly, it suggests that the Black religious revolution of the twentieth century, especially the innovation of these movements, is as relevant to the Black public as the arts, political, and feminist revolutions that rocked and shifted the Black public sphere.

## CHAPTER 1: THE CANONICAL BLACK BODY

While the introduction looked at the role of the "other" in the Black public sphere and why alternative or religious movements are important, this chapter looks at why the body is so important to new and alternative movements in the African American religious tradition. This chapter argues that central to the study of African American religions is a focus on the Black body and the production and engagement of canons on the sacred Black body within the Black public sphere. More than just an engagement of the Black body, this chapter looks at how Black religion, especially alternative ones, have been invested in the creation and circulation of sacred Black bodies and texts to engage and support that body. Through a critical engagement of the fields of Black theology and using the resources offered by Delores Williams's accounts of variety and experience and Vincent Wimbush's category of signifying, this chapter will argue how a return to the body provides resources and tools for not only theorizing African American religions but thinking about the production and creation of competing Black publics, including the important role of Black sacred publics.

## CHAPTER 2: BOUND NO MORE: BLACK SCRIPTURES AND THE BLACK WORKING-CLASS BODY

While a great deal has been written on the emergence and the development of Black publics, chapter 2 will focus specifically on the role of the Black Christian public and its relationship to the conscientious objection of Black religionists at the beginning of the twentieth century. Charles Mason, one of the founders of the African American Pentecostal Movement, is often remembered because of his role in the introduction and spread of biblical literalist movement and the Church of God in Christ being the largest Black Pentecostal movement in the United States. This chapter will look at this movement's theological argument that separates it from other Black Christian movements at that time as well as their evocation of religious freedom as a means to demand the full promise of democracy and citizenship for its primarily working-class adherents. It will address the fugitive nature of this movement as it relates not only to their invocation of alternative religious practices, but how they were critical in trying to provide bodily autonomy for a broad subsection of African Americans, most prominently working-class African Americans. In incorporating certain notions of respectability around dress and separation from particular normative cultural and religious practices, it was assumed that their options were limited, but this chapter will address how their novel use of canonical texts like the Bible and the Constitution offered a wide berth of bodily and sacred practices for their adherents.

## CHAPTER 3: DERACINATED DEMOCRACY AND THE BLACK DIVINE

The third chapter will look at the Father Divine Movement and its role in creating a new model of respectability through the reconfiguration of the categories of race and racialism. Specifically, the chapter will address Divine's relationship with other nationalist or proto-nationalist movements, like Marcus Garvey, and explore the ways that Divine argues for a model of reconfiguring democracy and the modern project through his specific attention to the working class. Like all of the movements explored throughout this text, Divine's attention to the bodies of his working-class Black adherents not only calls for renewed attention to the body but how disassembling imperial democracy can only occur through the mechanism of a racialized figure. Divine's call for an early form of a "post-racial" United States is predicated on the modern world being ready and able to accept a racialized divine figure and the full restoration of brown and Black bodies.

## CHAPTER 4: THE WHOLE BODY: ALTERNATIVE CHRISTIAN ECONOMIC SELF-DETERMINATION AND THE BLACK MADONNA

In this chapter, we will address the emergence of the Shrine of the Black Madonna in Detroit, Michigan, and its foray not only into theological and political encounters with the Black body politic, but their role in connecting religious fidelity with economic and cultural self-determination. Specifically, this chapter will address the ways that the Shrine of the Madonna sacralized the Black body and created new canons to support their middle-class adherents' cultural and economic identities through the vision of a Shrine. Specifically, the Shrine created a comprehensive model of economic self-determination that included the development of a publishing apparatus, the rise of self-sustaining agricultural communities, ad-hoc seminaries, and innovations in the fields of African American studies and Black theology. The entrepreneurial spirit of the Shrine and its collection of satellite shrines throughout Detroit and around the country introduced what could be seen as tacit acceptance of capitalism, but this chapter will explore how these visions of economic determination were tied to a radical repositioning of African history, African American communities, and new designs for what constituted democracy and African Americans' relationship to it. Finally, this chapter will look at how re-presenting the Black body, specifically the Black women's body, introduced new visions for the Black public's encounter with the empire.

## CHAPTER 5: TOWARD EMBODIED FREEDOM: CRISIS AND COLLABORATION ON THE MARGINS

Finally, I will argue that these movements develop a new language and protocol for freedom that happens on the margins of what has historically been designated as the Black church and the Black public sphere. These margins, however, did not have a marginal impact on the Black sacred and the larger Black sphere. Specifically, it will look at the evolution of the Black church, Black theology, and the projects of Black freedom as a result of these movements. This chapter addresses the collaborative, yet highly contested, spaces inhabited by these alternative movements and their central role in the articulation and struggle for Black freedom. Finally, the conclusion will address the risks and benefits of the canonization of the Black body, address why the Black body is critical to theorizing Black freedom, and return to the role of the Black body in the Black Lives Matter movement.

Overall, this book engages these traditions as religio-political movements molded in the crucible of American religious exceptionality, Black discontentment, and the development of a national and transnational lack radical politic. Furthermore, this book argues that Black theology, the Black church, and Black political formation are all heavily indebted to and shaped by alternative Christian traditions. This concept of alternative Christianity is an important distinction as it signifies a set of movements that either used the Christian narrative or are adjacent to it in a number of explicit and important ways, and this book emphasizes how these movements are invested in not jettisoning or ignoring Christianity or democracy, but looking for new methods and trajectories to attain freedom within these frameworks. In highlighting the depth and breadth of African American Christian communities of the mid-twentieth century and their communication with one another, the book provides a novel account of how the political and social imaginary of African American Christianity is informed by the political practices and canon formation of these traditions on the margin.[31]

## NOTES

1. "The Spiritual Work of Black Lives Matter," in the Black Lives Matter in *The Religious Dispatches*.

2. "The Burgeoning of the Black Lives Matter," *The Baltimore Sun*, 2017.

3. "The Black Church Is Dead," by Eddie Glaude in *The New York Times*.

4. Walter E. Fluker, *The Ground Has Shifted: The Future of the Black Church in Post-Racial America*, http://www.duke.eblib.com/EBLWeb/patron/?target=patron&extendedid=P_4500670_0. See also Raphael G. Warnock, *The Divided Mind of the Black Church: Theology, Piety, and Public Witness*, Religion, Race, and Ethnicity (New York, NY: NYU Press, 2014).

5. See also the womanist responses to the black church including Eboni Marshall Turman, *Toward a Womanist Ethic of Incarnation: Black Bodies, the Black Church, and the Council of Chalcedon*, 1st edition, Black Religion, Womanist Thought, Social Justice (London: Palgrave Macmillan, 2013); Kelly Brown Douglas, *Black Bodies and the Black Church: A Blues Slant*, Black Religion/Womanist Thought/Social

Justice (New York, NY: Palgrave Macmillan, 2012); Andrea C. Abrams, *God and Blackness: Race, Gender, and Identity in a Middle Class Afrocentric Church* (New York, NY: New York University Press, 2014).

6. See "Black Lives Matter Is Democracy in Action," in 2016 *New York Times* article and the article by Anthony Pinn in 2017 HuffPost on "Black Lives Matter and the Long Humanist Tradition." These articles highlight the humanist and democratic aspects of the radical, broad-based BLM movements, and often hold these values in contrast with their spiritual or even Christian values. Moreover, there seems to be a suggestion that this more democratic and expansive network of activists and participants represents a rupture with the traditional logic and models of the black public sphere. I argue that a long history of alternative movements, with alternative methodologies, and their deep and thoughtful engagements with the dominant factions of the black public sphere have always played a key role.

7. "The Spiritual Work of BLM," Patrise Cullors in *The Atlantic* (2016).

8. Douglas, *Black Bodies and the Black Church*.

9. See Keri Day, *Unfinished Business: Black Women, the Black Church, and the Struggle to Thrive in America* (Maryknoll, NY: Orbis Books, 2012). Day's analysis of the church's struggle against the erasure of black bodies and freedom is situated within the expansion of what had historically been constituted as the church and who was considered essential to its maintenance. The role of women and the emergence of alternative institutions to address the needs and concerns of black women and their bodies speaks to the expansive nature of this broad Christian tradition.

10. See Douglas, *Black Bodies and the Black Church*; Curtis J. Evans, *The Burden of Black Religion* (Oxford and New York, NY: Oxford University Press, 2008); Sylvester A. Johnson, *African American Religions, 1500–2000: Colonialism, Democracy, and Freedom* (New York, NY: Cambridge University Press, 2015). Additionally, this continues the important work that Bogues introduces that suggests that the attention to creating new canons is directly connected to the heretical tradition which is a deep and instructive part of the black public sphere. See Anthony Bogues, *Black Heretics, Black Prophets: Radical Political Intellectuals*, Africana Thought (New York, NY: Routledge, 2003).

11. Douglas, *Black Bodies and the Black Church*, xiii.

12. "An Act Concerning Slaves and Free Persons of Color," Revised Code 105 of The North Carolina General Assembly, 1831.

13. Julius Bailey, *Race Patriotism: Protest and Print Culture in the Ame Church* (Knoxville, TN: University of Tennessee Press, 2012), http://site.ebrary.com/lib/duk elibraries/docDetail.action?docID=10563936.

14. Theophus Harold Smith, *Conjuring Culture: Biblical Formations of Black America*, Religion in America Series (New York, NY: Oxford University Press, 1994).

15. See Theda Skocpol, Ariane Liazos, and Marshall Ganz, *What a Mighty Power We Can Be: African American Fraternal Groups and the Struggle for Racial Equality*, Princeton Studies in American Politics (Princeton, NJ: Princeton University Press, 2006).

16. Evans, *The Burden of Black Religion*.

17. See Ibid. as the first text that fully engages black religion and alternative religion as rightfully part of the discussion on the construction or re-envisioning of the modern project. Also see John L. Jackson, *Thin Description: Ethnography and the African Hebrew Israelites of Jerusalem* (Cambridge, MA: Harvard University Press, 2013).

18. Many have argued that the demand for full participation or integration was simply the repetition or a mimesis of normative religion, capitalism, and knowledge project. Many black political theorists have highlighted that this is not the case. See Bogues, *Black Heretics, Black Prophets*. This text argues that this is the case for black religion, especially alternative religions in the black sacred sphere.

19. Ibid. Also see Katie G. Cannon, *Katie's Canon: Womanism and the Soul of the Black Community* (New York, NY: Continuum, 1995).

20. Radical politics is defined as the set of acts that contest or challenge normative political participation. The radicality of black intervention is that it critiques the construction of blackness as "monstrous, other, and non-citizen." The radical politics is the rejection of politics as such and the creation of a counter-narrative that outlines a substantively new way of being in the world. This new way of being for the movements examined in this analysis cannot be understood outside of enchantment and religious formation.

21. Nikhil Pal Singh, *Black Is a Country: Race and the Unfinished Struggle for Democracy* (Cambridge, MA: Harvard University Press, 2004).

22. See Warnock, *The Divided Mind of the Black Church*. He argues that this idea of the black church is not only divided, but that there are questions about its function. He seems to suggest that these multiple roles or even the questions about the term mean that the church cannot be assumed to be solely or even primarily Christian. Also see Anthony B. Pinn, Stephen C. Finley, and Torin Alexander, *African American Religious Cultures*, 2 vols., American Religious Cultures Series (Santa Barbara, CA: ABC-CLIO, 2009).

23. This attention to the physical structures of the church does not intend to suggest that the "black church" should be instrumentalized as simply a physical space for black political or cultural speech, but I want to hold in deep tension the important notions of the black church's physicality, discursive flexibility, as well as a deep attention to the rituals and sacred texts.

24. Neil Roberts, *Freedom as Marronage*, http://chicago.universitypress scholarship.com/view/10.7208/chicago/9780226201184.001.0001/upso-97802 26127460.

25. Eddie S. Glaude, *Exodus!: Religion, Race, and Nation in Early Nineteenth-Century Black America* (Chicago, IL: University of Chicago Press, 2000).

26. See Charles H. Long, *Significations: Signs, Symbols, and Images in the Interpretation of Religion*, Series in Philosophical and Cultural Studies in Religion (Aurora, CO: Davies Group, 1999). Also look at the introduction of Vincent L. Wimbush and Rosamond C. Rodman, *African Americans and the Bible: Sacred Texts and Social Textures* (New York, NY: Continuum, 2000).

27. See Singh, *Black Is a Country*.

28. See Day, *Unfinished Business*.

29. See Dwight N. Hopkins and Anthony B. Pinn, *Loving the Body: Black Religious Studies and the Erotic*, 1st edition, Black Religion, Womanist Thought, Social Justice (New York, NY: Palgrave Macmillan, 2004); Anthony B. Pinn, *Embodiment and the New Shape of Black Theological Thought*, Religion, Race, and Ethnicity Series (New York, NY: New York University Press, 2010).

30. See the Anthony B. Pinn, *The End of God-Talk: An African American Humanist Theology* (Oxford and New York, NY: Oxford University Press, 2012). Of particular note in this text is his insistence to move beyond binaries of race, class, gender, and even spirituality which have limited the possible models for African American liberation. Also see Fluker, *The Ground Has Shifted*. Fluker suggests that the future of the black church will be impacted by new understandings of race and racialization and that the church's futures will be impacted by its ability to navigate new categories as well as new groups' relationship to these categories.

31. See Cannon, *Katie's Canon*. This text argues that the creation of a new set of sacred texts, practices, and symbols or a canon is the central concern of these new movements, their interaction with the black public sphere, and the larger project of black liberation.

*Chapter 1*

# The Canonical Black Body

## INTRODUCTION

A number of recent studies engaging African American religions have focused primarily on what has traditionally been called "new" African American religions. These studies are important not because of their focus on the chronological emergence of new religious movements, but how a focus on the new or the alternative impacts the study of African American religions and particularly how they help to frame the alternative Christianities studied in this account. From Sylvester Johnson's magisterial work on the long impact of the empire to Judith Weisenfeld's critical reappraisal of Black migration in the twentieth century, central to their analysis is the appearance and practice of new religions.[1] This focus on the new or alternative religious movements is important because of the ways in which the studies destabilize the emphasis or focus on Black Christianity or the Biblical scripture as the normative text for African Americans in place of what Weisenfeld calls a renewed focus on the adherents' construction of a "racial-religio" identity.[2] Furthermore, in these works there is a call to delve more fully into the ways in which African American religion is about the negotiation of empire, democracy, citizenship, and belonging.

In Sylvester Johnson's engagement of African American religion, he suggests that African American Religious Studies has as its call to take a more thoughtful and engaging account of the Western empire.[3] He argues clearly that empire both haunts and shapes the construction of African American religion and calls for theorists of African American religion to look more fully at the impact and importance of the thinking of the relationship between African American religion, state surveillance, and practices of belonging. Moreover, Vincent Wimbush, New Testament scholar and Director of the

Institute on Signifying Scripture, argues that religion, specifically African American religion, has been shaped by the practices of signifying on the dominant themes and ideas in the public domain. Blackness, for Wimbush, is a long history of signifying on, and interpolating of, the dominant regimes, practices, and texts. These significations lead to alternative expressions of democracy, Christianity, Christian-adjacent movements, and the appearance of new religious movements. Similarly, the work that is being done by Judith Weisenfeld and John Jackson all point to alternative religions as a means to understand African American religion and their relationship to the nation-state and empire.[4] The modern nation-state and the imperial practices and systems associated with the construction of the nation-state have destroyed and demonized the Black body, used exclusionary practices to deny the appearance and flourishing of the Black citizen, and constructed canons, institutions, and texts which prevent or attempt to limit the presence and persistence of alternative epistemological or philosophical irruptions.[5] All of these theorists' return to new religions, therefore, is as much about the resistance to dominant and normative religious systems as it is about Black America's encounter with a failed democratic system and the demand and articulation for greater participation.[6]

As a result of their work, the study of Black religion continues to decenter the role of Black Christianity qua Black theology and has begun to explicitly return to the archive and the experience of twentieth and twenty-first century African American religious experiences. In this chapter, the Black sacred sphere is defined as those organized spaces where African Americans gather to engage and interact with the sacred. This notion of sacred is an expansive term, and in this account, I understand sacred or sacrality as symbols, ideas, or a physical presence that disrupts, constrains, or reframes the everyday or the profane. The sacred is a disruption of epistemological and political practices that deny or occlude the other or an-other. Sacred does not, therefore, have to be connected with a divinity or otherworldly force, but it does supplant or challenge certain philosophical and epistemological understandings that deny its possibility. Therefore, Black religion is a production of African American communities' and institutions' construction of sacrality and their communication of the sacred via conversations, scripts, scriptures, and the production of new canons. Black theology, on the other hand, has focused on the engagement of African American Christianity and examining the philosophical and hermeneutical practices that are dominant in its production and evolution. This chapter will address the ways that, by closely attending to the production and engagement of the idea of the sacred in African American Christianity as well as alternative movements, provide insight on the role and deployment of the Black body and the Black body's relationship to Black participation in the modern moment/Black freedom.

While the return to the archive and experience are important for any accounting of African American religion, we will primarily focus on the canonical and critical role that the Black body plays in the construction of religion and African American religions' negotiation with empire and democracy. Furthermore, I argue that the Black body as sacred space is the central script or canon which is engaged, debated, and circulated within the Black public. While the Black public has been a heavily contested term, it is important to engage the critical role that the Black public has on/in the formation of the canon on the Black body. Some have argued that the Black public comprises those entities that have the power and influence to engage in the political and social sphere.[7] Many early theorists of the Black public imagined the leaders of it and the texts that comprised it as texts and persons whose main responsibility was to translate Black needs and concerns to a dominant audience or set of institutions.[8] As the term evolved, "the Black public" functioned as the dominant group among many Black publics that often seem to determine the hegemonic ways to address or unpack certain ideas of Black belonging. In this chapter, the Black public includes both the dominant groups as well as recognizes the important and insurgent role of alternate publics, which include, but is not limited to, alternative religions, radical political formations, and groups and institutions that challenged normative gender, race, and sexual identities. All of these groups are vying for attention or articulating differences of opinion among different groups of Black thinkers, discourses, and ideas.[9] Therefore, any thoughtful engagement of African American religion and the Black sacred sphere in the modern Western world must include the construction, deliberation, and deployment of the sacred Black body and the role it plays in the multiple publics outlined above.

The sacred Black body in this argument highlights the significant and signifying role that the Black body plays in the African American public and within the African American religious tradition. By highlighting its sacred dimensions, this chapter suggests that the Black body is doing more than just representing the African American experience. Rather, the Black body is seen as a meditation on or representation of the larger concerns of Black existence and Black humanity. This sacralization, or the process by which the body becomes the central motif and the creation of a public which circulates symbols and ideas (canon) simultaneously, is at the core of African American religion. The sacralization of the Black body stands as a religious response to the exclusive and colonizing practices of Western modernity and settler-based democracy. The circulation and negotiation of the sacred Black body, both physically and symbolically, is the means of challenging the larger public, articulating alternatives, and developing new models of participating (or new models of religion) in the broader world. What is new about this argument is not just the appearance or importance of the body, but how the body is sacralized and its construction is deeply embedded in religious communities and the construction of sacred publics. Therefore, as empire and modernity become more adept at its body-shaming, body-excluding practices, African American religions were creating counter scripts and canons that imagine worlds and spaces where Black bodies can be recognized as sacred and have the capacity and opportunity to flourish.[10] Thus, this attention to new religions/alternative religions and their insistence on the body is a way to chart the Black publics' demands for visibility and participation.

These visions for or concerns about the Black body, nevertheless, like most African American religions, see their impact on both the sacred and everyday.[11] Thus, African American religions are ones that simultaneously make claims about the sacred Black body, the physical realities of Black existence, as well as the Black body politic. As a result, the claim being made is that African American religion is about repairing the breach/disjuncture between the frayed and fragile relationship between Black bodies under the constraints of Western capitalism and failed democracy and a vision of full Black participation. Therefore, this chapter will look at the ways in which the methods of Black theology and alternative religious movements attempt to make space for the variety of African American religions and their engagements with the Black body. Secondly, this chapter will argue that it is the return to the body and the circulation of texts and ideas that sacralize the Black body that is engaged in the works of Kelley Brown Douglas and Delores Williams and their focus on gender and sexuality and Wimbush's project of signifying on religious traditions that is so important for this new direction. Finally, I argue that the engagement and creation of a canon on the sacred Black body is the primary goal of African American religions in the twentieth century. It will address the ways that a turn to alternative religions, a theoretical reconsideration of religious variety or multivocality in womanist and Black feminist thinkers, and a nuanced account of competing Black publics, including Black sacred publics, highlight the central role of the sacred Black body.

## THE FOUNDATION OF BLACK THEOLOGY

Black theology is a critically important method in reading and deciphering the role of African American religion in North America. While Black theology had at its center a primary focus on the concerns of Black Christian communities and readings of normative texts and scriptures, the method always pushed for new ways to address Black experience and to return to the archive of Black religious communities.[12] The Black theological method, therefore, has been, and in many circles continues to be, informed by a focus on certain communities of belonging that make it useful in reading certain patterns and practices, but it is often insufficient in its reading of alternative and popular religious movements. There is not the need or the call to jettison the Black theological method, but rather it is calling for the expansion of its method to include variety, dissonance, and variability as central to its method. It is following in the admonition of theorists of Black theology and Black religion like Anthony Pinn, Charles Long, emilie townes, Delores Williams, and other theorists to move beyond Christian orthodoxy and a limited view of the Black public and its inevitable recourse to the Black church. Anthony Pinn captures this best when he argues in his *Varieties* that "African American theological reflection troubles me because it limits itself to Christianity in ways that establish Christian doctrine and concerns as normative."[13] He then continues by asking, "how does theology address traditions that fall outside the Christian context, traditions that are contrary to, if not hostile toward, the basic claims of Christian faith?"[14]

Black theology has centered its analysis primarily on the reading of the Biblical text and on the role of Black Christian groups in their reading of that text. This movement to the Biblical text and Christianity was useful in that it unearthed one aspect of God talk and its formative role in the development of Black publics, both dominant and alternative. It suggested that Black Christianities and their engagement with Christian texts was essential in expanding what counted for and should be considered theological language.[15] In Anthony Pinn's and other theorists accounting of Black Theology, we are reminded that for all of its limitations it made visible and essential that Black American's relationship to Christianity could be and was quite often very different from other group's relationship to and interaction with the category of Christianity. Furthermore, Pinn suggests, and this is signaled throughout Black theological language, that it is not just Black Americans' relationship to Christianity but it is Black America's relationship to religion.[16] Religion plays a critically important role and once we take seriously that Black folk's theological efforts are not constrained by normative theological categories that the resources of African American religion begin to fully inform the production and construction of Black life.

It is this move away from the traditional theological categories or at least a critique of the limitations of those categories that make Delores Williams and her critique of Black theology so important. Williams' critique of patriarchy and certain constructions of Black Christianity, 25 years after the publication of her *Sisters of the Wilderness*, was premised not simply on a critique of male domination and male violence but also on the construction of knowledge that was intent on denying or occluding the full participation of other bodies. Therefore, it is instructive that Williams' intervention was not just an escape from the dominant or heterosexual gaze, but she was highlighting the complex identities and political formations that take place within new and resistant constructions of religion, gender, and race.[17] This impulse is in the earlier works of Black theologians likes James Cone and Kelly Brown Douglas, but they often name these other sources as a resource for African American Christianity (or what they often call the Black Church) rather than seeing the production of these discourses as the emergence of alternative publics, alternative religions, or the broad Black church tradition. The willingness to look far afield and to see the processes by which these discourses, sometimes in conversation with Christianity and sometimes not, open up venues for African American liberation and new variables in the field of African American religions is critical for this new method in African American religions. Black freedom and Black religion did not always have to engage or entertain Christianity in order to make a claim on the Black public sphere. Womanists, like emilie townes and Dianne Stewart, began the work of looking for those other religious movements and moments where Black freedom could be accessed and the sacred Black body was at the center of the discourse. Womanists have pointed theorists in the direction of accessing other sources to find these movements without necessarily returning to the Christian narrative. By invoking Black women's literature, Black women's experience, and crucially the role of alternative religious and spiritual practices throughout the diaspora, womanists have expanded the method by which we engage Black religions, the public within which these discourses circulate, and the possibilities of movements that are actively engaging the question of Black freedom and the sacrality of the Black body without recourse to Christianity.[18] The expansive nature of the womanist interrogation means that we are looking at much more complex and numerous accounts of religious practices and identities. This is a gesture toward the alternative or the unnamed that has often been rejected in response to the constraints or concerns with the hegemony of the Black church, Christianity, and Black religious respectability. The womanist concerns and ultimate dismissal of the logics and politics of respectability and the hegemony of the church and their ultimate recovery of the Black body open up a wider purview for discussion of not only African American religion but Black responses to the modern world.

## THE LIMITS OF NEW RELIGIOUS MOVEMENTS

Often times the quest for these other religious spaces have led thinkers of African American religion to explore other methodological paradigms. Cultural anthropology has been a fertile ground and it has opened the possibility of looking more fully at the multiple forces that shape Black life and flourishing.[19] In addition to anthropology, the field of New Religions or new religious movements has methodologically argued for an intervention that could be useful for the study and engagement of African American religion. This intervention, according to Weisenfeld, often places too great an emphasis on the new or the different. The methods of new religions look at the emergence of a new language, new patterns, the role of iconic and prophetic figures, and the ways that communities of people attempt to create a new language, scripture, and protocol to address the failure of the modern world view.[20] This description of new religion is useful in that it articulates the Black American struggle with modernity, but Weisenfeld and others want to resist the idea that these are new. Rather than focusing on the "new" nature of these practices, Weisenfeld and others all point to ways in which these movements are engaged in similar acts as earlier ones and that the descriptor of "new" may highlight a chronological distinction, but it fails to fully outline the ways in which this has been an essential aspect of Black religiosity since the middle passage. The focus, therefore, is not on the new, but on the continued use of religion, specifically all the alternatives made available in competing Black publics, as a way for Black bodies and knowledges to engage the broader public.

Similarly, the field of new religious movements has primarily been constrained by an attention to the nonnormative religious practices engaged primarily by normative bodies. This focus on normative whiteness often leads these studies to fail the litmus test of what religion means for marginalized and limited Black bodies. Jackson highlights the limitations of new religious movements in his evocative text when he suggests that if these movements are read solely as engagements with philosophical asides or eccentricities then that method is rendered negligible or not very useful for the theorizing Black religion.[21] Religion or African American religion is not a philosophical aside, but it is at the core of African Americans' engagement with democracy and participation in the modern world. African American religion is a world-mapping and world-making exercise or the negotiation and creation of a distinct public. In this examination, world-mapping is the process by which the constraints and norms of the current situation are evaluated and assessed, and world-making is the process by which new publics and discourses are created in order to disrupt the logics or constraints of maps that have been dismissive of Black bodies and Black freedom. Every analysis in African American religions must therefore attend to the world-mapping and world-making practices of Black religions and Black religious-affiliated movements. How do these movements not only attend to the structure of space, ritual, and beliefs, but how do they create the possibility of these projects in the realm and logic of Black bodies? How are they also engagements with citizenship, belonging, and empire? While both New Religions and Black theology open the possibility of thinking beyond the normative space of Black Christian communities, these methods have often marginalized or misrepresented the voices that will ultimately help us understand the nature and shape of African American religion more broadly.

## SIGNIFYING AS DISRUPTION OF "SACRED" PUBLICS

Signifying is the process by which a group or a person challenges, disrupts, or reformulates a normative script or set of ideas. This tactic or strategy is central to Charles Long, and eventually Vincent Wimbush and his understanding of African American religion. For Wimbush, African American is a series of significations on and around the canonical texts of whiteness and white supremacy. In Wimbush's fascinating text, *White Men's Magic*, he returns to a classic text in the Black public and its attempt to achieve full participation in the modern world, *The Interesting Narrative Life of Olaudah Equiano, or Gustavus Vassa, The African*. Thus, it is important to note that when Wimbush evokes the category of scripture and its relationship to Black world-making he does not begin with the Biblical text or even selected texts from the scriptural narrative, rather he looks at the world-mapping and making text of Olaudah Equiano.[22] His engagement of Equiano is illustrative for the study of African American religions in that its focus is on the production and deployment of an iconic, transnational text in the form of *The Interesting Narrative of the Life of Olaudah Equiano, or Gustavus Vassa, The African*.[23] The Equiano text is iconic in the same way that Wimbush argues that the Bible was for the construction of white identity. The Equiano narrative is deliberately a text about Black identity and the construction of Black identity that is signifying on and has been used to signify on modernity, empire, and the failed assimilation of the Black subject. Equiano is canonical not because it is an exhaustive account of Black existence, but it highlights the need for a text or the desire for a narrative (in Equiano's situation) that will provide a model for new world Black citizens.[24] Equiano's text is important in the ways that it constructs a mechanism for dealing with biblical and other scriptural texts, while at the same time becoming canonical and critical to the Black public. Equiano creates in the nineteenth-century world a space for his physical and discursive body as well as the movement of those bodies through physical and symbolic spaces. He is making a world that responds to the unique concerns and constraints of African American/African European migrants at that time.[25] His text is a canonical script for Black world-making or African American religion because at its center is the construction of Black identity and that identity's relationship to citizenship. This attention to Equiano is not as the adherent of mainline or normative Christian tradition, but rather as the creator of a dominant signification. Equiano challenges the "sacred" dimensions of whiteness and normative Christianity and offers an example of creating alternative scripts and making a world and engaging new publics through these texts and ideas. While Equiano does not explicitly disrupt Christianity or whiteness, his text and the slave narrative is used as a disruption. Equiano's narrative becomes the key mechanism to highlight the role of the Black body and the ways that it cannot be free under the constraints of western empire and capitalism. Equiano in many Black publics is not circulated as an exemplar of Black freedom or upward mobility, but rather it highlights the failure of the Western empire and early forms of democracy to truly be available to the Black body. Equiano's tragic narrative is one that reminds the reader and generations of world-makers that there must be a critical reappraisal or rejection of European Christianity, democracy, and empire.

Similarly, the second and third generation of Black theological thinkers, primarily using womanism as their method, have been known for their engagement and critique of normative Christian traditions. In Delores Williams' groundbreaking text *Sisters in the Wilderness* she is not only articulating the limitations of Christian scripture and the logics of dehumanization for Black women in many of these scriptures, she is also pointing out the possibilities of new and alternative religious and Christian movements. For Williams and many that followed after her, the resources for thinking about African American religion do not begin in the assimilation of mainstream religious modalities but the ingenious and subterranean responses to the question of the religious.[26] Williams' book, emilie townes' account of Brazilian religious practices, and Dianne Stewart's account of Jamaican spirituality point toward and are an inflection of the Black woman's variety, creativity, and desire for new and authentic spaces that map a world amenable to their bodies, needs, and demands.[27] This attention to the new is what Williams is outlining in this "midrash" or scriptural accounting of Tamar and her life after she exits the purview of the biblical writers.[28] Tamar for Williams is someone who, like Equiano, tries to follow the dominant script of the Jewish community, but by the end of the narrative, like many Black women in the modern era, Tamar has been physically and sexually abused, disposed of and rendered unfit to participate in mainstream political and religious spheres, and left to construct or at least consider the possibilities of a counter-narrative. Williams is articulating the central role of new religions or what Stephanie Camp has often called the "truancy" of Black women. The new or alternative religion provides an opportunity for "truancy" in that it offers a break or a respite from the dominant world system.[29] Often this break is short-lived or it seems to only speak to one area of a marginalized or oppressed person's life, but in reality this "truancy" works as a total restructuring of the marginalized person's body in relationship to the dominant space. Camp outlines how engaging the enslaved body in time and space allows us to see how the enslaved "claimed, animated, personalized, and enjoyed their bodies."[30] Camp is articulating the very genesis of Black religion with Black women's truancy from dominant spaces of white oppression and the reclamation of Black women's bodies.

In the case of Williams and the story of Tamar, the alternative religion is one that is required as a result of being jettisoned, rejected, or forgotten by the mainstream or normative tradition. However, Camp and her language of "rival geographies" or that of women's "third bodies" take on a much needed but qualitatively different intervention. Camp argues that while it may seem that women, especially Black women, stay in these normative spaces and that these models of periodic escape or the leaving while in place (consider polyamory) suggests that Black women are not wedded or tied to one dominant or normative way of creating and maintaining identity or religions.[31] In the claim that it is possible to love another women or it is possible to love a man and a woman simultaneously, Williams and others are highlighting the ways that alternative publics or new religions are not constrained by an allegiance to one text, one script, or even one God. Therefore, this attention to the alternative or the alternative that is adjacent to the normative tradition is what allows the womanist method and this method of African American religions to account for or engage movements that might seem to solidify mainstream notions but are actually doing other work. This is one of the important insights of womanist thought—the multivocality (the logic of signifying) of any one institution and the resistance to prioritizing/privileging one vision of freedom over the other.

Furthermore, the importance of the multiple or mutually constituting identities is exactly what womanist theorists were trying to outline in relationship to intersectionality and it is equally important in relationship to multiple religious identities. The fact that one adopts or engages one religious identity does not preclude him/her from adopting another one. The rejection of the puritanical, homo-textual impulse in the late modern era is critical to engaging Black women's religion and survival. The idea that more than one truth or that multiple truths could exist at the same time is experienced as anathema in the framework of normative Western culture. Nevertheless, Black humanity and specifically Black women's identity have tended to argue for a space for alternatives to the lie of an "abstract universal." The story of Black identity/religion has been the spectacle of and the demand for the new symbol, ideas, and literally the new subject or body.[32] The universal is displaced by multiple narratives, truths, and stories. This is the space that Walter Mignolo calls the "pluriversal" and in that space is the opportunity to reject the abstract universal of democracy, Christianity, and even religion which often elide and deny Black bodies and their experiences.[33]

## THE PROBLEMS AND PROMISE OF BLACK CANONICITY

The sacred Black body stands at the center of the Black canon and the set of scripts and institutions that engage and circulate these texts. Canonicity or the Black canon, however, does not have to be another model of exclusion and domination, but if canonicity is code for white supremacy or any type of religious or political hegemony, then it cannot operate in the service of Black freedom. Moreover, as Wimbush and Williams have so provocatively argued, epistemological and methodological hegemony are examples of this problematic form of canonicity as the politics of exclusion. In these cases, canonicity is a local project that has masqueraded as a universal project and thus denied alternative or other projects resistant to the dominant canon.[34] Vincent Wimbush in his critique of Biblical studies and Lewis Gordon, Black philosopher and thinker of Black existentialism, in his critique of the university system highlight the ways that canon, method, and epistemological privilege mitigate or prevent the full reading of African and African American expression.[35] Gordon continues that these biases or cul-de-sacs prevent the study of African American communities and the engagement of these communities as liberatory spaces. It is not surprising, therefore, that Gordon, Wimbush, and Williams all see the need to evacuate and create new methodological paradigms in order to do their work. Thus, the university or the discipline as the maintainer of a specific canon become suspicious or problematic. Nevertheless, this does mean that the term or the idea of canonicity needs to be evacuated. Canon as a colonial gesture or a maintenance of systematic oppression/exclusion must be abandoned, but the attention to texts that are circulated, sampled, and engaged in communities of belonging are central to understanding the project and logic of African American religious communities.[36]

As a result, Williams and townes in their evocation of Black women's experience or Wimbush in engaging the "textures, gestures and texts" of local communities are locating the subaltern or nontraditional ways in which canon is constructed, negotiated, and then used in communities.[37] This alternative canon is paramount, because it centers the concerns of the community members and provides insights into their vision and version of an alternative reality. Therefore, the canon is not just the text, but the creation, interpretation, and circulation of the texts in the community. Katie Cannon's groundbreaking work on African American Christianity and women's experience explicitly not only points to the role of text but also highlights the role of interpretation and ultimately its formative logic in specific communities.[38] The reading of Black religious communities from the position of new and alternative religions requires a renewed attention to what becomes canonical and who determines canonicity. Therefore, it is important to understand what work canon is doing for these communities. In many new religious movements, the prophet/founder and his texts become canonical. These texts are circulated as a means to make a broader argument about the transcendent or compelling narrative of the moment, but this circulation and the canonizing of language, ideas, bodies, and even songs function as a way to create a counter-script or narrative to the dominant discourse. Father Divine and the International Peace Mission Movement is a primary example of the canonical texts, symbols, and language as not just providing language or framing for the internal community of adherents or believers. Rather, new religious movements are providing language and ideology to counter and correct external canonical ideas and symbols. For Divine, the canonical vessel of his Black body being the divine not only provides theological orientation for the adherents, but in its sacralization and canonization of his Black body it responded to the impasse and the problem of Blackness and oppression in the twentieth century.

In the example of Father Divine it is clear that the canon or the new script functions as a counter-narrative over and against the erasure of Black bodies and the denial or surveillance of Black religious freedom. In many of these alternative Christian movements, the canon includes, but is not limited to, texts but most importantly reframes or resituates the sacred Black body. The Black body becomes the canonical corpus upon which Black flourishing and freedom are articulated. It is not a mistake that Father Divine is the actual body of the divine or that the well-fed, well-dressed bodies of the Black participants are so critical to these alternative movements. Furthermore, if the canon is en-fleshed in the actual body of Black leaders, participants, and symbols, the canon is extended by the response of other Black bodies to these symbols or ideas. In this regard, the canon is a repository of religious, political, and cultural responses to the fraught and compromised Black body. Therefore, it is not surprising that the leaders' bodies are venerated and actually stand in for the sacred Black body and that the physical repairing or presentation of the Black body become a central apparatus for the production of sacred space. Space in these movements becomes sacred by the appearance and resistance of the Black body in the forms of love feasts where Father Divine fed, engaged, and entertained his adherents, the protests of the Nation of Islam, and the parades of Marcus Garvey and his African nationalism movement. Thus, methods of African American religion must pay close attention to the ways in which the Black body is canonized and how the presentation or protection of the Black body is central to the world-making logic of African American religions. In this sense all Black publics that engage with the Black body are "Black sacred publics."

The Black or alternative canon, however, is one that is porous and flexible. The logic from the study of new and alternative religions and specifically from new frontiers in anthropology are useful as it foregrounds the fragility of the movement and the vulnerability of the people that practice it. The creation and protection of this canon and the use of methods to circulate and sample it become increasingly dangerous (political) in a world that devalues or attempts to erase Black life and needs. Thus, one of the first things to be evacuated when alternative movements move into the mainstream are aspects of their canon that challenge the status quo. In the case of African American religious movements, this attention and protection of the Black body is often de-emphasized or erased. The constant attacks on Black bodies and the continued return to the body is what makes many African American religious traditions suspect as they move to the mainstream. This is essentially the argument that Kelly Brown Douglas makes about the evolution of the Black church and its critical tension with Black bodies and Black physicality. As the Black church moves to the mainstream, the sacred and the physical Black body are de-emphasized or at least displaced from the center of analysis. Similarly, Divine's move away from the Black body at the end of his life occurs as a way to make space for a broader public, a set of adherents, and a growing disinterest in translating the critical role of the sacred Black body to the maintenance and protection of democracy.[39]

Again, this encounter with alternative Christian traditions forces us to explicitly return to the Black body as the quintessential space of Black religion. Black theology does this and has historically been involved in this project. James Cone in one of his later works, *The Cross and the Lynching Tree*, evaluates the critical and crucial role of the flesh for Black Christology and for Black religious identity.[40] Furthermore, other Black theologians that have focused on race like J. Cameron Carter, Brian Bantum, and Willie Jennings have all highlighted the fleshiness of the Black religious encounter.[41] However, this fleshiness stands in relationship to a theological category of the created being, whereas the method of world-making found in alternative religions helps us to understand the body as its own category. The Black body is not a mimesis or a substitute for the divine Christian body rather it is the real and physical body that must be engaged as a part of a new canonical tradition. In this regard, the Black body is sacred and profane and thus the Black body' sojourn through place and time often supplants the abstracted body of the dominant Christian or even democratic corpus. Wimbush's turn to Equiano is not simply a turn to a charismatic figure but it is the invocation of a Black body, albeit a tightly controlled one, and his sojourn through the process of world-mapping and world-making. Similarly, Father Divine's Black body is evoked to stand over and against the practices, politics, and logics that would attempt to erase it. Divine and his Black body is God, and he disrupts the normative notion that whiteness and sacrality are equivalent. The songs sung about Divine, the creation of his sumptuous meals, and even his unwillingness to be controlled by the logics of racialism all put the question of the body and a raced body at the center of his religion. Moreover, many of the womanist interventions have addressed African American religion at the level of the body because the body is the space in which we take seriously African American experiences of empire and their creative alternatives to it. Williams starts with a broken and bruised Tamar in the wilderness. Kelly Brown Douglas in her last work looks at the suppressed and dangerous ways that the body is negated in Black Christian communities. She then looks to blues women as a resource or a tool to return to the Black body.[42] These blues women are not just a signifier of the Black body's importance, but rather like Baby Suggs Holy, Shug Avery, and Tamar they designate the body as sacred in their ability to challenge the dominant regime and profane in their freedom to navigate their multiple identities as woman, Black, sexual being, and outside of normative religious practices. From Divine to Williams to the newest generation of Black theological thinkers, the Black body and the canonical accounts of the Black body, both the Black female and male bodies, are the texts and ideas upon which Black religion and Black public spaces must meditate and interrogate.

This dogged attention to the body and the creation of canonical texts and ideas around the sacred Black body is the centerpiece of engaging alternative Christian movements, both historically and in the present moment. Karla Holloway in her harrowing text on Black death and dying articulates this theme most provocatively when she argues that the central question of the twentieth century for African Americans (and I add African American religion) is "where is the body or who has the body."[43] While Holloway's text is often read as a meditation on Black mourning in the twentieth century, I argue that she is presenting the myriad ways in which Black communities deal with and respond to the fragile Black body. Therefore, she is not just recounting mourning stories but the creation and production of alternative publics, canons, and ultimately religions.[44] Therefore, the debates on who has the Black body, how the Black body should be handled, where the Black body should be engaged are all theological and religious questions. These public engagements or new public presentations of the Black body herald not just a new religion but an opening for new political and social formations (or a radical constellation of world-making movements). These are all questions that the alternative Christian movements had to answer.

In closing, the encounters and representation of the Black body in the modern moment is the articulation of a critical canon for African American religion. I argue it is the total container upon which African American religion rests. If the sacred Black body is central to the Black canon, it must not only be addressed, but it must be at the center of the study of African American religion. This book considers how the centrality of the body might shift what we count as African American religion. The Black Lives Matter movement and their focus on the bruised, harassed body, the Black humanist movements and their turn to Black aesthetics, the question of Black genocide and Black gentrification, therefore, all have spiritual and religious consequences.[45] The turn to the body is not new for the study of African American religion, but the focus on the production and circulation of canons and religions that respond to these new understandings and concerns about the Black body is. It is therefore not surprising that studies on Black respectability and Black freedom have focused on the movement and new parameters of the Black body, the logics of desire and the cartographies of Black space, and the opening of new modalities for gendered and sexual expression.[46]

## ALTERNATIVE AFRICAN AMERICAN RELIGIONS AS A MODEL FOR THINKING ALTERNATIVE PUBLICS

This attention to alternative African American religions, specifically the work of Wimbush and his theorization of Equiano, Father Divine and Black divinity, Delores Williams and her work on Tamar and Black women's religions all point to the construction and the engagement of alternative publics. When I use the term "alternative Black public," these are often members of those competing publics, but it is considered alternative because it exists on the fringe of the dominant public discourse. Often these alternative publics—sacred publics are usually a part of this group—are radically opposed to mainstream voices and providing options that are seen as distinct from normative voices. They are alternative not only due to their rejection of dominant tropes within U.S. society, but they represent the variety of alternatives for thinking about the relationship between the Black body, freedom, and religion.[47] These alternatives provide an alternative to modernity that are distinct and bring unique readings of the body and Black belonging to be debated within the Black public. They are not anti-modern, but deeply embedded in their critique, and public framing is a critique of the foundations of the modern world.

The alternative Black religious space outlines new trajectories for thinking about Black representation, Black citizenship, and ultimately Black visions for freedom.[48] These trajectories are important in that they challenge the mainstream and mainline itineraries that have masqueraded as dominant but are often in conversation and negotiation with these other models. This attention to these world-making movements are important as they must be read as comprehensive encounters with modernity, race, and modes of resistance rather than an escape from it. The movements are opening new venues for thought and therefore engaging in a public debate on what constitutes Blackness and Black freedom. This debate on the terms of Blackness and Black freedom must also be read as a debate on what constitutes Black religion and Black Christianity, and in this case what is the role of the Black body. This method in African American religions, by recourse to new religions, forces the theorist to always engage the relationship between Black freedom and flourishing and the role of Black religion.[49]

Weisenfeld outlines that the movement of Black bodies and their integration into new spaces and new ideas requires the creation of new liturgies, new scriptures, and new practices. These alternative religions or alternative Christian movements are just one example of this, but it is clear from this project that this attention to sacrality, location, and to the construction of new publics must not only be attributed to what has traditionally been seen as new religions, but this method must be applied to African American religion more broadly. This constructive and deliberative approach to African American religions point to its discourse, transactions, and world-making consequences.

The goal of re-engaging alternative religious movements in the Black public sphere is not to examine or re-evaluate under-theorized religious movements, but the goal here is to use the tool and resources of the alternative to think about the particular question of African American religion and the Black body. This Black body is canonical because it becomes the shared text upon which many of these movements can agree. While the nineteenth century depended on a religiosity divorced from the body, especially the Black body, or an abstract acknowledgment of the body, the twentieth century not only introduces the corporeal body as central to religious doctrine, but it makes the body and the restoration of a canonical body as an article of faith. The free and autonomous Black body was central to the canon. The argument here is that the liberated body and its elevation as a symbol of freedom and faithfulness begins to displace scripture and theological arguments. The presence and the persistence of the body and its fleshiness means that the body itself is a religious text and central figure that must be addressed within the theological and scriptural language of the movements.

The alternative Christian movements engaged the body, centered the role and appearance of divine beings, and began to recognize the veneration and protection of everyday bodies as a sacred rite. Many of these movements moved from an abstract discourse on bodies, where there was an explicit move from an abstracted divine being to a physical one that engaged the physical and political realities of its Black adherents. Oftentimes their leaders and/or their adherents were canonized as divine, and as a result, Black bodies and Black racial identities were seen as establishing a theological claim rather than simply a cultural construction. Therefore, the physical Black body was negotiated and debated whether or not it would be included in the permutations of Black religion, but how it would be included and valorized.

The twentieth century saw not only the introduction of Black sacred figures and Afro-divinities, but it also saw the circulation and the representation of Black images, the increase of Black theorists and thinkers on these images, and the increased prevalence of rituals and practices of representing and protecting the Black body. The Black body was sacred, and specifically the early Pentecostals identified themselves as saints, different from other bodies, and it was at the center of popular discourses on Africa, African culture, and African American culture. This canonization of the Black bodies and Black leaders did not just impact the vocabulary and syntax of religious movements and formation, but there was a similar shift in the popular domain or the broader cultural milieu. There was a new space and new models for thinking about the cultural significance of the Black body and the ways that it was positioned to participate in and be viewed by the broader public. As a result, the body became a symbol and a vehicle for something larger or more complex. This canonical Black body, therefore, plays the role of incorporating the lived everyday realities of the Black body as well the idealized/symbolic version of the Black body. This canonized Black body was an attempt for the body or this sacred reconstruction of the body to represent the historical narrative of the Black body as well as the complexity and fullness of the future possibilities. Therefore, it was canonical in that it offered a counter-narrative or a retelling of both a mythic Black past as well as the constellation of new vistas and opportunities. What does the canon do for these bodies, political futures, or new possibilities? This practice of canonizing the Black body was not simply a decision to focus on a renewed vision of the Black body but rather it was a decision to put the Black body and the realities and the concerns of that body at the center of the liturgy. As a result, it was considered a heretical tradition or a tradition that was radically re-conceptualizing the claims and major interests of the Black church as a theological and structural formation.

This canonical process and deep attention to Black aesthetics, lifestyles, and sacred spaces was a decisive break or radical repositioning of this new formation in relationship to the extant Black sacred sphere and the normative Euro-American church tradition. This chapter suggests that these communities are a part of complex heretical traditions and are noted for their explicit decisions to signify on traditional texts and concepts. More specifically, it is their signifying on Black bodies that is noteworthy. Particularly, in relationship to the Black body these models were challenging the notions of body-shaming, models of respectability, and the ability of Black bodies to be recognized and engaged through all aspects of the ecclesial and democratic spaces. The Black body was literally written into the sacred texts and made to be a part of the liturgical calendar. There is this inclusion that transformed the body into the subject of the religious inquiry, the site of the salvific message, and ultimately is positioned as an idea and object worth veneration. The Black body and the embodied Black experience are at the center of the Black worship experience and new tools, texts, and rituals are developed to engage this intervention.

While there had been earlier moments in the life of the church where the Black body and experience stood at the center of Black Christian traditions, the twentieth century witnesses the explosion of these communities and the re-emergence and reconfiguration of older traditions that attended to the body. While this book and chapter focus on new traditions, throughout the twentieth century there was a significant restructuring of older and extant traditions that were compelled or interested in rethinking their relationship to the Black body and rituals or cultural practices were the body was centered. This canonizing of Black bodies was an introduction of new themes in contemporary church movements, but it was also a re-imagining of the longer Black church tradition and Black church history. The canonization included re-engaging earlier avatars of Black sacrality and integrating these histories into new movements and communities. The inclusion of these earlier figures was an assent to their theological or cultural contributions as well as attending to the lack of full democratic participation that narrowed the expression and freedom of Black adherents. The canonization was not just the inclusion of the body, but it was that the affirmation of the Black body gave people the opportunity to reimagine Africa as a sacred beginning and the Black body as having theological and political import. It was the introduction to a new way of not only being religious, but it was a new way of being a modern subject. These alternative movements and this method of addressing their interventions helps us to rethink our engagement with more traditional religious movements. Therefore, reading the rise of socially conservative Black evangelicals at the end of the twentieth century becomes a much more compelling exercise when we use the tools and methods of alternative publics and the canonization of the sacred Black body to understand their engagement of Black respectability, their use of the body, and their relationship to citizenship and empire.[50] The attention to these alternative communities opens up myriad and nuanced debates around Black life, Black flourishing, and Black citizenship that are often imagined on the sidelines of many of these movements, but when engaged more explicitly we are provided a window into a growing debate on what constitutes Black participation in competing publics. The overarching argument here is that the methods by which we attend to African American religion matter. If we focus on African American religion as projects that ossify a long history of the hyper-spiritualization or the narrowing of religious trajectories of Black and brown people, then our study of religion will often function as a mechanism to support that argument. However, if our focus on African American religion is to address the complex and nuanced ways that it maps the world and engages with other social structures to make room for new ideas and newly emerging bodies, then the study of African American religion and this book will provide new insights into citizenship, democracy, and the complex and diffuse logics of Black freedom.[51]

## NOTES

1. See Judith Weisenfeld, *New World a-Coming: Black Religion and Racial Identity During the Great Migration* (New York, NY: New York University Press, 2016). Also see Johnson, *African American Religions, 1500–2000*.
2. Weisenfeld, *New World a-Coming*.
3. Johnson, *African American Religions, 1500–2000*.
4. Evans, *The Burden of Black Religion*.
5. See Cornel West, *Prophesy Deliverance!: An Afro-American Revolutionary Christianity*, 1st edition (Philadelphia, PA: Westminster Press, 1982). West provides a thoughtful and critical accounting of African Americans exclusion from the Western imperial project.
6. Jackson, *Thin Description*.
7. See Evelyn Brooks Higginbotham, *Righteous Discontent: The Women's Movement in the Black Baptist Church, 1880–1920*, 1st Harvard University Press pbk. edition (Cambridge, MA: Harvard University Press, 1994). See her discussion of the Black counter-public. I am arguing that the alternative publics are what make up the Black public or what Higginbotham calls the counter-public.
8. Ibid.
9. Michael C. Dawson, *Black Visions: The Roots of Contemporary African-American Political Ideologies* (Chicago, IL and London: University of Chicago Press, 2002).
10. See Douglas, *Black Bodies and the Black Church*. Note the important work that Brown Douglas does on the imperial design to shame and denigrate Black bodies and how the shame around Black bodies and sexuality impact African American religion and African American Christianity in her theorization.
11. Dawson, *Black Visions*. Dawson's understanding of Black visions is important as he is situating Black visions of Black bodily transcendence with a deep archive of Black visions for freedom. These visions include within them an attention to the particularities of Black political and social relations as well as a transformation of the larger economic, political, and social system.
12. See the limits of the Black theology as an interpreter of Black humanist and Black artistic rhetoric. See Anthony B. Pinn, *Noise and Spirit: The Religious and Spiritual Sensibilities of Rap Music* (New York, NY: New York University Press, 2003).
13. Anthony B. Pinn, *Varieties of African American Religious Experience* (Minneapolis, MN: Fortress Press, 1998), 48–50.
14. Ibid., 86.
15. By world-mapping, I am referring to Tom Tweed who suggests that religion is primarily about crossing and dwelling and that these itineraries and journeys are a critical part of mapping the world and carving out niches and opportunities for creating meaning and identifying opportunities for participation in the political and religious space. For Tweed, like John Jackson, where one is and what that person is doing is critically important to understanding the role and goal of religion. See

Thomas A. Tweed, *Crossing and Dwelling: A Theory of Religion* (Cambridge, MA: Harvard University Press, 2006).

16. Anthony B. Pinn, *Moral Evil and Redemptive Suffering: A History of Theodicy in African-American Religious Thought* (Gainesville, FL: University Press of Florida, 2002).

17. See the definition of womanism in Alice Walker, *In Search of Our Mothers' Gardens: Womanist Prose* (San Diego, CA: Harcourt Brace Jovanovich, 1983).

18. See the introduction of Stacey M. Floyd-Thomas, *Deeper Shades of Purple: Womanism in Religion and Society*, Religion, Race, and Ethnicity (New York, NY: New York University Press, 2006).

19. See Marla Faye Frederick, *Between Sundays: Black Women and Everyday Struggles of Faith* (Berkeley, CA: University of California Press, 2003); Jackson, *Thin Description*.

20. See Edward E. Curtis and Danielle Brune Sigler, *The New Black Gods: Arthur Huff Fauset and the Study of African American Religions*, Religion in North America (Bloomington, IN: Indiana University Press, 2009).

21. See Jackson, *Thin Description*.

22. *In White Men's Magic*, Wimbush is careful to note the importance that the Bible has for creation of maintenance of white supremacy-based settler democracy and how that canonical text has relevance not only for those that have power in that matrix, but that it also has resonance for those that are seeking it. Other group's interest in and approach to the biblical text was not because of a particular allegiance to the biblical narrative or even any structural or theoretical overlap with earlier or indigenous religions, but purely because of the power that those in power accrued as a result of their relationship to the text.

23. Vincent L. Wimbush, *White Men's Magic: Scripturalization as Slavery* (New York, NY: Oxford University Press, 2012).

24. In Henry Louis Gates' introduction to the Harvard Edition of the Equiano slave narrative, Gates argues that Equiano is an important text, because of its circulation among different publics but also the ways in which its structure and format become canonical for the genre of slave narratives. This genre in Gates's analysis is crucial for a particular telling of the new world Black's desire not only for freedom but for its opening of constructive and imaginative possibilities for Black contributions to the new world public. Equiano is not looking for a space outside of modernity, but he is clearly critical of modernity and sees the intrusion of the Black body as both a disruption and an opportunity for something new.

25. While Equiano can be read as the proto-typical African American subject, his references to his explicit African past as well as his movement within the Americas and Europe complicate what might be assumed as a stable identity. I think it is best to assume that Equiano is best understood as a new world citizen who is attempting to make sense of both his African culture as well as the American and European cultures that he came to be a part of. His narrative is one that heavily relies on the impact of this movement on his body and his relationship to other bodies.

26. Delores S. Williams, *Sisters in the Wilderness: The Challenge of Womanist God-Talk* (Maryknoll, NY: Orbis Books, 1993).

27. Emilie Maureen Townes, *Womanist Ethics and the Cultural Production of Evil*, Black Religion, Womanist Thought, Social Justice (New York, NY: Palgrave Macmillan, 2006); Dianne M. Stewart, *Three Eyes for the Journey: African Dimensions of the Jamaican Religious Experience* (New York, NY: Oxford University Press, 2005).

28. See Wilda Gafney, *Womanist Midrash: A Reintroduction to the Women of the Torah and the Throne*, 1st edition (Louisville, KY: Westminster John Knox Press, 2017). Additionally, it is important to reflect on the scriptural resistances and exegetical strategies deployed by womanists and the Black theological thinkers. Also see Renita J. Weems, *Just a Sister Away: A Womanist Vision of Women's Relationships in the Bible* (San Diego, CA: LuraMedia, 1988).

29. See Stephanie M. H. Camp, *Closer to Freedom: Enslaved Women and Everyday Resistance in the Plantation South*, Gender and American Culture (Chapel Hill, NC: University of North Carolina Press, 2004). While Camp's work is illustrative of Black women and everyday resistance to the physicality enslavement, Camp is also important for thinking about the ways that this resistance and sabbatical makes room for the flowering of new religious traditions, the critique of hegemonic formations, and the celebrating of new modes of resistance in the midst of their current resistance. Camp is not read as model for thinking about religion, but her work is important for thinking about the philosophical and epistemological space needed to create new mappings of the world.

30. Ibid.

31. Alice Walker's definition of womanism has been instructive to many generations of womanist and Black feminist thinkers. It remains instructive for thinkers of alternative religions because of the emphasis that it places on fluidity and discontinuity. See Walker, *In Search of Our Mothers' Gardens*.

32. I use the term "spectacle" here, because I am arguing that the disruption of white supremacy and the lie of abstract universals in the form of white culture are often experienced as a radical and explosive interruption by the mainstream. For the Black body to articulate itself as a part of the body politic or to see itself as the canonical scripture of African Americans is a spectacle or a disruption of the normative representations of the Black body. See Walter Mignolo, *The Darker Side of the Renaissance: Literacy, Territoriality, and Colonization* (Ann Arbor, MI: University of Michigan Press, 1995). Also see "Spectacular Blackness."

33. Walter Mignolo, *Local Histories/Global Designs: Coloniality, Subaltern Knowledges, and Border Thinking*, Princeton Studies in Culture/Power/History (Princeton, NJ: Princeton University Press, 2000).

34. Ibid.

35. See Vincent L. Wimbush, *Theorizing Scriptures: New Critical Orientations to a Cultural Phenomenon*, Signifying (on) Scriptures (New Brunswick, NJ: Rutgers University Press, 2008); Lewis R. Gordon, *Disciplinary Decadence: Living Thought in Trying Times*, The Radical Imagination Series (Boulder, CO: Paradigm Publishers, 2006).

36. It is important to note here that canon and scripture both have the imprint or impulse of hegemony, but Cannon, Gordon, and Wimbush are also suggesting that

there are alternative means of deploying these discursive frameworks that can work for the benefit of the marginalized and oppressed.

37. Wimbush, *Theorizing Scriptures*.

38. See Cannon, *Katie's Canon*. This text alongside Delores Williams highlights that the critical feature of African American religious identity is the creation of new canons, traditions, and ethics that fully respond to the needs and concerns of African Americans as full humans and citizens.

39. Evans in his text often highlights the short life span of Black religious movements and he suggests that their continued claim to Black lives and flourishing place them in direct opposition with the mainstream logics of democracy and capital.

40. James H. Cone, *The Cross and the Lynching Tree* (Maryknoll, NY: Orbis Books, 2011).

41. J. Kameron Carter, *Race: A Theological Account* (Oxford and New York, NY: Oxford University Press, 2008); Willie James Jennings, *The Christian Imagination: Theology and the Origins of Race* (New Haven CT: Yale University Press, 2010); Brian Bantum, *Redeeming Mulatto: A Theology of Race and Christian Hybridity* (Waco, TX: Baylor University Press, 2010).

42. Douglas, *Black Bodies and the Black Church*.

43. Karla F. C. Holloway, *Passed On: African American Mourning Stories: A Memorial* (Durham, NC: Duke University Press, 2002).

44. It is not surprising that the last chapter of Holloway's text is the sermon delivered over her young son's body. Maurice Wallace's closing eulogy functions to highlight that Holloway's text is as much a history of Black religion as it is a history of African Americans' response to death and dying.

45. See Pinn, *Embodiment and the New Shape of Black Theological Thought*.

46. Both Treva Lindsey and Brittney Cooper's works on the Black body both reference the important role of Black religion as a means of creating these codes and parameters of Black respectability. These "experiments" with the Black body can be argued as the opening or transgressive acts that inform the basis of a new religious movement. "Crunk Feminism" is therefore the opening salvo of not simply an ideological or disciplinary interruption, but it is the foundation for a new engagement with the body or a new religion.

47. See Higginbotham, *Righteous Discontent*; Frederick, *Between Sundays*.

48. Evans, *The Burden of Black Religion*.

49. The point that ethnography can only provide us so much is critical to John Jackson's *Thin Description* and is very important for theorists of Black religion to not already predetermine the issues and publics upon which Black religions intersect. This tension is at the heart of Jackson's analysis, and he is trying to warn us to use new religions or any methodology as a way to enter into the conversation of Black publics and not determinative of it.

50. Frederick, *Between Sundays*. See also Johnathan Walton and Kate Bowler as folks that are seriously looking at the production of Black evangelicals in the last half of the twentieth century.

51. Jackson, *Thin Description*.

*Chapter 2*

# Bound No More

## *Charles Mason, Black Scriptures, and the Working-Class Body*

### INTRODUCTION

Charles Harrison Mason, founder of the Church of God in Christ (COGIC) movement, testified before Federal Investigators in 1918 immediately following his arrest in Lexington, Mississippi, for "obstructing the draft." This was twenty years after the official founding of his Christian movement and ten years after he parted with the original founders to focus on a radical reinterpretation of "glossolalia" and create the Pentecostal movement with the most decisive footprint among African Americans in the Southeastern United States.[1] While this movement is often characterized by its focus on spirit-filled expressions of Black piety, a critique of commercialized culture, and the formal dress of its adherents who were called "saints," this chapter will address how Mason's re-visioning of Black respectability/protest shaped his reading of the Biblical text and particularly Black Christianity's relationship to armed forces and more largely the project of democracy. This chapter will discuss in depth that Mason's real threat was not to a disruption of traditional theological concerns or the invention of new denominational spaces, but rather Mason's intervention was a new way of being Black and religious in the twentieth century. In his testimony before the Military Intelligence Division, Mason dressed in his traditional Black suit and flanked by three bishops of his church ministry opened his questioning with this statement:

> Let us not reserve this moment for an accounting of conscientious objection or even a clarification of my sympathy with the Kaiser, but let us realize that democracy and black folks' participation in democracy is at stake. This is not a war for black people and this is not a war for black Christians.[2]

This opening statement is important for two reasons and the remainder of the chapter will address these two reasons. First, the text argues that a certain form of respectability/protest and Blackness are tied to a new understanding of citizenship. If one is to be Black, Christian, and respectable then one is forced to resist unjust laws and particularly any unjust law that maintains the logic of violent hegemony that had been and continued to be central to the U.S. democracy's treatment of African Americans. Secondly, I would like to argue that it is not only a particular construction of Black Christianity that is important in our analysis of Mason's statement, but I would like to suggest that it is the circulation of Mason's texts and ideas that are central to this analysis. Overall, this section suggests that Mason, like Divine and Cleage, began to provide a logic (a way of thinking) and a liturgy (a way of practicing) for Black religious subjects and their relationship to democracy. This logic and liturgy shapes not only the nascent COGIC movement but also is central to a burgeoning Black religious renaissance that was looking for language and logics that would support a Black religious subject and radical Black theological project in the making. While Mason does not introduce nor advocate for a racialized understanding of the divine or even see himself as a part of the Black radical political tradition, he begins to suggest a model for reading history and texts in a way that suggests that Christianity's, especially Black Christianity, encounter with democracy must challenge and resist democracy's exclusive, violent, and hegemonic formations.[3] Mason is a prophet of protest, but the nature of his protest is often misread as insider language or having minimal impact on the larger Black public. This chapter will highlight the ways that Mason's resistance and protest provides important language and methods for the long Black freedom movement, Black protest, and especially their reformulation in the twentieth century.[4]

Mason at the time of this statement is fifty-four years old and for the last ten years had been in the entrepreneurial stretch of building and maintaining a religious organization which was primarily made up of Black working-class migrants to urban areas in the South. The COGIC movement was primarily composed of newly urbanized Blacks in the New South with limited educational attainment and relatively compromised economic and social mobility. Different from Baptists and other movements that were made up of working-class Black southerners, the COGIC movement was independent, theologically, economically, and denominationally, from any previous Euro-American tradition. While many other Black church organizations and denominations had relative economic and organizational autonomy, their theological and ritual framework had been decided or heavily informed by Euro-American forbearers or traditions. Mason's independence from ecclesiastical and cultural/social oversight is what made him and his movement a concern to the broader public and the maintainers of Christian and democratic hegemony.

Therefore, it is not surprising that the early stages of his movement and the experiences of his followers are marked by intense racial violence and incessant instances of surveillance and resistance by governmental and ecclesial officials. Prior to Mason's encounter with the federal government in 1918, Mason and his associated leaders experienced a number of interactions with local and state officials, white religious leaders, as well as locally organized mobs or "militias" who wanted to control this "menace."[5] Mason very early in this leadership role is demonized and criminalized as both a theological fraud and a political problem that needs to be controlled or ultimately removed from the public sphere. Recognizing the precariousness of his position in relation to local government officials, Mason in early 1917 sent a letter to President Wilson outlining his position in relation to the war and was in the process of sending emissaries to Washington, DC, to hand deliver the letter and try to attain certain protections as a religious group as well as an aggrieved citizen. Nevertheless, Mason was imprisoned in 1918 with his emissaries en route to the District of Columbia with only the backing of a relatively nascent movement, but he persisted as he saw the possibility of impacting other African American centered religious movements at that time.[6] While his and COGIC followers' conscientious objection are at the center of the testimony, it is interesting to note who constitutes the Black public interested in this particular discourse. Not only was Mason's imprisonment but his delegates' attempt to meet with President Wilson and his testimony to the intelligence officials were reported widely in mainstream newspaper and periodicals of note. Additionally, it filtered through a wide variety of Black local, regional, and national periodicals. Mason, during his imprisonment and testimony, was supported and received funds from a wide variety of leaders and organizations in the Black public, including the National Association for the Advancement of Colored Peoples (NAACP) and the National Baptist Convention (NBC). Interestingly, these movements that just a couple of years prior, including the General Baptist Missionary Association of Mississippi, had argued that Mason was an outsider and marginal figure and that the COGIC movement was a misreading of the biblical text were now standing in support of Mason as he made this argument about Black citizenship and its relationship to the war industrial complex. Even the Black intellectual public that was shaped by a growing number of theorists of Black life and experience were critical if not dismissive of these new Black Christianities. Du Bois in his groundbreaking text *The Philadelphia Negro* talks about the failure of some Black church denominations to impact the public square and to uplift the race, and he particularly highlights the role of spirit-infused churches like Mason's.[7] Du Bois and others had determined that Mason and his movement were inconsequential to Black and U.S. history and ultimately an insufficient model of social protest and racial uplift. Du Bois does not just disparage the liturgy or ritual practices of these new Black Christianities, but he argues that there is no protest and no real social transformation for its members. Ida B. Wells also argued that "a weak and uneducated clergy lacked the respect of God, self and community betrayed the principles of truth, honesty, and self-respect."[8]

It is therefore of great import that Mason's testimony becomes one of the central pieces or what others might identify as an article of faith of Black religion and Black civil religion in the twentieth century as he articulates the very parameters of Black political participation and the limits of a coercive and hegemonic government.[9] Mason's testimony in this regard precedes Elijah Muhammad, Malcolm X, and Muhammad Ali's requests for waivers in light of religious conscientious objection. Mason sets the model for Black religious intervention and protest as a means for interrogating the possibilities of democracy. Mason and his movement are therefore consciously setting a course one might argue for civil disobedience at the beginning of the twentieth century, in whatever form that it might emerge, as a religious practice and a means to test or highlight the real capacity of democracy to accept the resistance and full inclusion of Black bodies. Most importantly, Mason is highlighting the relationship between Black religion and political dissent. Mason's intervention highlights that this was not just a religious group dissenting from military service, but that this was a predominantly Black movement that was involved in the dissent. Moreover, the Black nature of the COGIC movement did not escape Mason who preached an early form of inter-racialism, but he saw that Blacks being at the vanguard of this conscientious objection movement was important for Christianity as well as the larger Black public. In the FBI files on the church and Mason, the role of its Black leader and its attention to Black Christians was highlighted: "It is clear that Mason and his followers felt it to be of far reaching significance that one of the great religious movements of the twentieth century was founded by a member of the African race."[10] Mason, regardless of language and historiography that reads him as apolitical or removed from the larger Black freedom struggle, was critical to setting the parameters of Black religious protest in the twentieth century, creating a new scriptural canon for Black resistance and providing these venues of protest and radical dissent to a much larger swath of the Black public.

## MASON AND SCRIPTURE

It is of particular note that as Mason addresses the Military Intelligence Division that he invokes seven scriptural references and two additional African American canonical texts. Mason in this regard provides a clear model of the role of not just biblical scriptures but provides a tour de force of the use of scripture or Africana canonical texts to implicate and provide alternatives to the logics of white Christendom as well as the logics of exclusive democracy. It is clear that the audience of the testimony is not the Military Intelligence Division as Mason never explicitly addresses the concerns of the selective service, obstructing the draft or even the current soldiers fighting in the multiple regions around the world. Rather the audience of these comments is the nascent COGIC movement, the Black Christian community, and the larger African American public. Mason is eager to provide a rebuttal to the misrepresentations of his movement and its relationship to the nation-state, but he is also eager to provide a new way of resisting the state through the lens of his alternative religious movement. He, therefore, begins his scriptural engagement with an analysis of the following text:

> [5] The next day the rulers, the elders and the teachers of the law met in Jerusalem. [6] Annas the high priest was there, and so were Caiaphas, John, Alexander and others of the high priest's family. [7] They had Peter and John brought before them and began to question them: "By what power or what name did you do this?"
> [8] Then Peter, filled with the Holy Spirit, said to them: "Rulers and elders of the people! [9] If we are being called to account today for an act of kindness shown to a man who was lame and are being asked how he was healed, [10] then know this, you and all the people of Israel: It is by the name of Jesus Christ of Nazareth, whom you crucified but whom God raised from the dead, that this man stands before you healed.[11]

After invoking this text, the same text used by Frederick Douglas, David Walker, and Howard Thurman, he signals that he is an astute student of the Black canonical tradition and the Black radical Christian tradition and moves to consider a model for African American democratic participation through the lens of Christian witness.[12] Mason then concludes with using a particular reading of glossolalia that attempts to link spirit immersion and speaking in tongues as not an outlying Christian practice but rather as central to the democratic project and Black Christian's interrogation or revision of it. Glossolalia in this reading and particularly Mason's reading of Acts 4 is a reading of radical participation, access, and opportunity in the Christian and democratic world. Moreover, he is arguing that glossolalia has particular theological and ritual import for marginalized communities. It is this moment that difference and racial and economic hierarchies are erased and that new models and ideas, often dissonant and creative, are made visible in the public sphere. Mason sees his vision and the voice of his working-class adherents as a part of these dissonant and creative voices that might be able to challenge the current social and political system. The Memphis Commercial Appeal even highlighted how the idea of speaking in tongues was not reserved for the leadership or just the religious elite, but "the test was applied to the congregation. If the members of his church could not speak and understand the language, they were not sanctified and could not be saved."[13]

Mason argues that glossolalia (or speaking in an insider, community-mediated language) and egalitarian participation are centrally linked to the democratic project and more specifically offer practices and opportunities for African Americans and other disenfranchised subjects to participate in it in a wide variety of ways. He therefore centers Black subjectivity, the body of the African American solider, and particularly his version of Black Christian protest as not the antithesis of democracy by way of some religious ecstatic tradition or some rejection of democratic capitalism via communism or socialism, but he suggests this is precisely the type of participation at the center of radical participant-based democracy. In these comments, he argues that the COGIC adherents are "saints" and a "witnesses of a new era" in a number of different places. His language of sainthood is one that is not used as language of withdrawal, but it is used to invoke their appointed status as messengers and interlocutors in the current moment. Therefore, his comments do not uphold the current system of democracy but rather provide an alternative response to it. Mason, however, is clear to not align himself with communism or what might be seen as an enemy or anti-American sentiment, but he invokes and identifies himself as a patriot with a deep desire and commitment to United States-based democracy. Here again, Mason references the Christian text of faithfully being a Christian and rendering to Caesar what is Caesar's. Throughout the testimony he signals his fidelity to his U.S. citizenship and stemming the critique of any treasonous behavior. While many associated Mason and his movement as pro-German or Socialist, Mason and his cohorts made it clear that their allegiance was with the United States. A statement provided by one of Mason's members suggested as much when it read,

> We herewith offer ourselves to the President for any service that will not conflict with our conscientious scruples in this report, with love to all, with malice toward none and with due respect to all who differ from us in our interpretation of the scriptures.[14]

Furthermore, it is not a surprise that the final encounter with Mason by the Military Intelligence Division is not to question his ecclesial or theological competencies or even to critique his exegetical prowess, rather Mason is asked whether he believes in democracy.[15]

His vision and version of democracy is so radically different from the prevailing construction of violent, racist settler-based democracy that it is virtually unrecognizable to those questioning him. Specifically, Mason's argument that Black men via Black soldiers and their conscientious objection should have the same rights, privileges, and options afforded all other members of democracy. In Mason's eyes, his movement's desire to reject participation in some "worldly" activities was not a rejection of democratic participation, but for Mason, the ability to decide when and how to participate was precisely the hallmark of the democratic project. Mason believed that all legal democratic activities should be seen as just and made available to all citizens regardless of race and religion. Therefore, the right to conscientiously object as Black citizens or to separate from worldly activities was a radical intervention for African Americans, and it placed Mason and his movement as one of the more nuanced calls for African American religious self-determination during the first half of the twentieth century.[16] This call is important as it constructs a clear argument, at least for Mason, that religious freedom and self-determination were hallmarks of American democracy and something that Black Americans, or any American, should have that opportunity to engage. While Mason was arguing for religious self-determination and the right for a group to resist, Mason was also a part of a broader movement that was skeptical of the war, its reliance on working-class Black bodies, and overall government/society's lack of consideration about the equality of its Black citizens.

While the official statements made by Mason suggested that he was primarily concerned with the protection of conscientious objection and African American's access to that, other statements made by Mason and his members suggest that he was at best ambivalent about the war and at worst critical of the war complex that identified war as central to democracy. Mason argued in a sermon in 1918 that "there was no reason for the Negroes to go to war," and in this selection he makes no argument about religious freedom, rather he seems to argue that African Americans should have the right to resist. In many ways, Mason is attempting to marry his deep religious convictions with the current state of the treatment of Black Americans. For Mason and his followers, these ideas cannot be disarticulated. Freedom to serve God for Blacks at that time was predicated on a different relationship to democracy than had been previously constructed. Mason was explicitly calling for a rejection of the status quo and this included a rejection of Christianity's status quo as well as the status quo acceptance and involvement with all aspects of the state apparatus, specifically democracy. As other COGIC members who testified to federal authorities suggested, the COGIC movement was willing to participate in democracy, but only to the degree that it would not interfere with their "conscientious scruples."[17] Some have narrowly read this statement to suggest that COGIC was only resisting service on the terms of non-violence, but reading the depth and range of Mason and the organization's statements, it is clear that there were other reasons and other activities that they might not being willing to support. Most clearly, it was not just their fighting in the war, but the war more broadly was an issue for Mason and many other members of the Black sacred public sphere. In the next section, we will see that many aspects of participation, from buying war bonds to even supporting any activity of the war (e.g., the Red Cross), were being debated and that Mason and his movement were actively involved in helping African American religious communities to negotiate the language and liturgy of conscientious objection and the impact of envisioning alternative democratic spaces. Mason and his movement's relationship to these issues were not always perfectly correlated as Mason was invested in critiquing democracy and providing alternatives for his adherents while not endangering their well-being and inciting additional scrutiny of his movement. Therefore, it was possible for Mason to simultaneously advocate, or at least accept, the purchasing of war bonds for his members and the larger Black public, while publicly highlighting his deep tension with Blacks fighting and the war in general.

## MASON AND THE PROBLEM OF THE WHITE MAN'S SCRIPTURE

In addition to its impact on the Black public and Black religion, Mason and the COGIC movement had a lasting impact on the white Pentecostal movement. From 1907 to 1914, Mason, being legally incorporated and chartered in Tennessee, was able to ordain a number of white American ministers as well as issue credentials to a number of ministers throughout the region. As a result of this arrangement, these white ministers were enabled to perform the rituals and experience the benefits of being officially connected to this nascent movement. However, these white ministers and their churches were only associated with Mason for a short period of time. In 1914 in Hot Springs, Arkansas, the white ministers and their congregation began a predominantly white Pentecostal denomination, the Assemblies of God. Given the realities of segregation and the overt racism of that time, the only qualitative distinction between the Assemblies of God and Mason's COGIC movement was the Assemblies' racialized language. It is clear that the short-lived multiracial, egalitarian movement was now giving way to a status quo Jim Crow inscribed model. Mason, therefore, responded to this separatist model by not arguing for Black separation but highlighting the failure of both segregated white churches as well as segregated African

American churches. He positioned the COGIC movement as one that was arguing for radical egalitarianism not only in the public square but also the sacred sphere. Again, for Mason the ability for African Americans to be seen as fit in both places was crucial to his vision for a renewed vision of democracy. After the defections of the white ministers and the creation of the Assemblies movement, Mason spoke about a vision for the church and the larger society where the logics of white or Black exceptionalism would be discarded for a radical unity that was dependent on the reorganization of the structures of democracy.

While Mason argued for a vision of radical unity, he was unwilling to limit the influence of his church members in order to appease the concerns of the white supremacist ideology. Most importantly, the Pentecostal tradition, especially under the deployment and evolution of Mason and Jones, offered a great degree of autonomy and freedom to its Black working-class leaders and participants. The split of these movements seemed like an inevitable result of the reigning segregation of that time, but it was also clear that the Hot Springs Convention and the eventual Assemblies of God movement was actively dedicated to a set of practices that not only supported many of the theological underpinnings of Pentecostalism but also the tenants of white supremacy. The Assemblies of God movement created language and practices to assure that whiteness and specifically white male identity were central. A number of theorists have written about the construction of the white imagination in the creation of the Assemblies of God movement and their eventual break from a more multicultural leadership model.[18] Less has been written about the private and public statements that Mason and COGIC made with regard to the eventual breakdown of the original multiracial category of the Pentecostal movement. Moreover, it is clear that the failure of the multiracial Pentecostal experiment heavily impacted Mason's orientation to the Black church and the larger project of democracy. Mason understood the pernicious role of racism within his Christian community as well as the larger framework of the country, and he saw his version of Pentecostalism as a way to invoke the fitness of African Americans to participate in religious as well as nation-state communities. Thus while many critics and members of the Black sacred public argued, "In essence, COGIC, to a large degree, had adopted the values of as well as religious standards of Western behavior."[19] It is clear that it had not adopted the problematic value of white supremacy or Black inferiority. Therefore, in many ways, Mason was much more aligned with the other African American social and religious leaders of his time as he argued for a social uplift and a reorganization of the public sphere, but without sacrificing the religious and cultural particularities that were unique to African Americans in the New South at the beginning of the twentieth century.

## SCRIPTURES AND COMMUNITIES OF CONSCIENTIOUS OBJECTION

In 1895, the general assembly of Mason and Jones' Pentecostal movement adopted the following statement in a section entitled "Political Government,"

> We believe that the shedding of human blood or the taking of human life to be contrary to the teachings of our Lord and Savior, and as a body we are averse to war in all its various forms. We herewith offer our services to the President for any service that will not conflict with our conscientious scruples in this respect, with love to all, with malice toward none, and with due respect to all who differ from use in our interpretation of the Scriptures.[20]

It is important to note here that Mason and the COGIC movement not only state their conscientious objection, but nevertheless pledge their fealty to the President and, in such, his and the organization's deep regard for and commitment to democracy and democratic participation. He is highlighting that Christian resistance was not an absolute withdrawal from the public domain but that certain types of scriptural readings, and particularly African American scriptural readings, understood democratic participation as contingent and often resistant toward mainline Christian and popular understandings. Nevertheless, he offered an alternative to participating in the public domain, and he highlighted that the withdrawal from certain aspects of the public domain did not mean withdrawal from democracy. Furthermore, this alternative response or "righteous resistance" was one that circulated within the Black sacred public or what could also be described as the African American religious imagination.[21]

First, it is important to note that the idea of conscientious objection was not something new to Christian movements or new Christian movements at that time. Mason and his followers were among a wide subset of Christians and Black Christians that evoked this language at this particular historical moment. Many of the holiness and Pentecostal groups at this time made a claim of conscientious objections. There were a number of Quaker, Christian Science, and Jehovah Witness movements that were making these same appeals to the federal government. Additionally, in the surveillance papers of the FBI, many of the movements and their leaders were either called in for questioning or explicitly named in the federal documentation. Furthermore, there were a number of Black organizations that had expressed a concern with the war apparatus or the building up of global military presence on the back of Black and working-class soldiers. While these African American and radical organizations were not making a claim to conscientious objection on religious grounds, the FBI materials and the larger discourse suggested that there was resistance to this war from a variety of groups. Mason's response to the questions of the Intelligence Division was not surprising nor did they differ explicitly from what other religious movements who had been asked similar questions by this body. However, one of the main differences was Mason's nuanced and evolving response to this issue over time, and the ways that Mason's response was connected to larger networks of Black religious and political identity. Mason becomes a cause de celeb not because he resisted armed service but because his resistance or critique of armed services was so deeply connected to a critique of U.S. democracy and Black Americans' relationship to that democracy. Mason's critique of U.S. democracy was intensified because Mason's critique was different than the traditional responses of most Black Christian organizations.

The Black sacred public and many of the leading African American religious leaders were critical of the emotionalism and piety in the Pentecostal and holiness movements, and these leaders argued that certain forms of Black religion were preventing African Americans from being accepted into the democratic public. This left Mason in tension with the Black elite, and it highlighted his particular articulation for radical religious freedom and that Black working-class citizens should be able to participate in democracy without forsaking or changing their cultural and religious particularities. While Mason was in agreement with many mainstream organizations about the goal of attaining full citizenship for working-class African Americans at this time, Mason believed that full civic recognition should not be dependent on the acceptance of religious or even secular norms. Mason also was invoking a deep history of religious freedom and the right to conscientious objection, and he was also highlighting a deep suspicion with the current project of democracy and the overall treatment of African Americans. The NAACP and the NBC, two quite distinct organizations, immediately responded to Mason not on the question of what this meant for Christian readings of the Bible, but rather what it meant for Black organizing, the history of Black protest, and the larger project of integrating Blacks into the larger public. Mason, therefore, was forced to circulate and further explain this position among Black Christians as well as within his own denomination. While his statements to the investigators were well-known articles of faith for the larger Black public, Mason's interrogation of democracy and Blackness led to Black Christians' re-evaluation of their relationship to the United States' and particularly COGIC's relationship to democracy and their role in political protest. Mason at this time was taking a step that was out of line from most Black religious organizations, and it was clearly a distinctive move from the earlier years of COGIC. Mason saw his movement as central to the reorganization of Black communities, Black economic development, and new modes of participating in and resisting democracy.

While the doctrinal statement of 1895 is quoted often, it is Mason's popular 1918 sermon "The Kaiser in the Light of the Scriptures" that was circulated, parsed, and engaged widely in the Black sacred public. This sermon made an explicit argument that Black respectability/protest as Mason understood it was deeply embedded in scripture and Mason was committed to engaging this concept within his movement and the larger sacred Black public. Mason, unlike the claims made by many early and mid-century readers of his movement, was not trying to escape the questions of the Black public and its relationship to democracy, but rather he saw a response to it in the biblical scriptural, the Black religious tradition, and the extra-canonical excess (revelations of the spirit) made available through engagement with the divine. Black subjectivity and respectability were not limited to the confines of the church or the movement but rather demanded a comprehensive appraisal of Black well-being and flourishing in the larger society. Black respectability for Mason could neither be reduced to a type of religious expression or access to economic upward mobility. Moreover, Black respectability was not summed up by Mason and his adherents' modest dress and rejection of certain commercial and public activities. Therefore, it is incorrect to assume that Mason simplified Black respectability to a set of fashion choices or even the project of African American economic or ecclesial self-sufficiency. For Mason, Black respectability and Mason's understanding of "black protest" were linked to the full participation of Blacks in any or all aspects of the democratic process. Black respectability was the right to dissent and even to withdraw from the public sphere and still be seen and treated as a citizen.

Mason begins his exegetical encounter with the Kaiser's declaration of war with Romans 14:17 when he states, "Surely he did not pray thy Kingdom come, because the Kingdom of God is righteousness, peace, and joy in the Holy Ghost." He identifies that Black suffering and the conditions of war are similar in that they both highlight the absence of the qualities and characteristics that are associated with the Kingdom of God. This absence or the lack of Christian values used as a critique of Kaiser could also be read as a critique of white Christians, the U.S. government, and the prevailing conditions for African Americans at that time. Kingdom of God language, as it is used in this sermon, was not Mason invoking a model of quietism or an evacuation of the public domain but a call to explicit and specific action in relationship to Black bodies, especially the vulnerable bodies of the Black working class. Righteousness, peace, and joy had real world implications for Mason, his movement, and their critique of the modern world in the midst of an international conflict. Similarly, Mason is arguing that peace and righteousness had real, embodied meaning for African Americans at that time. Mason in this text and in responses to this text suggests that the Kingdom cannot be experienced where certain bodies carry the burden of protecting the interests and borders for others. Here he is both critiquing the project of the military industrial complex, acquisitive capitalism and its impact on the working class, and the nation's complicity with unequal application of freedom and participation for racialized bodies. This critique of acquisitive capitalism and his movement's withdrawal from and critique of consumptive culture often led people to associate Mason and his working-class movement with rising interest in the Communist Party among Black working-class groups. The communist ideologies, especially the emerging Black communists alongside the UNIA, were often making nationalist claims and the call for Black self-determination that were dependent on secession from the United States or some form of repatriation. Mason's call was not for racial separatism or even a racially oriented/organized nation-state, rather his was a call for a religious self-determination within the constraints of capitalism and modern society. Mason is suggesting that a radical vision of the kingdom should account for and listen to the concerns of Black people, especially poor Black men who were fighting for the American empire and the extension of democracy.

This language of "kingdom" or the "Kingdom of God" is important, because it is a term that was and has been heavily debated in the Black sacred public. Thurman used the "kingdom" language as a means to evoke the possibility of what later became MLK's "beloved community." Even cultural figures like Garvey use the Kingdom to highlight the possibilities of Black organized and led autonomous nation. Furthermore, Father Divine talks about the "kingdom" as a means to radically erase the economic and social disparity that emerged during these times. Mason, however, invokes "kingdom" to expose the depth and possibility of Christian community within the constraints of democracy. Mason's engagement with "kingdom" language was a response to those that argued that Mason's understanding of kingdom was unnecessarily insular and overly spiritual. There was a critique that Mason's group and its theology were advocating for a withdrawal from the public domain. Mason's evocation of kingdom was a direct response to this, and it highlighted Mason's nuanced engagement with both the Christian public and the Black sacred public. Mason wanted to make space for the unique theological understandings and ritual practices of his group which were different from and critical of normative cultural practices. Additionally, COGIC wanted to advocate for and enable certain expressions of religiosity while simultaneously highlighting that this was not apolitical or an act of passive withdrawal from the democratic practice. In his bi-weekly publication "The Truth," he talks about the "kingdom" and spends a great deal of time talking about the meaning of "in the world and of not of the world." In these moments, Mason is specifically targeting Black religious and cultural organizations that have designated him as apolitical and a detriment to Black advancement. Mason highlighted his differences with mainstream Black Christian organizations. While *The Truth* pinpointed the theological differences and complained about the growing factionalism and denomination, Mason and Jones, as they were still together during the publication of this text, highlighted the growing loss of autonomy for the local church. Mason and Jones, along with other critiques and concerns, highlighted that the loss of local church authority not only prevented culturally distinct practices, but they saw it as an affront to the working-class populations that made up the majority of their churches. This "usurpation of power," as Mason phrased it, into the hands of upwardly mobile Black ecclesial leaders led to the silencing or erasure of other voices. Mason, in particular, argued that this erasure was premised on the removal of certain groups from the Black public or the creation of fragmented Black public, African Americans fit to participate, and those who were not ready or unfit. The early Pentecostal movement was therefore breaking from the other Black sacred groups because of the ways that these groups not only marginalized their theological logics and cultural practices of Pentecostals but also questioned their readiness, specifically working-class Pentecostals, for democracy. While Mason and Jones were wary of the overt protest and social accommodations that the mainstream Black movements were suggesting, Mason did not see that as a call for Pentecostals to fully evacuate the democratic process but rather to engage the democratic process and larger society on their own terms.

For Mason, like other movements at that time, Black respectability had two specific categories embedded in it. First, like the African American women's movements of the nineteenth and twentieth centuries and outlined so powerfully in Higginbotham's classic text and most recently in the work of Black feminist historians like Treva Lindsey and Brittany Cooper, respectability was centered on upward mobility and access to the economic largesse of the post-industrial age[22]. It was about economic inclusion, the erasure of caricatures of Black unfitness, and rewriting African Americans into the larger social project. In many ways this first understanding of Black respectability was squarely lodged on the masses of African Americans moving from the South to industrial centers or moving from rural areas to more urbanized ones. The burden of respectability, therefore, fell on working-class Black folks, many who made up these alternative religious movements, to successfully enter and integrate into a racist and exclusive economic and social system. Secondly, respectability was about fitness to participate in the democratic system. The quest to achieve that fitness was marked again by educational, social, and economic metrics, and the ability to participate took on different roles in the history of the country. During the Revolutionary War period and continuing to the Civil War, Black respectability was often measured by assimilation to Euro-American culture and values as well as fealty to nation-building projects like engagement in wars, public works projects, and participation in civic rituals. However, participation in the most discrete sense was not optional, but rather it was enforced and heavily surveilled while often only offered to a small portion of the population. Proving one's fealty or readiness to fight or vote was the bar that one had to overcome. Therefore, Mason's understanding that citizenship and the respectability associated with citizenship as more than just the right to participate, but it was the right to dissent and still be seen as a central part of the Western project were seen as outside of the norm. Under these definitions, Mason challenges the norms of respectability in two discrete and important realms. First, Mason sees respectability as a mechanism to challenge the range and flexibility of Christianity and Black Christianity.[23] At this point, Black respectability was assessed in a number of ways from the organization of the Black household and marital status, the ability to access education and gain employment, and finally in the assimilation of normative western practices and rituals. Therefore, the controlling of Black religion and expressions of Black religion were key components of Black populations being seen as rationale, modern, and fit for participation in public society. Moreover, the control of and constraints of the Black body, especially in public spaces, were critical nodes in assessing or enforcing Black fitness. Theologian Kelly Brown Douglas has argued that

> inasmuch as the blackness of the black church is predicated upon responding to the need of black bodies, the black church is a body-centered church. The black church at its best is an institutionalized response to the calls of black bodies. For the black church to adopt a narrative that denigrates or diminishes the primacy of the body in any way is to adopt a narrative that is by nature anti-black.[24]

Moreover, this control was not exerted by explicit maneuvers by external communities or institutions, but often religious respectability was enforced by the Black sacred public who sought to remove any trace of African indigenous or "less civilized" worship practices from Black sacred places. As such, there was a call for Black religious spaces to be both anti-African and anti-body, and this meant the removal of emotionalism and embodied worship practices and rituals. The Pentecostal movement was a direct affront to this evacuation of "less civilized" or controlled worship practices. Mason and his movement could be read as body affirming at least for heterosexual men and women within the allowed rituals of the movement.[25] The body, the Black male and female bodies, was central to COGIC's spirit-inflected Pentecostalism, and thus the movement was seen as a troubling site of irrational, retrograde Blackness. We see this body-affirming logic in Mason's sermon "Is It Right for the Saints of God to Dance?":

> Dancing shows that we have victory. Dancing of the people of God is to be in the Spirit of Jesus only, for as in Jesus only can we rejoice and praise God. The people of God do not dance as the world dances, but we are moved by the Spirit of God . . . The children of God dance of God, for God and to the praise and glory of his name.[26]

Mason here is affirming the Black body and its ability to be fully embodied within the constraints of the Black worship service. From dance to the speaking in tongues, Mason informs a logic of affirming the Black working-class body and his or her full participation in sacred spaces. This affirmation of embodied practice is one that challenges some of the surveillance and controlling of Black religious subjects as well as provides an opening for these affirmed bodies to see their value in public and political spaces.

## WOMEN, RESPECTABILITY, AND THE CHALLENGE TO NORMATIVE BLACKNESS

While Mason and COGIC were known for a number of interventions, it was the particular intervention of female leadership and governance that suggested a beta, if not comprehensive, test of the limits and/or possibilities of full participation/inclusive democracy. Different from many other Black churches at that time, the COGIC outlined a comprehensive and radical interpretation of female participation. Anthea Butler's work on women and their role in the COGIC church is essential for understanding their central role in the evolution and development of this denomination.[27] Additionally, I would like to suggest that Mason's critique of failed democracy via COGIC's theological arguments and ritual practices led to a critique of the operation of the Black church and the variety of Black Christian institutions and the role of Black women in these spaces. Furthermore, the prevalence and numerical majority of Black women in these Pentecostal institutions required that COGIC and these movements decipher creative ways to integrate them into the practices and rituals.

Butler argues that women worked in the crevices of the COGIC movement and then innovated parallel, and sometimes hidden, structures to make room for their concerns, to construct their own version of respectability and to resist their tragic alienation from the American project. I suggest, like other Black Christian movements, that the women in the COGIC circulated Mason's language and critique of democracy to argue for a more comprehensive expression of democracy that would include them both inside and outside of the movement. Their circulation of Mason's texts and their use of these texts to critique both the movement and the larger project of democracy points to the elasticity of Mason's work and its use in a variety of venues. This is particularly seen in the ways that the women's auxiliary sometimes functioned as a mirror of the male-dominated COGIC institution, but at other times central to the women's auxiliary was a critique of the exclusivist and materialist practices of the official COGIC apparatus. The female adherents saw themselves as "saints" as much as they understood the other male adherents to be, and thus their practice of sanctification had multiple levels of critique embedded in them. There was a clear suggestion of female equality and thus sanctification did not just make the female adherents simply wives or respectable, but rather it opened the door for their radical participation in the movement as well as the larger society. These women were, therefore, also making claims about democracy and the space for Black women in the Black sacred sphere and the sacrality of the Black female body.

In addition to the women's auxiliary's critique of the male-dominated structure and the absence of true egalitarianism, the women's auxiliary also was intent in transforming and experimenting with the role and function of the Black woman's body, specifically the Black working-class women's bodies. There was a desire to recreate the Black women's body as not just a site of culture or reproduction, but there was the model of restoring all the possibilities of democratic participation to Black working-class women and enabling those bodies to be active participants in democracy. While Mason and his leaders often visibly focused on the male soldier and the rights of African American men to participate in mainstream public life, the women's auxiliary articulated for the radical participation of the whole community, especially Black women. Their focus on respectability therefore was not on exteriority or sartorial appointment as a way to signal Black women's fitness for Christianity but rather exteriority, respectability, and full sacred participation to articulate one's experience as a fit for democratic participation.

## MASON, BLACK CHRISTIANITY, AND ALTERITY

Mason proposes a challenge not just to the Kaiser, democracy, and the war apparatus, but he also proposes a challenge to the reigning Black progressive Christian tradition and that tradition's relationship to Black autonomy and freedom outside of the territorial United States. Mason in his engagement of the war industrial complex is as much talking about the limits of war and the war industrial complex as he is prodding the Black sacred public to revisit its role and relationship to the failure of democracy. Mason's call for a prophetic re-imagining, therefore, is looking for models and alternatives that will help African Americans and Black Christianity rethink their role in shaping public spaces in the United States and beyond. Mason and the COGIC does this in two ways. First, Mason resists a model or models of Christianity that are linked to reinforcing western norms and values. Put more simply, Mason wants to retain the decisively Black and embodied characteristics of the COGIC movement. Secondly, Mason wants to expand the reach and shape of Black Pentecostalism and thus provide a model of religious autonomy and agency to Blacks throughout the diaspora, specifically the Caribbean and Africa. This expansion meant that the reach of the Black sacred public exceeds the territorial boundaries of the United States and leads to new and porous definitions for what constituted Black freedom and participation.[28] Mason's reach is expanded and this increase is not simply from the perspective to gain more followers, but we see Mason actively considering the broader impact of state-sponsored violence and inaccessibility of Black freedom to Black bodies throughout the diaspora. While Mason and COGIC's expansion to the diaspora often included paternalistic and hegemonic ideas about African and Caribbean cultures, it still argued for the autonomy of the Black body and Black religious organizations. Additionally, it provided these "satellite settings" with texts and models within which to rethink their relationship to democracy and civic participation, and it connected them to a network of Black religious institutions that had a relative degree of religious and economic autonomy. While it is clear that Mason was not arguing for a Pan-African movement that elevated African culture and ideals, he was suggesting that the missionizing efforts of his church would provide greater freedom, both bodily and civically, and autonomy to Africans throughout the diaspora. What distinguished Mason's expansion to the Caribbean and Africa from other movements' expansion were the ways that Mason empowered local leaders and churches to be equal participants in the growing global communion of COGIC saints. Therefore, it is not surprising that Mason's critique of the Kaiser can be read as a critique of empire, the nation-state, as well as the larger logics of state-organized violence.[29]

While Mason embraces the radical possibilities of the U.S. nation-state and is creatively articulating for models of a modern nation-state, he was not satisfied with the U.S. nation-state as offering the only model or even the ideal model for Black participation and Black freedom. Therefore, like Divine and Cleage, Mason pushes beyond the boundaries of the U.S. nation-state and even the parochial notions of what constitutes freedom and democracy.[30] Mason and his evocation of a transnational communion of saints, specifically the early inclusion in 1923 of the Caribbean and Africa as part of the COGIC district is the first sign of Mason looking for alternatives to the constraints of the nation-state as well as Black Christianity. Moreover, Mason continues that the dissent from the nation-state was not an evacuation of it, but rather it was a call for a more nuanced account of options and possibilities for Black political legitimacy. In this way, the availability of other transnational or extra-territorial options shaped the possibility of thinking more expansively about options in the United States and abroad.

Thus, when we engage Mason's critique of the Kaiser we also see him gesturing to a critique of empire that calls for communion with Black Christians and Black religious movements domestically and around the world. Mason, in this sense, is a critical part of the expansion of a transnational, diverse Black sacred public. Therefore, it is important to not only recognize the critique of the Kaiser that Mason makes in his 1918 speech, the development of a transnational church that emerges with branches throughout the Caribbean, but also the ways that a particular critique of the war industrial complex becomes a central aspect of the Black sacred canon. Muhammed Ali, formerly known as Cassius Clay, asks the question fifty years after Mason, "what has the Vietcong done to me?" Ali aligns himself with the rejection of certain forms of democracy and empire that enables and foments forms of violent subjugations that had been circulating in the Black public sphere. From Mason's critique of World War I to the critique by Thurman in his *A Way of Life That Is Worth Living* to Malcolm X's "War and the Ballot Box" to King's evocation of the imperium at his final speech in Mason's church, Black religion has been deeply connected and committed to a reimaging of democracy and specifically democracy's relationship to war.[31] We have a confluence in the Black public, and particularly the Black religious public, that is heavily informed by these alternative movements, that Black Christianity and democracy are not consonant with war-mongering and the raging exceptionalism of imperial violence. Ali's Speech and King's Speech at Mason Temple in Memphis, Tennessee, provide compelling evidence. They highlight that African American resistance to the war industrial complex is not just informed by a pedantic read of scriptural texts and it is not just to hold democracy hostage for its implied and real violations of Black political legitimacy, but it is a connection of the African American freedom struggle to the larger transnational freedom struggle.

His critique of empire and the colonial project or at least the colonial project's unwillingness to accept certain forms of Black religiosity are all read as anti-American by the federal government or an impediment to Black progress by mainstream African American Christian traditions. King, Ali, and Malcolm X all directly connect African American suffering to the global suffering of the marginalized and the oppressed and therefore are direct descendants of Mason's critique of not just Black suffering but the relationship between Black suffering and imperial/colonial economic arrangements. Therefore, Mason's question in his 1916 sermon, "What Have the Germans

Done to Me" resonates as a rhetorical tool and canonical turn of phrase to think about the violence endured by Black soldiers as well as the violence impacting the Africana diaspora and other marginal groups in relationship to a growing imperial military complex.[32] It is therefore interesting to note that Mason's expansion to the Caribbean was met with the same type of suspicion and concern as the initial founding of the church. Primarily, many of the Caribbean-colonial governments saw Mason's movement as a threat to their political stability as well as offering the marginalized new options for protest and democratic participation for their most vulnerable citizens. Mason is elevating or at least attending to the sovereignty of the other as a means to introduce a global and transnational politics into the language of this relatively small and regional Pentecostal movement. Mason similarly suggests that by linking African American suffering to suffering around the world that there is a possibility to not only disrupt the problematic imperial logics of the U.S. democracy but also those logics throughout the world.

## MASON AND THE BLACK CHURCH

Mason very early in the development of his movement found himself, his movement, and his scriptural reading practices in conflict with the mainstream Black movements at that time. In an early magazine article on Mason and his movement, Mason is alternately described as a "hoodoo leader" and out of touch with mainstream Black America. Just twenty-five years after the publication of his text, *The Philadelphia Negro*, Du Bois similarly describes Mason and his cohort as backward and behind the times.[33] Mason and the Pentecostals, it was argued by progressive Black movements, risked setting back the Black church and the Black public that was trying to rehabilitate the Black church. Mason, therefore, found himself squarely on the outside of the normative Black church and took it partially as his responsibility to name and negotiate the limits and liabilities of the Black church as he saw them. This becomes especially important as Mason and COGIC highlight the ultimate freedom that a "discarding of the secular" provided Black folks.[34] In this vein, Mason makes a compelling argument about the role of the Black church or the other Black church, and he highlights the opportunities that separatists' movements provide African Americans at that time in history.

First and foremost, Mason is renowned for his preaching and institutionalization of radical egalitarianism in the early stages of the COGIC church. In many ways, this radical egalitarianism in terms of access to leadership and advocacy, but also in terms of access to all types of socially and economically positioned African Americans in the radically changing south, placed Mason in a unique position from the mainstream Black church. Upward mobility and respectability were not the leading values of this movement and therefore integration, access, and the role of capital played a far different role for Mason than it did his peers in the Black Baptists and Methodists movements. Furthermore, the work of Anthea Butler, *Women in the Church of God in Christ*, highlights the nuanced and asymmetrical approach COGIC took toward the growth and encouragement of female leadership and participation and its critical accounting of the upwardly mobile Black middle class and their engagement with consumer goods, participation in liberal economic and political culture, and their acceptance of whiteness and white interpretations as good and standard.[35] It is the voice of Mason's wife at the women's convention in 1927 who clearly articulates a distrust for certain versions of Black Christian malaise:[36]

> Black women must lead their families and their homes and not be consumed by the evils of the stores and who will be dressed the best on Sunday. We are all saints, regardless of how much money or education we might have.[37]

It is clear that she assigns the failure of the Black middle class not only to a failure in their theological and scriptural practices but also their rejection and negation of all Black bodies and the knowledge that some of those unsuspected Black bodies can bring to their acquisition of holiness. This disruption of the mainline ideological, theological, and political argument and arrangement of the Black church placed the COGIC in a unique position to not only create an alternative version of the Black church but to set parameters for thinking about alternative versions of respectability, upward mobility, and ultimately democracy. Mason cements the importance of the Black working class in his vision of an enlivened, sanctified democracy when he outlines his vision of Black America and the larger American polity in light of these beliefs. In a speech given to the second general session of the COGIC in 1936, Mason states that we are "disinherited but not without value."[38] He highlights that these workers and nonelites contribute not only to the city of God but also the secular city. He talks about the role of Christian economic development, leadership inspired by Christian values, and the radical worth of all individuals. "If we can create a thriving movement shaped and led by farmers, sharecroppers, and janitors, then we can lead our cities, states, and this country."[39] Mason delivers a clarion call for the gatekeepers of the Black church, the civil rights leadership, and the larger limits of representative democracy to give a second look to the Black Southern masses and their possible contributions to the larger public. And as Mason makes these points, he addresses the concern about his movement's internal and separatist nature. He provocatively suggests that the "saints" turn inward, not that their solutions or prayers would only impact them, but their inward gaze is to bolster an imagination that is not shaped or tainted by the fear or ignorance of the world.[40] The revolutionary model of COGIC was to imagine models or ideas that would ultimately provide new solutions for the problems of race, class, and the illegibility of the Christian witness to the majority of America's democracy. Mason exclaims, "Our church does not just have a message for us, but there is a message for all that will heed to the Word and His Spirit."[41] Therefore, it is not a surprise that Mason, who did not quote many theologians, spoke persistently about two theological thinkers of the late nineteenth and early twentieth centuries—Howard Thurman and Booker T. Washington in his sermons and writings.[42] Mason's version of the "social gospel" felt that it only worked if the workers and the appointed spreaders of the gospel were not the enlightened rich or white Christians, but if the enlightened were any or every person who had access to sanctification and a public space with which to share his or her teachings. Mason as a radical, untrained prophetic voice put a great degree of his emphasis on what Thurman called the disinherited and what Gramsci would theorize as the organic intellectual. Organic in this case was a leader that had a native relationship to the spirit of God and the plight of marginalized or unseen peoples. Mason's telling of his own narrative and the narrative of COGIC often followed this logic. He was an unlettered leader with a native and "precocious" relationship to the spirit of God and was deeply connected to poor and marginalized Black folks in the American South. Mason's reading of scripture through the lens of his alternative movement became his central argument for the creation and maintenance of spirit-inspired public domain or democracy. While Mason infrequently spoke about explicit democratic institutions and was often suspicious of elected officials and their "clamor for acclaim," in his most noted editorial after the defeat of James Johnson, a Black candidate for the city council in Memphis, he argued that,

> Furthermore, he suggested that there is a role for "inspired" leadership, and that person must not be overly indebted to the politics of integration or segregation but rather the possibility of egalitarian participation.[43]

Therefore, it is not surprising that years later that the dominant Black preachers take explicit pages from Mason and the anti-war movement as King's famous speech on Vietnam at the Riverside Church and his last speech in Mason temple speak to the changing shape of the Black church, its relationship to Christian doctrines, and white nationalist doctrines of manifest destiny. Mason, in the latter stages of his career, is not only integrated into the Black church, but he has shifted the language that the Black church is using to talk about the role of the war industrial complex, the working class, and even the possibilities of American democracy. Mason's call to reimagine the Black church is now at the center of what is the norm of Black religious identity—a deep suspicion of the state and the goal of using deeply Christian workers to transform democracy.

## MASON AND THE POWER OF THE PRESS

Mason utilized the press, including the global press, and the pulpit to make his arguments about the failure of democracy, the problem of war and empire, and the need for religious self-determination and freedom. The Black press was not just a means to circulate key historical data but it was an important, if not essential, node of the Black public and the Black Christian public. Therefore, it is not a surprise that Black presses were essential spaces among the elite, the working class, and the religious adherents to deploy and engage competing constructions of American public life.[44] The COGIC is no different. One of the most compelling archival features of Mason's movement was its focus on recording and rehearsing the production and performance of Black Pentecostal beliefs and conferences, but also the interaction between Black Pentecostal belief and the frame of freedom. Local presses, including denominational presses, and national and transnational writings functioned as the space in which Black subjectivity is contested. Eric Gardner's text *Black Print Unbound* makes this precise point.[45] Periodical culture is the space of Black life and Black determination. This culture is the unmasking of the Black imaginary and the spaces in which Black life, even Black theology and religion, become debated and rearticulated for mass consumption. The fact that Black religious movements placed such a great emphasis on the periodical is precisely because they were trying to impact the everyday and the public sphere. These alternative movements do exactly this in relationship to a critique of mainstream productions of Blackness and Black identity. Mason like other Black religionists at this time uses his denominationally supported periodicals, magazines, Sunday school curriculums, photo albums, and press releases as a means to communicate consistently with its public and to shape particular language about Black existence and Black flourishing. This is not unique to Mason, but it is of great importance for Mason and movements like his, as unlike more mainstream movements, that these periodicals and publications often served as the only texts consistently and carefully read by its followers. From the very beginning of his ministry, Mason used the pamphlets to argue the theological position of COGIC, to highlight their position to the nation-state, and to chronicle the growth and impact of this working-class movement. While the press was a way to circulate ideas and mitigate issues internally, the press was also a mechanism to make their organization and practices visible and legible to a critical Black public. The press and the archives were a means of legitimating the reach, scope, and impact of the movement. Therefore, it functioned to support the claims of the size of the organization and it also proved that this working-class organization had the ability to communicate and engage in the modern world.

Mason was never invested in ignoring the Black public or the larger concerns of mainstream society, but he wanted to do this on his own terms. Mason accomplished this by engaging with the two audiences of the periodicals. That first audience was an internal one that needed information on theological matters, logistical concerns, and the overall state of the movement. Therefore, for this first and primary audience, there were sections that highlighted Mason's sermons and the specific concerns of the women's auxiliaries. Furthermore, the periodicals were actively engaged in publicizing major events, conferences, revivals, and fundraising campaigns that were essential to the ritual and cultural calendar of the movement as well as key sources or revenue for the movement. Mason understood the periodicals and bulletins, provided to churches for free, as a source of free advertising and a means to increase the excitement around events happening within the larger movement. Furthermore, COGIC was one of the first movements to produce an ad-supported bulletin that included paid-for advertisements by local and regional businesses. These advertisements paid for the printing, circulation, and maintenance of the bulletin's operations, but they also functioned to highlight Mason's relationship with the broader Black public. While Mason's movement had been unfairly characterized as theologically and politically insignificant in its early stages, the organization's relationship with local and regional businesses told another story. Mason and the organization were actively involved in supporting the broader Black economy, providing economic and educational opportunities for its members and specifically revitalizing the Black Memphis economy. Mason was thoroughly modern in his construction of a transnational, economically sustainable organization with a variety of press organs, and much of this was to legitimate the organization and its members' place within the Black public sphere.

Furthermore, thefounding of the denomination's seminary in the late 1960, Charles Mason Theological Seminary, in Memphis, Tennessee, was predicated on a model that would increase revenues for the church but also provide a model of respectable upward mobility. The seminary was constructed primarily as a space to educate adherents who were interested in entering the ministry. However, in addition to religious education and supporting the reproduction of church leaders within a controlled environment, the seminary imagined itself as an alternative educational opportunity for the working-class membership as a continuation of Mason's commitment to the denomination and its particular demographic. The seminary admitted students with a varying degree of educational backgrounds, and its alternate path to post-secondary education as well as a mechanism for church and communal leadership were lauded by church adherents as well as the Memphis community. Therefore, the seminary was a key component of providing opportunities for Mason's working-class adherents and competing with the other African American religious movements at the time. As a result, much of the movement was dedicated to repositioning the Black Pentecostals in relationship to the other African American religious movements at that time. The movement's economic sustainability/productivity was significantly increased during this moment as well as the integration of the movement and its members into the mainstream.

## MASON, A. PHILIP RANDOLPH, AND ALTERNATIVE BLACK PUBLICS

Mason's interaction with the Black public was not limited to Black church and his long history with other Black denominations. Mason was also involved with labor organizing and other progressive Black movements as his resistance to the war complex as well as growing influence over a large number of African Americans made him of particular interest to a number of leaders and organizations. These interactions highlight Mason's deep impact on the Black public and the ways that he was deeply imbricated in constructing and theorizing other alternatives for thoughtful models of democracy for African Americans. Mason met with A. Philip Randolph on June 1932 during the height of the great depression and in the middle of a deeply contested conversation in the Black public around Black survival, Black labor, and the role of Black bodies in the securing of democracy and domestic safety in the war encounters. While Randolph was arguing for a large scale, interracial, and transnational movement that brought together the concerns of labor and Black political organizing together, Mason was uniquely and specifically interested in the role of autonomous Black agencies in the growth and development of autonomous economic development. He argued that independent Black churches provided a model for thinking about economic development and for preparing African Americans for roles in the larger economic system. While much of Mason and Randolph's conversation focused on Mason's support for the unionization of Black workers, Mason, in this case, wanted to argue for his understanding of absolute freedom for the democratic citizen and the Christian conscience. He argued to Randolph that while he supported unionization and the integration of formerly all-white unions, he felt that the freedom to participate in a union should be the right of any democratic citizen and that right should be afforded by the African American citizen.

Furthermore, he argued that members of his congregation made their political decisions based on their religious and spiritual conscience and that there should be no democratic rule or racial-cultural imperative that contravened the right of the religious conscience. Mason was clear that the right to participate in the public as an ethno-religious citizen or what he would call a "saint" was critical to his understanding of Black Christianity and Black citizenship.

In addition to meeting with Randolph, Mason spent a great deal of time working with the Memphis Labor Rights Commission. Again, this highlights that Mason's involvement in re-visioning and critiquing democracy did not emerge only through explicit theological language. Rather, Mason's vision for radical forms of democracy emerged in other venues. He was actively involved in the Memphis labor movement, the coalition for economic mobility, and he was the co-convener of the Memphis Business Association. All of these roles highlight or resist any simple model of consigning Mason as exterior to or uninterested in the machinations of democracy. Most importantly, one of his noted speeches or letters was one that took place outside of his role as leader of COGIC and it did not deploy scripture or denominational language in order to make a claim about the importance of democratic participation. In December 1954, seven months after the landmark *Brown v. Board of Education* decision, Mason and the general assembly sent a letter (drafted by Elder James Feltus) to the U.S. Supreme Court commending its decision that "separate education facilities are not inherently equal." Four years later, Mason was once again probed by the FBI and accused of "stirring up racial tensions." Mason's fluidity in the creation of an alternative movement while simultaneously constructing a vision for democracy positions him as an innovator and outlier in the Black religious sphere.

## WAITING FOR A NEW WORLD ORDER

There was no question that Mason and his cohorts were looking to another means for the expression of Black religion and Black freedom. Mason's debates with other religious leaders were often read as critiques of denominationalism or issues around the main theological concerns that were central to the growing understanding of Pentecostalism and Holiness. However, this final section will suggest that at the core of Mason's critique and debate with other Black religious leaders was a concern over the use of scripture to engender Black visibility and representation in American society. Alongside, the groundbreaking work of Anthea Butler, I argue that Mason is suggesting a new way to think about Black presence and participation that was in contrast to the dominant models of Black integration into the mainstream religious and economic centers. Mason's engagement with the A. Philip

Randolph, the NAACP, white Pentecostals, the Black Baptists Alliance, and the African Methodist Episcopalian movement all highlight a particular attention to scripture, the role of women, and the nascent idea of Black cultural and religious autonomy that stood in contrast with the mainline denominational models espoused by the Black Baptists and Methodists. Mason's expulsion from the mainline white Pentecostal revival and his eventual break from other interracial Pentecostalism movements led to the development of what Mason would outline as Black Pentecostalism and autonomy. The suggestion here is that Mason not only diverged with normative (read white) Pentecostal readings of scripture, but he was also a divergent reader of scripture and the modern project of Backness during the middle of the twentieth century. He was invested in creating the conditions for a more diverse and accessible democratic canvas that could make room for new expressions of Black religion.

Mason argued that the goal of Black religion, specifically Pentecostalism, was to provide Black believers the ability and the freedom to speak freely and uniquely about their relationship to the divine and how that relationship to the divine was paramount for the construction of social communities. The idea that Mason was focused on other-worldliness or that the group term applied to the COGIC movement, the Black saints, was a body negating or denying practice misreads Mason's consistent focus on the real Black body, the Black body politic, and the sacred Black body. For Mason, creating spaces for working-class Black men and women to express a variation of spirit-infused, African-inflected religion was an intervention and response to the exclusionary practices of other African American and Euro-American Christian movements and denominations as well as the larger project of democracy. While the Black body was still under internal surveillance and there were restrictions on what the Black body should or should not do within the confines of the COGIC movement, there was never a denial or erasure of the Black body or the experience of Black suffering. In many ways, the COGIC experience allowed a wider variety of Black bodies to participate in their community and the Black sacred sphere. Furthermore, the fullness and the diversity of these bodies were seen as capable and often presented as idealized vessels for sacrality, including Black women. The Black ecstatic body within COGIC was the sacred body that not only had unmediated and direct access to the divine, but this body was validated as being the quintessential expression of Black disruption to both mainstream or broader constructions of the modern. The creation and elevation of the Black sacred body or the "saint" was a means to not only challenge the dominant narrative of Christianity, but it gave those bodies a more pronounced impact on the discourse of democracy, citizenship, and the agency of individuals, especially marginalized individuals. Therefore, the Black public, the larger public, and their response to Mason and his movement are clearly at the center of this analysis. Mason has enlarged what constitutes the Black public with his focus on the working-class Blacks of his movement; he has redefined the nature of Black protest and the importance of religious freedom in this protest; and as a result he created a movement that desired to shift the Black public and alter its relationship to modern democracy.

The new world order that Mason inaugurated was one that offered true religious freedom to African Americans and new religious movements, moved working-class African Americans from the periphery to the center of the Black public, and argued for economic and social solutions that would benefit a diverse range of democratic participants. Mason in this regard upended the traditional intervention of the Black church and offered an alternate and unique response to democracy. His evocation of the sacred nature of the Black working-class body, the role of his conscientious objection, and the flexibility of his sermons and actions throughout the Black public sphere highlight his important role in shaping the nature of protest, specifically African American Christian protest, throughout the twentieth century. His version of democracy and protest are much messier and flexible than what had traditionally been outlined as the path to the full participation of African Americans. Moreover, Mason radically challenged what should or could be the norms of that participation. Mason and his saints were decidedly agnostic as to the benefits of assimilation and if or what that assimilation should look like. Mason called for a broader and dynamic vision for Black participation that imagined space for Black Pentecostals but ultimately demanded that there be free and full expression of Black identity. Furthermore, Mason provided new liturgy and logic for African American religious organizations to move beyond denominationalism, the limits of Black protest as a means for assimilation, and to create new religious spaces and experiences that were open to Black autonomy. Mason makes space for a wide berth of new Black religions where Black identity and the sacred Black body make claims on Black participation as well as the long history of Black religion. Therefore, the movement's relationship to the state, its construction of economic and social centers of development, and ultimately its expansion outside the borders of the continental United States all point to the critical role of its outward facing impulse. Mason, therefore, is outlining in his sermons, speeches, and institutional press organs as much about his movement as he is about the changing shape of the twentieth century. These movements have often been consigned to outside of modernity, but I argue that this movement, like many new religions in the twentieth century, highlight a specific focus on the Black body and their specific attention to Black humanity's relationship to the modern project.

## CONCLUSION

Black Pentecostalism, especially Mason and COGIC, was challenging the shape of twentieth century Black Christianity as much as it was connecting to a larger set of practices that had historically and in that present moment informed the shape of African American religious liturgy.[46] Secondly, with his critique of the war industrial complex and his desire to resist participation in World War I and World War II, Mason argues for a particular reach and shape of normative American participation. Mason is suggesting that respectability is measured by the extent by which one can dissent and still be seen as a part of the group. He continues that the Pentecostalism movement should not only be seen as a vital part of Black Christianity and have access to all the rights and privileges of religious freedom but that the Pentecostalism movement highlighted the depth and range of democracy and offered religious freedom and political dissent to a much larger range of people. The Black Pentecostal movement and specifically Mason's COGIC movement, by making inroads to the Black working class and reconsidering the shape of what was considered the modern, Pentecostals' descriptions of God and religious experience, in fact demonstrate how these religious innovators were not just active participants in religious modernism but in fact on its leading edge. No other religious group would come to define Black religiosity and piety in the modem period as Pentecostals would. Their influence extended beyond cultural expression to more intellectual domains of how Black people thought of themselves, their relations with the larger (white) society, and the divine[47]

The Black Pentecostals were therefore not only religious innovators, but they were innovators of the modern moment and African Americans relationship to that moment. Therefore, it is critical to read Mason's dissent as not simply insider theological language or differentiating between different sects of Black Christianity, but it is important to see Mason as a theorist of democracy and Black bodies' relationship to that democracy. His model of respectability or Black radical participation is then measured by African Americans' ability to resist and participate in the democratic state on their own terms. His model of protest was to prove the elasticity and breadth of the African American public. This is a much more nuanced read of democracy, Black participation, and the means of Black access to freedom and flourishing than what is usually applied to Mason. Most often, the discourse on Mason is his relationship to class and economic or cultural empowerment that his movement afforded adherents. While the economic and social spaces afforded by working-class men and women inside the movement are quite impressive, this focus on respectability as radical democratic participation or the elasticity of Black protest addresses the way that Mason enables different ways for African Americans and institutions to address the problem of imperialism and a failed democracy. Mason is figured here as a public intellectual who is debating the progressive Blacks of that era and particularly a public critic of the failures of democracy who uses the logic of Pentecost and Africana scripture/canon as an explicit response to its failings. The public presentation of Pentecostal scripture is presented as both a critique of certain forms of Black Christianity as well as a critique of the reigning political format that sought to exclude Black bodies as well as their ideas in the public debate. Thus, it is important to recognize alongside Michael Dawson, a political theorist, that Black visions of freedom and resistance were quite broad and these visions came from unexpected places and prophets.[48] More importantly, Mason and his critique outlined the diversity and variety among Black and Black religious visions for freedom during the first half of the twentieth century.

## NOTES

1. Glossalia is traditionally understood as the access to, and the conversing in, a divine language. It is colloquially called the "speaking in tongues" and it was a central component of Pentecostal belief and was a critical aspect of the Pentecostal revivals and practice. Mason's focus on glossalia and it being a sign of faithful belief is what set Mason apart from other Pentecostal movements and what eventually led to his break from the movement that he founded with Jones in 1898. This chapter accepts that their primary disagreement was strictly a theological one, and therefore this chapter will not address the role that their different political orientations or relationship to the Black public played in this break.

2. Mason, "The Notes before the US Foreign Service Committee," 1937. This version of the notes includes not only Mason's statements to, and correspondence with, the committee, but they also include his reflection on this particular moment and how it impacted the growth and development of the COGIC.

3. While Mason was neither a part of a Black radical nor the progressive tradition during the early years of the COGIC movement, he clearly invokes language that is connected to the long history of Black autonomy and agency. Furthermore, unlike Du Bois, the NAACP, and the Communist Party, Mason is looking for a clear religious path for Black freedom and autonomy. I often use the term religious self-determination to not only highlight the right to choose one's relationship and to practice it freely and uninhabited but also to highlight the role of religion in achieving freedom. This quest for autonomy, in itself, functions as a break from many other smaller Black social and religious movements at that time and functions as a critical innovation for Black religion at the beginning of the twentieth century. Mason argues for the possibility of democratic participation as well as full racial and religious autonomy.

4. In addition to being connected to a long history of Christian language being used as a means of protest, Mason also innovates in a number of ways and therefore

creates language for the burgeoning Black religious renaissance of the twentieth century. He, therefore, is a central part of the long Black freedom struggle as well as critical alternative religious movements in the twentieth century that radically reshaped the Black sacred public. See both Singh, *Black Is a Country*; Curtis and Sigler, *The New Black Gods*.

5. The language of menace comes in a newspaper article in the Memphis Plain Dealer. It is interesting that menace is used not only to describe Mason and this nascent movement, but that it was a particularly politically fraught term that was used to underscore Mason's threat not only to religious decorum, but his threat to the political and economic worldview of the South.

6. In 1918, the COGIC had self-reported having over 100,000 members, while the Baptists and Colored Methodists at that time claimed to have over 1 million followers. At this time, the COGIC movement was still considered to be a relatively small and politically insignificant Black religious movement.

7. See W. E. B. Du Bois and Isabel Eaton, *The Philadelphia Negro a Social Study*, Publications of the University of Pennsylvania Series in Political Economy and Public Law (Philadelphia, PA and Boston, MA: Published for the University and Ginn Distributor, 1899), microform. This text is critical for the ways that it not only places the burden of failed assimilation of African Americans into twentieth century democratic society on Black religion as well as white supremacy. Du Bois is unflinching in his concern with and the need to totally revamp certain aspects of the Black church, particularly what he calls "unlettered, holy rollers."

8. Todd Steven Burroughs, *Warrior Princess: A People's Biography of Ida B. Wells* (Brooklyn, NY: Diasporic Africa Press, 2017).

9. The shape and form of Mason's testimony is echoed in the language of Muhammad Ali and Malcolm X's rejection of the war industrial complex and their unwillingness to serve in the armed forces. It is important to note that Malcolm X's father Rev. Little was an early conscientious objector and a preacher in a Pentecostal church. This reminds us that this practice of resisting the selective service or drafting of Black soldiers predates Mason and his movement. Moreover, this argument suggests that Mason is not the first, but that his deployment of Black canonical texts in a public manner heavily impacted and shaped the continuing negotiation and use of conscientious objection throughout the twentieth century.

10. The FBI Files on Charles Mason, 1917 Interviews and Investigations.

11. Acts 4:5–12, NRSV.

12. See Frederick Douglass in *The Narrative Life of Frederick Douglass, an American Slave* (1845) as well as *My Bondage and My Freedom* (1855). Also see David's Walker use of this scripture in his *Appeal to the Colored Citizens of the United States* (1848). Both Walker and Douglass argue that central to democracy is an internal and shared language that is protected and held among the most faithful adherents of the group, and they connect this shared identity and practice to a central conceit of the early church and the larger Christian community. The failure to attend to the community is deep abrogation of not only one's personal responsibility but the larger community's moral code. Glossolalia, as Mason and the COGIC see it, is a heightened moment of this shared language and moral responsibility, and he argues

that the twentieth century's call for global democracy and freedom is likewise a heightened moment for the United States to live up to its moral claims.

13. "Fanatical Worship of Negros Going on in the Holiness Church," *Commercial Appeal*, 1907.

14. Testimony of George Bacon in Mason's FBI File (1917).

15. Mason's FBI File (1917).

16. Religious self-determination is the right to religious freedom and the ability for the religious freedom to be the hallmark of one's relationship not just to the state but the larger democratic project. Mason becomes the hallmark for leading with religious self-determination, which was a right available to U.S. citizens and one that was subsequently used and riffed on by other "black gods" in urban centers. We particularly see this focus in the Nation of Islam and Father Divine's movements.

17. From the section on "Political Government" in the 1895 General Assembly Meeting of the Pentecostal Assemblies, 1895 (Church of God in Christ Archives, Memphis, TN).

18. Grant Wacker, *Heaven Below: Early Pentecostals and American Culture* (Cambridge, MA: Harvard University Press, 2001).

19. Calvin White, *The Rise to Respectability: Race, Religion, and the Church of God in Christ* (Fayetteville, NC: University of Arkansas Press, 2012).

20. From the section on "Political Government" in the 1895 General Assembly Meeting of the Pentecostal Assemblies, 1895 (Church of God in Christ Archives, Memphis, TN).

21. The idea of "righteous resistance" was not unique or new to Mason. As I mentioned earlier, this language is also found in David Walker, Frederick Douglas, Anna Julia Cooper, as well as Ida B. Wells. Their formulations of righteous resistance often did not make as clear and absolute break from the normative concerns of democracy. Mason, on the other hand, says that his resistance should allow him to dissent regardless of the options or considerations afforded by African Americans. Even in the midst of absolute equality and the fair treatment of Black citizens and Black soldiers, Mason is arguing that he and his followers should have the right to dissent. Mason, in this regard, is using language similar to the Garvey movement which sees itself as offering African American citizens' alternate options while they negotiate the limitations of democracy.

22. See Higginbotham, *Righteous Discontent*. Additionally, Treva B. Lindsey, *Colored No More: Reinventing Black Womanhood in Washington, D.C.*, 2nd edition, Women, Gender, and Sexuality in American History (Champaign, IL: University of Illinois Press, 2017); Anthea D. Butler, *Women in the Church of God in Christ: Making a Sanctified World* (Chapel Hill, NC: University of North Carolina Press, 2007); Melissa V. Harris-Perry, *Sister Citizen: Shame, Stereotypes, and Black Women in America* (New Haven, CT: Yale University Press, 2011); Brittney C. Cooper, *Beyond Respectability: The Intellectual Thought of Race Women*, Women, Gender, and Sexuality in American History (Champaign, IL: University of Illinois Press, 2017).

23. Black Respectability has often focused on the ways that certain constructs of gender and class impacted Black women and their role in the public sphere. Higginbotham, Lindsey, and Perry all highlight this in their work. Higginbotham

is noteworthy because of her focus on women and religious institutions. Her work alongside Butler shape my understanding of respectability as not just a means for integration or assimilation into a dominant worldview, but rather respectability as a means or a model for revolt, insurrection, and alternative models of formation.

24. Douglas, *Black Bodies and the Black Church*. Nevertheless, Douglas argues that this body negation or erasure was central to the mainstream African American churches in the eighteenth and nineteenth centuries.

25. See Clarence E. Hardy III, "'No Mystery God': Black Religions of the Flesh in Pre-War Urban America," *Church History* 77, no. 1 (2008). Also see Ashon T. Crawley, *Blackpentecostal Breath: The Aesthetics of Possibility*, 1st edition, Commonalities (New York, NY: Fordham University Press, 2017).

26. Mason, "Is It Right for the Saints of God to Dance," *The Truth*, 1927.

27. Butler, *Women in the Church of God in Christ*. This is a groundbreaking historical text that provides a cogent and expansive account of Black women's participation. Butler suggests that their participation, agency, and efficacy is linked primarily to the unique and less surveilled homogenous spaces that women occupied. I agree that much of the women operated in separate and autonomous spaces and it could be assumed that Mason spoke as much for them as he did not. However, Butler also argues, less explicitly, that it was not just the spaces but the imaginative work that women did with Mason, his use of the scripture, and the larger tradition's theological category to make room for themselves and their issues.

28. Mason is not unique here as there has been a great deal of work on African American religious movements and their mission activities in the direction of the diaspora and Black Atlantic. Again, what makes Mason and COGIC unique is that this movement is one that clearly identifies the Black body as unique and precious in relation to religion and democracy. While Mason and COGIC often bought into paternalistic accounts of African and Caribbean culture and religion, the missionaries brought their embodied and "body-affirming" practices to the Caribbean. Additionally, in light of Mason's call to rethink protest and respectability, the COGIC brought its critique of Western imperialism, acquisitive capitalism, and the war machine to these places. Therefore, alongside their introduction of Christianity and this new religious movement, COGIC provided language for Black autonomy and a critique of certain forms of colonialism.

29. Again, this critique of empire and the larger question of a transnational critique have been a deep and distinct part of the African American public. We see this in the African American and the global response to the Haitian Revolution as well as the varied and complicated responses to African recolonization projects. Nwankwo identifies this as an emerging "black cosmopolitanism" and while many have read Mason and his movement as insular and nativist, this section attempts to highlight his cosmopolitan and world-making practices. See Ifeoma Kiddoe Nwankwo, *Black Cosmopolitanism: Racial Consciousness and Transnational Identity in the Nineteenth-Century Americas*, Rethinking the Americas (Philadelphia, PA: University of Pennsylvania Press, 2005).

30. Father Divine espouses a concern with spaces that exceed the United States throughout his career as he travels throughout the Caribbean to expand the reach of his movement. Specifically, his rejection of both normative racial identifiers leads

Divine to look to other movements outside of the United States. Cleage, on the other hand, is clearly a part of a transnational pan-African movement that is looking to expand African Americans' understanding of the sacred beyond the United States as well as traditional Euro-American theological categories.

31. See Howard Thurman, Walter E. Fluker, and Catherine Tumber, *A Strange Freedom: The Best of Howard Thurman on Religious Experience and Public Life* (Boston, MA: Beacon Press, 1998).

32. Mason, "COGIC and the War," 1916 reprinted in *The Whole Truth*.

33. Ibid.

34. This discarding of the secular has often been read as Mason's rejection of modernity, but I argue that it signifies a particular version of secularity and modernity. Mason's version of modernity has always been an enchanted one that was not shaped or constrained by emerging theories of the secular.

35. See Butler, *Women in the Church of God in Christ*.

36. Ibid.; Bruce Ellis Benson and Peter Heltzel, *Evangelicals and Empire: Christian Alternatives to the Political Status Quo* (Grand Rapids, MI: Brazos Press, 2008).

37. EW Mason, COGIC Women's Convention Bulletin of 1927.

38. Mason, COGIC 2nd General Session Program, 1936.

39. Ibid.

40. Mason, *The Power of the Church*, 1931.

41. Mason, *The Spirit of the Work*, The COGIC Guidebook, 1929.

42. Thurman, *Jesus and the Disinherited*, 1941.

43. *Memphis Appeal*, "James Johnson Defeated," 1946.

44. Eric Gardner, *Black Print Unbound: The Christian Recorder, African American Literature, and Periodical Culture* (Oxford: Oxford University Press, 2015).

45. Ibid., 125.

46. The pastiche of religious practices and rituals was not unique to African American religious systems, as the question of religious practices was also being circulated throughout white evangelicalism and the second great awakening. While many of the embodied and emotional practices that made up African Pentecostalism were prevalent in a number of Euro-American Christian groups, the burden of respectability weighed much more heavily on African Americans and their desire to achieve full access to the rights and privileges of democracy. Therefore, the notion that African American religion, specifically African American Christianity, included aspects of African indigenous and other forms of embodied practices further disqualified African Americans from full and equal citizenship.

47. Hardy, "'No Mystery God'."

48. Dawson, *Black Visions*.

*Chapter 3*

# Deracinated Democracy and the Black Divine

## INTRODUCTION

In 1931, George Baker, known as Father Divine by his adherents, is called before a sitting judge in Sayville, New York, in order to provide the validity of his identity and to address a number of housing and zoning restrictions. It is clear by the language of newspapers and popular accounts that the judge as a state actor has a vested interest in the disciplining and controlling of both Divine, his movement, and their unwillingness to acquiesce to state maintenance and surveillance. In the local and state-wide newspapers, he is called "charlatan" and "rabble rouser," and a local supplement to the *New York Times* even uses another local African American religious leader to defame Divine and his followers. While the outcome of the case ultimately works out in the favor of Divine after the judge unexpectedly and "prophetically" dies during the court case, this example is just one of the many ways that the state and resistance to the state and state surveillance were a central part of this alternative Christian movement. It is therefore important to note that Divine and the early twentieth century Africana prophets were not simply perceived as a threat to Christianity or African American public space, but they were seen and engaged as threats to the political order of settler-based democracy. As a result, their movements within their local communities, their conversations with nationalists inside and outside of the state, and the thrust for economic autonomy were all heavily surveyed and adjudicated in the court of public opinion and in actual court rooms. As this chapter will argue, Divine and his movement had to negotiate the murky waters of nationalist movements and the call for racial unity as well as the constant surveillance by the state as the movement attempted to create economic, political, and cultural alternatives for their adherents. Furthermore, I will argue that Divine and the prophets and their nascent organizations are profoundly engaged in the process of constructing a counter-modernity that is simultaneously critical of nationalist/proto-nationalist movements like Garvey but wary of democratic citizenship as the ultimate goal of modern life. Furthermore, this chapter will argue that they belong in the category of Black theology and theological theorizing because they suggest that a certain form of God talk is critical to the development of Black citizens' relationship to the state and the creation of alternatives to mainstream Christian and democratic participation. Divine as a provocateur of modernity and astute user of scriptural texts helps to reframe Blackness and Black participation in the creation of sacred modalities and their relationship to the nation-state during the first half of the twentieth century. Most importantly, they highlighted new ways for Africana bodies, particularly Africana Christian bodies, to participate in the modern public sphere.[1]

## FATHER DIVINE AND ALTERNATIVE BLACK CHRISTIANITY

The critical texts on Father Divine have well documented his stories of origination and the implications of a number of different theological streams that impacted the development of the Peace Movement in the 1920s and the 1930s.[2] It is clear that Father Divine, born in 1876 as George A. Baker, Jr., incorporated Pentecostal, Methodist, and New Thought teachings and practices into the Peace Movement. The Peace Movement was most widely known as a positive thought movement that eschewed traditional racial categories, prohibited sex among its participants, and created community houses, or Peace Houses, throughout the United States that provided shelter, food, and ritual to those that either wanted or needed to exist in the traditional mainstream modern discourse of that age. The movement started in 1923 by George Baker and a small multiracial group of adherents has been described alternately as a deviant and troublemaker in critical texts like *Black Gods of the Metropolis* and Horshor's *God in a Rolls Royce* and as part of a broader discourse on the rise of new religions during the rise of the industrial age.[3] Theorists of religion have argued that this prophet fits into the logic of the New Thought movements and the new religions that were coming to the fore in a number of marginalized groups in the nineteenth and twentieth centuries. This chapter, however, will look at Divine and his Peace Movement as the result of larger dissatisfaction with the narrow notions of Black nationalism and American citizenship, and using the language of divinity, race, and class to participate in a larger Black public sphere and to challenge the shape of that public sphere that seemed to be dependent on the construction of narrow racial essentialism which Divine and his follows often challenged.

## REARTICULATING THE BLACK CHRISTIAN PUBLIC

Father Divine has primarily been rendered and remembered as a Black Prophet or Black "God," but those notions of Father Divine tend to underplay his role as not just a critique of race and racialism but as a critique of the modern moment. Father Divine and his movement were actively engaged in national and transnational debates on the role and impact of race, citizenship, and Christianity on Black peoples. Race and its problematic role in denying "raced" people the option or opportunity to participate in the public sphere is a central concern of the movement. Divine and his movement were asking, how can Black people (and consequently all people) fully participate in the benefits of the modern world. The colonialist or imperialist construction of race and the scriptural projects that justify racial oppression had to be explicitly and immediately addressed. Therefore, it is no surprise that the Peace Movement's foundational document highlights that, "Thoughts are things! If we dwell upon them we will become to be partakers of them, automatically. Therefore, we hardly use the word that is commonly known as race, creed, or color among us."[4] Divine and his movement identify race and racial essentialism as an untenable burden for the deployment and flourishing of American democracy. Now, Divine is not new in this concern, but his movement's response to these concerns talks about a third way that is neither nationalism nor acceptance of the dominant regime but that is characteristic of alternative Christian movements of the twentieth century.

In addition to outlining the role and goal of creating alternate space within the United States to engage and create an alternative modern project, it is also clear that Father Divine is doing two other things that are of great importance for this analysis. On one side, Divine is clearly challenging the logic of orthodox Christianity and more importantly the logic, ritual, and scriptural cues of Black protestant Christianity in the United States. On the other side, Divine is engaged in a larger debate on what constitutes an acceptable engagement and shaping of the Black public. In particular, Divine's engagement with other Black gods in the Black diaspora articulates ways not only to shape the construction of race and diaspora but also ways in which to construct new modalities of Christianity. Therefore, this section will focus on Divine's and the Peace Movement's engagement with Marcus Garvey and the UNIA as an example of the variety and the competition with Black publics, and it will also highlight Divine's engagement with other alternative Christian movements, specifically Black-led Christian movements, as a way to highlight how

Divine and his movement see scripturalizing or the creation of sacred texts and the divine as a space within which to rearticulate the modern moment.

In many ways, Father Divine and the Peace Movement emerge as a response to the deradicalization of the Black church that was happening at the beginning of the twentieth century.[5] The Black church movement in many instances, especially under the auspices of orthodox denominations like Methodists, Episcopalians, and Baptists, had adopted the logic of the modern moment accepting a second-class status for African American subjects and attempting to participate in the burgeoning capitalist marketplace. The goal of the Black church and the primary public that it heavily influenced was to achieve a level of middle-class respectability in the midst of the tumultuous age between and during the world wars. Thus folks like Divine, Daddy Grace, and Wallace Fard of the Nation of Islam emerge not simply as a response to the Black masses, but they emerge as a constitutive piece in the reshaping of the Black public sphere, specifically the Black Christian public sphere. In the earliest days of his ministry, Divine constituted his ministry as a response to the destitution of Negro migrants in the Southern United States. Much of his focus was a rejection of the racial hierarchy of the American project, particularly the American South, and to provide through his fusion of New Thought, Black Protestantism, and Pentecostalism a vision of social, economic, and political progress for the Black underclass.[6]

> God's second appearance on earth was in a form of Jew and that now he comes in the form of a Negro. He told them that he was going to bring the world to an end before long and that those who do not believe on him will be lost.[7]

## FATHER DIVINE AND ALTERNATIVE BLACK PUBLICS

Along with a number of other Black religions and cults developing during the early twentieth century, Divine and his movement were involved in the reconstruction of mainstream Christianity and particularly its relationship to African Americans newly migrated from the South. The evolution of a number of Christian projects that relied on the Christian scripture, but ultimately engaged in a reframing or re-imagining of the Christian witness, dotted the urban landscape. From the Hebrew Israelites to the Temple of the Gospel of the Kingdom to the evolving holiness and Pentecostal movements, the evolving shape of Black religion, specifically Black Christianity, was a part of a larger discourse on what shaped the Black religious diaspora and who had the power to determine the boundaries of that Christian discourse.[8] While the Hebrew Israelites were arguing for a Afro-Jewish diaspora and the Nation of Islam, and the Moorish Science Temple argued for Afro-Islamic diaspora, and others like Garvey and Blyden argued for the creation for cultural diasporas, Father Divine was in many ways creating a distinctively Afro-American religious diaspora that was focused on articulating a mechanism for Black Americans and other groups to be stitched into the fabric of the American story. Divine in his opening love feast at his Sayville campus articulates the distinctively American narrative of his movement when he articulates why the term "Negro" was used:

> For the specific purpose of bringing about a division among the people, to belittle and lowrate those that were of a darker complexion, by calling them not African by nature, neither an Ethiopian, neither an EGYPTIAN, but by calling them something that they never were.[9]

Furthermore, not only Divine does identify the Peace Movement as an articulation of the American narrative of upward mobility and exceptionality made possible through positive thought and correct relationship with the divine, but he suggests that it is done not through evocation of Black exceptionalism but through a critique of the state and its reliance on superficial class and racial distinctions.[10] Thus, Father Divine and his doctrine of integration and nonraciality function as a critique of the reigning discourse of Black exceptionalism or separatism. He explicitly rejects Black nationalist projects as well as other Black Christian movements that refer to and rely on the evocation of racial identifiers. However, this rejection of racial identifiers and his critique of the traditional Black church did not suggest that Divine and his followers were uninterested in the racial discourse of that age. More explicitly Divine and his movement sees their critique of Black exceptionalism, traditional Black Christian modalities, and especially Garveyite movements as congruent with a critique of white supremacy and the reigning racial apartheid facing Black subjects in the United States. It is in this way that Divine and the Peace Movement are expanding the dialogue on modernity while extending their understanding of normative Christianity.

In creating an alternative public space that was open for all bodies, his theological focus was on human anthropology. He focused on the body and the beauty of all the bodies involved in the movements, specifically the Black bodies. This elevation of the body and the permanence of the body sought to stand in contrast with the ways in which Black bodies were often considered impermanent, ugly, and often expendable. R. Marie Griffith is correct in her argument that Divine desired to reimagine the body and center the body as a part of his religious vision.[11] Therefore, it is clear that his version of new thought-inflected Christianity serves not only as a reflection on the role of Black bodies in the public discourse, where again he supports the idea that Black bodies are not exceptional but that they are radically equal. Equal, to the degree, which the reincarnation of the divine would come in the form of the corpulent Black body of Father Divine. Furthermore, in this instance Divine is engaged in creating a Christian discourse that not only re-imagines Blackness but also engages the question of the modern moment. He suggested to his followers:

> I am a free gift to mankind. Of the plenty abundance which I have I give to you freely. I ask of you only faith. I take from you nothing. I take your sorrows and give joy. I take your sickness and give health. I take your poverty and give you peace and prosperity, for I am the spirit of success and health.[12]

His alternative Christianity in this regard is not just the evocation of a latter-day prophetic figure, but it also serves to critique the very conditions of the modern moment that imperil all bodies and specifically Black bodies. It is noted time and again that his new thought trajectories do not simply suggest personal or individual uplift, but in line with the logic of the traditional Black church model, he suggested that his presence and this construction of Black identity functioned to correct the Black public as an equal and important part of the American public.

This critique of modernity and therefore modern Christianity took place in three discrete ways. In the most immediate way, the Peace Movement was a critique and re-evaluation of the racist character of the modern moment. Divine argued that the failure of the modern moment was a failure to politically, socially, and religiously eradicate racial bias from modern discourse. The evocation of racial categories, the continued acceptance of racial hierarchies, and the persistence of racial segregation had led to spiritual, corporeal, and political disease. His movement forbade the use of racial categorizations, argued for the removal of racial hierarchies in social interaction, and actively recruited and developed a multiracial religious community. According to Lincoln and Mamiya, Divine's movement stood as one of the few religious movements that explicitly called for a multiracial community and the importance of this multiracial interaction for the ultimate health and salvation of the community.[13]

In addition to his critique of the racial categories of this age, Divine was also known for his explicit critique of capitalism. While his relationship to capital and capitalism changed over the course of his life, Divine, ultimately, was critical of any form of capital that created conditions of suffering and oppression. While Divine's critique of the New Deal might be read as ultimately calling for capitalist markets to remedy the problem of the Depression era, Divine was suggesting that the conditions that created and maintained the oppression and suffering that came alongside that depression could not be remedied by government handouts but by a re-appropriation of the wealth in society. While many theorists have focused on the communal nature of Divine's movement and the renunciation of individual wealth, it is important to note that Divine and his movement was critically involved in creating business cooperatives in the burgeoning space of emerging black cities, specifically Harlem.[14] The chain of laundromats run by the female adherents of his movement were seen not as a rejection of capital or the modern moment, but a reorganization of the modern and especially the role of women and Black women in the modern moment.

Finally, Divine's critique of the modern project was also a critique of the colonizing impulse of the United States both internally and externally. While Divine existed in the midst of both Black nationalist and back-to-Africa movements, Divine sought to reorganize the modern public sphere by calling for a radical rearticulation of power. While Divine argued that separatist and nationalist modality inevitably doomed Black bodies to sickness and failure, he ultimately rejected a colonizing impulse that would deprive the modern world access to variety and diversity in terms of cultural, political, and religious options. While Divine rejected race and racial language, he did not reject the burgeoning Black culture that was emerging during the Harlem Renaissance or the larger Black culture that shaped him during his time with the Black church. The love feasts and the privileging of what has traditionally been called soul food, the call and response testimonies that were the central ritualistic feature of his love feasts, and ultimately the creation and integration of music that organized his worship space. Visitors to the love feasts and to Divine's sermons often noted the import of the songs and the merging of politics and the divine in the construction of these musical narratives.[15] As Divine gained more and more access to the Black Christian public, it was often his rearticulation of soul food and soul music in the form of cosmopolitan spiritualities that often highlighted Divine's special attention to the bodies, needs, and desires of his primarily Black female adherents. Father Divine was often noted and reported as saying that "I did not come to save the soul . . . but I came to save the bodies of children of men," and it is clear that this was a critical part of his affirmation of the particular bodies in his movement and critique of Black Christian public that failed in this regard.[16]

## DIVINE AND THE BLACK INTERNATIONAL PUBLIC

In addition to creating a counter-Christian public, Divine was also involved in the creation of counter-public as it related to Black identity and especially Black exceptionalism. Divine primarily known as an anti-racialist did not just create this in conversation with other religious worldviews, but in contrast with the language of Black exceptionalism that was a part of the Black public sphere. While Divine and the other "Black Gods" have been virtually ignored by diaspora studies and only tangentially engaged by Africana Studies, Divine was a crucial part of the renaissance of Blackness at the rise of the twentieth century. While the discourse on production of Blackness has paid attention to economic, material, and religious factors, scholars of African American studies and scholars of Africana studies have ignored the import of these alternative Christian figures more broadly. However, when we return to the contested space of Blackness and racial representation of the twentieth century, the Black gods are not just present but vitally important. Especially important is the figure of Divine. Divine is mentioned again and again on both local and international settings. Throughout the pages of local newspapers, Divine comes into conflicts with local communities and preachers, and throughout larger national and internal organs Divine is debated within the context of Black nationalist and internationalist discourse.[17] It is particularly noteworthy to highlight that Divine appears in a variety of texts associated with the Harlem Renaissance from writers as diverse as Hurston, Claude McKay, and James Van Der Zee.[18] The famed Renaissance writer Dorothy West following other Harlem renaissance writers' fascination with prophetic religious figures included interludes on Divine in "The Living Is Easy." In that text Divine and Daddy Grace are alternately described as a "savior" and a "charlatan." West exclaims that, "he saved Black Americans at the expense of their reputation."[19] She highlights the complicated ways that Divine was both engaged as a totemic figure that highlights a nativist approach to these Black gods but also as a political actor who changed and impacted local and national protections of Black bodies and interests.

Not only was Divine clearly part of a growing public sphere that was engaging the creation of alternative religious and Christian modalities, but Divine was also a part of Black public sphere that was engaging the concept of race, Black exceptionalism, and the role of Blacks in the larger political and public struggle. While a number of theorists have addressed the ways in which the urban cults competed with one another for the needs and interests of primarily Black congregants in urban cities, it is important to note the ways in which Divine was constructing an alternative version of Black political participation through his use and deployment of race and the role of his nonracial movement in the political process.

Particularly noteworthy is the exchange between Marcus Garvey and Father Divine in the 1920s as they both attempted to shape the Black public sphere and the role of race and specifically racial language within that sphere. Divine was known for his refutations of race and the use of racial language in his movement. In many of his speeches he spoke of the crutch of racial language and racial ideology among Black Americans. He was known for starting his speeches with the following admonition to his followers and the larger public, "That out of one blood God created all the nations to dwell upon the earth. He came to bring them all together in One".

While Divine clearly rejected the mantle of race, he was surrounded by Black nationalist movements like the Nation of Islam, the United Negro Improvement Association (UNIA), and even the National Association for the Advancement of Colored Peoples (NAACP) that were elevating and outlining the import of race as not only a political concept but for the Nation of Islam as a theological framing and for the UNIA as transnational envisioning of Back-to-Africa Utopia. Furthermore, the discourse on Black exceptionalism and racial identity was shaping literary discourses, the rise of Black popular music, and the emergence of internal discourses on Pan-African (ethnic and racial) identities. Divine stood in stark contrast with the dominant narrative of the early twentieth century Black public as he rejected the politics of racial language and argued that it was preventing Blacks and other believers in shaping a useful and meaningful alternative religio-political project. In the *Black Man*, Garvey argued that the theological argument of Divine was suspect:

> There is no god but One Almighty Being of Heaven, wherever Heaven is. He is the Creator of the universe. Man is but a small part of his creation, and Father Divine is but man. He is physical flesh and blood and of spirit just like another human being and if it is true that he assumes the role of God, then he must be mad or a wicked contriver of deception.[20]

Alongside questioning Divine's divinity, he also questioned the racial ideology that stood at the center of Divine's alternative to the modern world. While Garvey had constructed a proto-nationalist plan dependent on the ideas of Black exceptionalism, specifically the maintenance and propagation of Black people, Divine was articulating a vision of the modern world that exterminated the concept of race, pushed for a radical vision of integration, and ultimately suggested that race difference would be erased. Garvey saw Divine's worldview "constitute[d] a gross attempt at race suicide, leading to the complete extermination of the Negro race." Divine's nonracial Utopia was premised on the positive thinking of all individuals that was not dependent on or impacted by what he considered the negative logic and optics of race. He argued in many of his sermons and the journalist organs of the movement that "there is no so-called blood of some special race. Blood is blood, Spirit is Spirit, Mind is Mind!"[21] He further continued that using racial and ethnic language carried with it "the germs of segregation and discrimination."[22]

He believed that this raceless, genderless world would offer Blacks and particularly Black women new ways to participate in the modern world. Thus, while many theorists have focused on Divine's seeming evasion of race, what is most noteworthy is his suggestion that the removal of race and gender is what would allow for Blacks to be seen and treated as human beings. Thus Divine inaugurates a way to enter into the transnational discourse that both supplants the language of race but still provides for the visibility and presence of Black bodies, specifically Black women. It is therefore important to highlight that during the height of Divine's movement that his evacuation of race did not function as simply a symbolic or rhetorical gesture, but it has been argued that it was Divine's way of bringing together discourses on a multiracial view of Marxist thought and a means by which to participate in the political process.

During the height of his movement, Divine was not only involved in creating an alternative Christian public, but he was imagining new ways for Christians and Black Christians to participate in the democratic process. In response to the New Deal and the failure of this government intervention to respond to the bodies and concerns of those central to his movement, Divine organized a set of speeches, songs, and practices around the idea of the call for Righteous Government. This call for Righteous Government that became a central point of the Peace Movement in the late 1930s was most forcefully a critique of injustice, suffering, and the horrors of capital that allowed for Divine to center the experience of his followers, most Black women, as not a "ghettoized" rallying cry but ultimately suggested that they spoke for the universal concerns of the working poor. In this way, Divine is challenging the notion that construction of a marginal or isolated cultural movement or ideology was needed to put the concerns of poor people and especially Black folks at the center of his analysis. Ultimately his tactics are central to creating a Black public that sees the possibility of remaking the modern moment within the shape of a multiracial space.

By the end of the 1930s, the debate between Garvey and Divine has begun to wane as a result of the growing irrelevance and marginalization of the Garveyite movement as a result of Garvey's deportation from the United States. However, at this point Divine has not only reshaped the construction of Black Christianities with his model of re-imagining the limits and possibilities of the Christian worldview, but Divine is also heavily involved in the international space. In 1936, he is actively involved in creating and lobbying for an anti-lynching bill that again highlights his focus on his bodily needs and has taken a more active role in local and national elections.

This attention to the attacks on Black bodies was critical in the ways that even though Divine divested from the logic and language of race, central to his movement was the creation of a model and organization that protected the interest of the most vulnerable. It is therefore not surprising that his Righteous Government agenda was interested in finding candidates who were either committed to Divine or willing to support his movement's platform. One other article of faith in the movement's platform was Divine's interest and focus on an anti-lynching bill. This attention to a Black flesh was emblematic of a movement that suggested that its central concern was not Blackness in a simplistic or limiting sense. Divine wanted to create the conditions under which surveilled and constrained Black bodies could be free without using the language of race.

## DIVINE AND THE WORKING-CLASS SCRIPTURE

While Divine was actively involved in the transnational sphere and was critical of other prophetic figures and alternative Christian movements at that time, Divine was also deeply engaged in constructing devotional and religious materials as well as opportunities for its working-class adherents, both men and women. The devotional materials as well as Divine's commitment to certain aspects of communist ideology are important to engage as they show Divine's particular attention to a subsection of the Black public, the Black working-class, and their relationship to the politics of race and respectability. Most specifically, Divine outlines in the devotional material an attention to marginalized working class bodies, their real and felt sufferings, and provides a model or set of texts to connect them to new models of economic autonomy and development. In this section, I will particularly look at the ways that these devotional materials circulated and were particularly purchased for new and working class adherents; how the devotional materials intended to differentiate between African Americans in this movement and the more traditional Black church movements, and how the model of economic communalism was connected to a new politics of belonging and resistance that was distinct from the civil rights and Black nationalists' focus on racism and racial identity.

The hallmark of many of these movements and the Black church in general was their overall accessibility to the Black public. While many of the African American migrants to these new churches in newly urbanized areas or in the American north were impacted by a clear code of respectability, Divine and others were invested in a radical openness to the widest variety of participants. This access included removing restrictions on dress, decreasing the dependence on consistent giving, and also not requiring or enforcing a high degree of social mobility. Divine's commitment to class equality and accessibility was most clearly evidenced in his protection and validation of working-class bodies in sermons and public engagement and in the written devotional material created for these groups. The devotional materials along with the recorded and taped materials of Divine's sermons were the most easily accessible aspects of the Peace Movement's community. These devotional materials functioned as a type of scripture for Divine and the most ardent participants. The devotions were intended to be read or listened to daily and they were constructed so that even the most basic or rudimentary reader could engage and respond to them. The devotional materials were circulated among the core participants as way to introduce the sacrality and theology around Divine, to coordinate particular understandings of ideological and political concerns, and to illustrate the movement's relationship with the traditional Black church and other new religious movements at that time. While the devotionals functioned to educate and create community, they also operated as one of the central means to attract new members to the Peace Movement.

Of particular note is the way that the devotional material was primarily created for the adherents of the Peace Movement, but they were also circulated to the larger Black public and were distributed by a number of other organizations. These materials were also noteworthy in the ways that they were gendered and politicized, in that they responded to the critical issues of the day. First, it is noteworthy to explore how the devotional materials were divided between the male and female adherents of the movement. The materials not only responded to the questions and concerns of the bodily comportment, but they also outlined the ways in which Black male and female bodies should understand the import of Divine's body to their own. In particular, the devotional materials highlighted the ways that the theology around Divine's sacrality was deeply connected to the movement's understanding of the adherents' bodies. The devotional materials, therefore, focused on three items: celebrating the body and all of its varieties; the relationship between Divine's sacrality and participation in the democratic system, and the hope for a new world.

While the devotionals were constructed with the working class, new migrants to the urban North, in mind, the relationship between the movement and the communist party was also in response to Divine's politics as well as being responsive to the needs of these adherents. Divine was explicit that aggressive capitalism and crony democratic politics were not meeting the needs of this demographic, and therefore the devotionals not only attended to the theology of the movement and created accessible language for the dissemination of Divine's belief to the broader public, but it also began to incorporate language borrowed from the communist party to articulate other ideological and philosophical models usable by this group. Most specifically, Divine's devotionals addressed the problem of capitalism and the need for communal and collectivist response to the current moment.

## CELEBRATING THE BLACK WOMEN'S BODY

Three-quarters of Divine's followers were Black middle-aged women. These women were a part of a cohort that migrated to the north after World War I looking for opportunity as well relief from the dictates around certain norms of respectability and codes of genteel behavior. He offered to give these women and the rest of the followers release from all their troubles: "Rest from your lacks, wants and limitations. Rest from your sickness and diseases. Rest from your oppressions and depressions . . . Rest from your segregation and your discrimination."[23] He specifically spoke to the type of bodily trauma experienced by Black migrants and Black women. He argued

> They have not thought much on the REDEMPTION of the body . . . but this was the Mystery for which I came . . . to REDEEM your Bodies from misery and sorrows, from woe and every other undesirable condition, that you might have the VICTORY.[24]

It was the redemption of their physical realities that separate this movement from others at this time. Black Harlem and New York had become the new frontiers of Black life and Black freedom. The freedom that Divine was offering was not only the freedom to escape the essentialist attachments and genteel constructions of the racially segregated South, but it was the removal of racial identity and the need to confirm to racialist expectations anywhere, including Harlem. He was imagining a new world where racial identity was no longer a factor in their religious, political, economic, or social practice. "Put off the old man with all his deeds," he said, "EVERYTHING you had before you knew ME—things that are animate or inanimate—will cause you to be identified with your infirmities." He warned, "if you even have a hat or a pair of shoes you had before you knew ME, these things are identifiable."[25]

In the *Spoken Word*, he is speaking explicitly not of cultural and religious practices but the stubborn and pernicious practice of racial identification. He told his Black followers,

> there is no such a nation or a race of people as "Colored." There is no such a race of people as "Negro" as you may call them. Over the ages, he said, black people had lost sight of their divinity."[26]

"You have visualized the negative. Visualized yourselves in poverty, lacks, wants and limitations, visualized yourselves as the preys to the prejudiced minds of our present civilization, to be segregated, as the expressors of segregation. You have visualized those detestable tendencies and you have imposed them upon yourself."[27] Divine suggested that Black Americans were vulnerable, because they had bought into a system that narrated their inequality and their inability to fully participate. His critique of the modern problem of race is similar to Du Bois's, but the Du Boisian double consciousness is more than just a philosophical question or issue. Divine is arguing that it requires a real transformation of the Black experience.

Divine says that, "I came to give you REAL NAMES," he said, and "real Emancipation."[28] "The time has come for a house-cleaning," he wrote, "the human family must undergo a complete shake-up, a drastic revision and readjustment of the entire social structure."[29] He particularly made this new structuring of the world available to Black women and working-class Black segments of the popular. Therefore, the Peace Mission differed from these other movements not only in its more limited sphere of influence, but in its more expansive vision: the Peace Mission sought not the enactment of particular economic or social measures but the entire reordering of American society. This reordering meant that Black women's body and participation were more evident in the life of the movement and their freedom and mobility was prioritized. Working-class Black women and their ability to earn a respectable wage was at the center of the movement's priorities. He wanted these adherents to be able to fully participate in society, and Divine believed that this was predicated upon the removal of conditions that mitigated that. For Divine, this included the removal of racial stratifications and the end of economic systems that were connected to their dehumanization. Divine was active in trying to erase the emergence of "slave markets" for domestic and day laborers and introducing a fair minimum wage that would erase their dependence on the state or their need to accept stereotypical constructions of Black identity. By 1936, 76 percent of Black female workers were employed as domestics. The *Liberator* newspaper described the scene of female domestics as follows,

> Propped up against store walls at street corners they stood. The women will occasionally rest weary bodies on old discarded grocery boxes. In their hands they hold a brown paper bag. In that bag is their promise of comfort for the day—a dry piece of bread for lunch, also a few torn bits of work clothes. The men carry their pails and cleaning rags and often they will turn their pails and use them as chairs, while waiting for a possible employer to come along and offer the beggarly wage of seven and one half cents for cleaning a window.[30]

While much of this critique of the slave markets was led by the Communist party, Divine and other movements began to attend to these problematic constraints faced by Blacks, particularly Black women, in the labor market. As a result, by the end of 1934 he established the principle of a minimum weekly "living wage" for all followers in work outside the Movement. He reminded his followers,

> You should not work for less than ten dollars at the least. Why should you demand it? It is because you are honest—because you do not desire to be as

you have been. You do not desire to be a thief again. You do not desire to leave your old bills unpaid. You do not desire to get means in a dishonest way, as you have been doing.[31]

Thus, Divine's discourse of removing the "old man" was not limited to a disavowal of racial categories, but it included Divine's commitment to his adherent's disavowal of the economic order and their marginalized relationship to it.

## REORDERING OF THE BLACK MIDDLE CLASS

Father Divine also began to lay down guidelines on the "evangelical" standards that he expected the followers to observe in all the enterprises bearing the Movement's name. The idea of "evangelical" standards was the way that Divine articulated his language for reordering the public sphere and African Americans' relationship to it. Specifically, his reordering was a critique of the reigning project of capitalism, a reordering of the values of the Black middle class, and a repudiation of the logic of respectability that informed much of Black religion and Black middle-class culture. Divine argued that the "evangelical" standard was to value everyone and to make room for them regardless of race and social status. He rejected the individualism and the search for private profit that had motivated many Black business and religious ventures in Harlem. He told his followers that they should not go into business with the sole aim of making money. They should go into business, instead, to serve and benefit others. By helping others and by bringing new standards of justice into economic affairs, they would gain their own reward in material success and self-respect. But Father Divine declared:

> I have come to let you know and to let them know God is as much in the Flesh and on the material shall Rule and have Dominion over and in the affairs of men, the same as they supposed Him to be in Heaven. "We are not studying about a God in the sky," he said, "we are talking about a God here and now."[32]

By arguing that God was a historically, embodied reality, Father Divine saw himself as breaking down the barriers of class and status and bringing about "the exhaltation of the least and the levelling of all racial and class enmity." He continued,

> Once upon a time it was a disgrace for the wealthy to participate or associate with the poor class of people and different races . . . but through My

Condescension . . . the great conversion and the great lifting are actually lifting the races from every angle expressible and bringing each and everybody on a common level. The scripture is also fulfilled.[33]

The idea of poor populations, specifically poor populations of color, as equal and integral to the creation and maintenance of the public square was radical, and Divine was not only imagining the poor as equal but was suggesting a model to bring them to the economic and social table. The leveling of the social and economic field meant that new models were introduced and this particular focus on equality and access for all groups were integrated in all aspects of Divine's movement. The accessibility of his movement to all classes, the rejection of particular surveillance of dress or behavior codes, and the creation of economic enterprises and projects embodied the central values of the movement. As a result, Father Divine turned accessibility, high quality goods, and exemplary service as an article of faith and a matter of obedience within the Movement. He argued that these evangelical standards rather than tying the adherents to unattainable class or racial codes provided adherents a new venue for citizenship. Furthermore, it was not just class distinctions or prevailing racial apartheid of the era, but Divine argued that many norms and values maintained by Black organizations were detrimental to the well-being and the freedom of African Americans. Divine claimed that traditional forms of religion, including African American led religious movements, had been used to "keep you in poverty . . . to bind you in slavery."[34] The "you" engaged here were those enslaved by a class and racial system that prevented them from fully participating and seeing the value and equality in their neighbor. This class and racial critique, therefore, required the destruction of a narrow construction of the middle class, specifically a Black middle class, where individual wealth or social accumulation was exchanged for the communal restoration of fair and sustainable conditions for everyone.

## THE RIGHTEOUS GOVERNMENT AND THE CRITIQUE OF LYNCHING

This attention to all Black bodies, regardless of economic status, extended to a critique and particularly to the violent attacks, mob violence, and lynching on Black bodies that shaped the African American experience of the twentieth century. While Divine divested from the logic and language of race and racialism, central to his movement was the creation of a model and organization that protected the interests of the most vulnerable, specifically lynched Black bodies. One specific article of faith in the movement's platform was Divine's interest and focus on passing a federal anti-lynching bill; he was committed to educating his adherents and gathering signatures to represent the "will of the American people" against the continued practice of lynching.

This attention to a Black flesh was emblematic of a movement that suggested that its central concern was not Blackness in a simplistic or limiting sense. Divine wanted to create the conditions under which surveilled and constrained Black bodies could be freed without using the easy path of race or racialism. In Divine's engagement with the Scottsboro Boys trial, it was clear that the movement was bringing attention to marginalized Black bodies and even assenting to the Black spiritual tradition in its engagement with the trial and the public debate. Divine's Movement created a song entitled "The Scottsboro Boys Shall Not Die." This song was sung to the tune of "Mary, Don't you Weep, Don't You Moan" and the song highlighted the unmerited suffering of the boys and their unfair imprisonment by arguing "compelled to lie in a dirty cell / For long years in a Southern hell." The song highlighted that Divine wanted to actively engage this issue and continued, "Alabama shall lose illegal fights / When prosecuted for human rights" and that Divine saw this as a human rights issue and not merely a racial concern. The song concluded by arguing that Father Divine and his movement would intervene. Thus intervention, however, was not limited to the Scottsboro case, but it was central to his garnering support for the broader vision of the "Righteous Government" platform. Father Divine wrote personally to President Roosevelt, state governors, senators and congressmen as well as members of many local political organizations, and he invited them to attend the local convention. As a sign that his concerns were broad and they were not reserved for certain religious movements or only to those who represented particular demographics of the Black public, Father Divine invited a number of religious groups and organizations ranging from the Bahaists, Theosophists, and Anthrosophists to the Federal Council of Churches. Alongside the explicit critic of lynching that highlighted Divine's concern with certain bodies, the remainder of the platform highlighted Divine's goal of a broad and expansive vision of democracy that was not controlled or overly determined by privilege. Father Divine and the movement advocated free, universal public education; the abolition of capital punishment; the abolition of political patronage; appointment and promotion on the basis of merit; laws to end lynching and prevent discrimination and segregation because of race or religion; and a national commitment to pacifism and international harmony. Deeply embedded in this platform was a commitment to addressing issues that primarily plagued his Black constituency but also critical to the formation of what he understood as a more just society and democracy. Moreover, Divine has created an alternative discourse in the public sphere that has eschewed the provincialism of race and argues for a larger platform that will enable participation in the public sphere that emerges through the denial of the body (vis-à-vis race) as an alternate model for participation.

## A NEW VISION FOR THE MODERN CITIZEN

While Divine was not totally dismissive of capital and some of its logics, he rejected any form of capital that would exclude or hinder access for all participants. While his visions of capital and democracy were already radical, to suggest that this could reach to the masses, particularly Black women, was beyond the discourse not only of U.S. democracy, radical Black groups, and the communist party. He was articulating a model of governance and inclusion that would radically change the modern structure. This attempt to encourage, sometimes cajole, candidates to affirm and begin to enact the Righteous Government platform was to introduce not an evasion of the modern society but a radical restructuring of it. This was a plea to not reform the modern era but to provide a new model for it with Black bodies being equal and integral aspects of its reformation. The Righteous Government sought a world governed by God's laws, where individuals would work for the greater good of all. This was not a demand for recovery or relief programs organized by the federal or state government, but it was a newly structured society where these programs would not be necessary. While the NAACP and other liberal organizations dedicated to the needs of Blacks of this period argued for set asides and relief programs, Divine felt that their short-term solutions highlighted a limited understanding of the holistic vision of the righteous government and ultimately wouldn't ensure long-term protections for the most vulnerable populations.

The Peace Mission was critical of handouts or set asides that adopted or were enjoined to the logic of racial identity or racialization as an organizing framework for the modern era. By using the terminology of "God's laws" or greater good, Divine and the righteous government movement were shaped by an approach that was linked to a new way of incorporating the marginalized and the oppressed into citizenship. While Divine understood that his policies would benefit his predominately Black movement and that his bully pulpit was made up of Harlem, a critical epicenter of Blackness, he was staunchly committed to using a model of not just de-emphasizing racial categories or markers but asking his parishioners to move away from racial justifications. He refused to join the NAACP and Urban League, and other Black identified movements, to push for racial set asides or even to insist that Blacks, as an aggrieved racial group, would receive appropriate federal and state relief that was created in response to depression and the inability of the state to meet the needs of the masses. Divine and his Righteous Government platform envisioned an egalitarian society where racial distinctions would decrease and ultimately be eliminated. This critique of race simultaneously separated him from many of the mainline Black progressive movements while adjoining him to Communist movements that wanted to focus on uplifting working class groups.

This focus on erasing markers was evident in Divine's language and the devotionals that were circulated in the movement. Many of the devotionals required that folks not only refuse to engage in racially coded language, but the devotionals also highlighted the new names and the new identities that the adherents inhabited within the movement. These new names were representative of their fidelity to the movement as well as their relationship to a new way of being in the world. These names also allowed African American participants to be divorced from histories of broken families, the plantation economy, and even previous debts and records. There was an opportunity for the adherents to reinvent themselves in the relationship with the state, familial relationships, and relationship with the larger society. The Peace Mission was invested in creating a sacred worship space which was enthusiastically identified through the feasts, speeches of Divine, and the devotional culture played out in the magazines and newspapers of the movement. While the magazines and the newspapers played a significant role, it was also the reconfiguration of the public domain and space. Divine understood the hotels, barbershops, dining establishments, and a slew of community-based enterprises created by and for his adherents as sacred spaces and as evidence of a new era. He believed that giving the "best to the least" or providing an entrée to modern citizenship and well-being was the introduction of the Kingdom of God. For Divine, this was a reordering of the modern project and settler-based democracy and its accessibility to as many people as possible. In this regard, Divine's deracinated democracy was also a sacralized one that believed that the full participation of society's people required a sacred love or reimagining of their relationship to God, America, and democracy. Thus, Divine is as much a prophet of democracy and modern citizenship as he is a religious innovator and a totem for the divine. His millennialism was not connected to the end of the American empire but the reformation of it. Divine believed that American exceptionalism was necessary but that it needed to be redeemed or saved from its logic of racism, racialism, and acquisitive capitalism.

## CONCLUSION: AN ALTERNATIVE TO RACIALIZED DEMOCRACY AND CIVIL RIGHTS

While Father Divine and his movement were often imagined as a critique of modern racism and the elevation of a universal discourse that could accommodate the needs and concerns of Black Americans, this chapter hopes to look at the ways that Divine argues for an alternative democracy that is not only amenable to new religious modalities but fully attending to the needs and full integration of Black bodies. Like the Church of God in Christ, Divine is similarly challenging the narrative of orthodox Christianity while at the same time engaging in the project of constructing an alternative Black public. Moreover, Divine emerges in the crucible of the reconstruction of African American and Christian identity, while at the same time engaging the role of the Black body and its relationship to the state and the broader political apparatus. Divine's vision of democracy and his critique of racialism and acquisitive capitalism similarly made him a figure that was also rendered inside and outside simultaneously. He is a figure that sets the stage for the continued disruption of the Black public and the fragmenting of the Black church. Divine is both tethered to the long tradition of the Black church as well as arguing for a way to reimagine sacrality, the body, and Black identity in the middle of the twentieth century. His notion of Black citizenship is one that required that African Americans move beyond the norms of Christianity, democracy, and race and that specifically Black folks and their visions for the modern are no longer limited by race, creed, or color. "The time has come for a house-cleaning," he argued, "the human family must undergo a complete shake-up, a drastic revision and readjustment of the entire social structure." This drastic revision and readjustment had a profound impact not only the adherents of the Peace Mission, but the larger Black public and the shape of Black religion for the remainder of the twentieth century.

## NOTES

1. See Arthur Huff Fauset, *Black Gods of the Metropolis: Negro Religious Cults of the Urban North* (Philadelphia, PA: University of Pennsylvania Press, 1971). Also pay attention to the important work by Curtis et al. that engages the rise of Black prophetic figures; however, the connection of these Black prophetic figures to Black theology and a larger Black Christian public are not fully addressed. Curtis and Sigler, *The New Black Gods*.

2. See Robert Weisbrot, *Father Divine and the Struggle for Racial Equality*, Blacks in the New World (Urbana, IL: University of Illinois Press, 1983); Jill Watts, *God, Harlem U.S.A.: The Father Divine Story* (Berkeley, CA: University of California Press, 1992); John Hoshor, *God in a Rolls Royce; the Rise of Father Divine: Madman, Menace, or Messiah*, The Black Heritage Library Collection (Freeport, NY: Books for Libraries Press, 1971).

3. See Hoshor, *God in a Rolls Royce*; Fauset, *Black Gods of the Metropolis*.

4. *The Spoken Word*, 4 January 1936, 27.

5. The deradicalization of the Black church at the beginning of the twentieth century has been outlined and re-engaged by multiple theorists, most notably Gayraud Wilmore in his classic text. See Gayraud S. Wilmore, *Black Religion and Black Radicalism: An Interpretation of the Religious History of Afro-American People*, 2nd edition (Maryknoll, NY: Orbis Books, 1983). I, however, would argue that Wilmore and even Lincoln support this thesis by narrowly identifying the Black church through the lens of the mainline traditions. Once the Black Christian public is broadened to include the variety of projects that are engaging or rearticulating the New Testament narrative of Jesus Christ, it is clear that this is not necessarily a period of deradicalization, but a period of rethinking the stability and usefulness of the Christian. Black Gods like Fard, Divine, and Grace all exist as important innovators in creating an alternative Christian public that takes seriously the flexibility of sacred texts and the creation of new sacred ideas in the modern era.

6. Watts, *God, Harlem U.S.A.*, 19–26.

7. Jill Watts, "'This Was the Way': Father Divine's Peace Mission Movement in Los Angeles During the Great Depression," *Pacific Historical Review* 60, no. 4 (1991).

8. Glaude, *Exodus!*, 33.

9. *The Spoken Word*, 30 November 1935, 20.

10. Of particular note here is that Divine and his engagement of the Black Christian public sphere attempts to provide alternatives for Black Americans that will allow them not to divest from the normative public sphere but also to engage as a sacred citizen.

11. R. Marie Griffith, "Body Salvation: New Thought, Father Divine, and the Feast of Material Pleasures," *Religion & American Culture* 11, no. 2 (2001): 153.

12. *New Day*, 30 March 1935, 17.

13. C. Eric Lincoln and Lawrence H. Mamiya, "Daddy Jones and Father Divine: The Cult as Political Religion," *Religion in Life* 49, no. 1 (1980).

14. Beryl Satter, "Marcus Garvey, Father Divine and the Gender Politics Of," *American Quarterly* 48, no. 1 (1996).

15. Robert Allerton Parker, *The Incredible Messiah: The Deification of Father Divine* (Boston, MA: Little, Brown and Company, 1937), 27–37.

16. *The New Day*, 15 March 1936, 35.

17. Watts does a fine job engaging the interactions that Divine has with local Black congregations and communities as Divine's movement spreads and begins to challenge the power and orthodoxy of local Black churches. Watts and others also begin to look at the role of Divine on the national and international levels, and I will continue their interventions by addressing the import of Divine's critique of modernity and the creation of a counter-public sphere.

18. Benjamin Kahan, "The Other Harlem Renaissance: Father Divine, Celibate Economics, and the Making of Black Sexuality," *Arizona Quarterly: A Journal of American Literature, Culture, and Theory* 65 (2009).

19. Ibid.

20. Robert A. Hill, Marcus Garvey, and Universal Negro Improvement Association, *The Marcus Garvey and Universal Negro Improvement Association Papers* (Berkeley, CA: University of California Press, 1983).

21. *The New Day*, 24 November 1945, 7.
22. Ibid.
23. *World Herald*, 21 January 1937.
24. Ibid.
25. *Spoken Word*, 26 September 1936.
26. *Spoken Word*, 19 May 1936.
27. *New Day*, 16 November 1939.
28. *New Day*, 21 October 1937.
29. Ibid.
30. *Negro Liberator*, 15 June 1935.
31. *Spoken Word* 1 (18), 16 February 1935.
32. Ibid.
33. *New Day* 1 (10), 23 July 1936.
34. Ibid.

*Chapter 4*

# The Whole Body

## *Alternative Christian Economic Self-Determination and the Black Madonna*

### INTRODUCTION

On May 26, 1967, the image of the Black women's body was installed in the sanctuary in the Shrine of the Black Madonna. Six months prior to the installation, the design for the Madonna was created by Glanton V. Dowell and inspired by the poem "Black Madonna" by Harold G. Lawrence. It was designed after the image of a historic African American woman, and it was intended to be a certain height and length in order to fill the entirety of the shrine. The original commission was to create an image that would inspire awe and deep reverence for Black culture, especially the Black woman. One of the earlier versions of the Madonna was rejected because it was both not religious enough and not African enough. This Black Madonna, though decidedly Western in the composition of the painting and the first Black Madonna in the United States, was in conversation with other Black Madonnas around the world.[1] There was a clear negotiation of Blackness and sacrality that had to be effectively addressed in this one image. Cleage argued at the installation of the image and the opening of the Shrine that the idea of the church or the Black church was outmoded. He said,

> We reject the traditional concept of church.... In its place we will build a Black Liberation movement, which derives its basic religious insights from African spirituality, its character from African communalism, and its revolutionary direction from Jesus, the Black Messiah.[2]

The poem and its gestures toward Africa, as both the birthplace of humanity and Christianity, also played a critical role in this newly emerging community:

You were beautiful when your apparition formed, from Tanga mud and rift. Rocks of Rhodesia, Kush Ethiopia, Sahara Sands and Maya Mounds, And Grottes de Enfants preserved your image.

You modeled at the Pharaoh's throne; Mother of Horus, Mother of Krishna, Mother of all! In dark virginity.

You, lost for a while, In cadence with the crescent star. Continued in obscured worship of the North, Among many who never knew your birth Yet still adored you.[3]

In Lawrence's poem and Cleage's opening call to the Black community they offered a combination of new ideas alongside vocabulary and symbols that had previously been engaged within the Black sacred community. An engagement of African spirituality had been engaged in previous religious communities and the concept of African communalism had been a long part of the Black freedom struggle, but the new idea that Cleage and his cohorts offered were the concepts of the "Black Madonna" and the "Black Messiah" within the Black public sphere and the recovery of an African-centered Christianity.[4] It was the combination of these ideas that were relatively new to the Black sacred and Black public sphere. The idea of a Black messiah had been introduced in other settings and within other ideological constraints, most notably the Nation of Islam and the Garveyite movement.[5] Cleage's Black messiah, however, was designed for African American Christianity, and it was a clear response and interruption of what Cleage called the "moribund framework of the post–World War II and Southern-based civil rights movement."[6] His new model was expansive in that it called

> to build a black communal society which can protect the minds and bodies of Black men, women and children. Calling for community control of institutions in the inner city, as a model for self-determination in economics, politics, and above, all religion.[7]

This expansive framework was centered on the Blackness of the messiah and the Madonna, the liberation of African Americans and their communities, and a new Christian or a new religious framework that could accommodate this. Cleage recognized that this was a disruption and thus he argued for an aesthetic, theological, and political framework to accompany this. The Shrine, the Black Madonna, the radical Black community, and Cleage's theorization of the Black messiah became the canonical texts and mode of articulation for this departure from the normative Black church. The deep dissatisfaction with traditional Black religious communities was evidenced not only in his explicit critique of their institutional methods, but Cleage's call for a new version of an African-centered Christianity witness. Yet, in spite of all of these things, Cleage was never divorced from the long history of the Black church or the Black Christian tradition.

*The Black Messiah* and the attendant theological discourse were intended to outline an ideological response to the concerns and issues facing African Americans at the time, but it was also a mechanism to differentiate Cleage's movement from other Christian movements at that time. His critique of the Black church framework, which was similar to his critique of King and the Southern civil rights establishment, was that it was too wedded to a politics of accommodating whiteness and did not account for the reality of the African American experience. This critique was most clearly articulated in Cleage's response to King's iconic speeches at the Detroit and DC marches in 1963, "You can hope for change, but it must be predicated on realities and not what we dream of."[8] While this and other interactions suggest that there was deep enmity or even a radical difference between the two figures, there was actually greater theologically overlap than what has been generally argued. Nonetheless, the theological overlap did not lead to any considerable overlap in their methods or the language they used to construct their response. Cleage pointedly and repeatedly uses the language of "Black liberation" and revolution suggesting that the way forward was a radical departure from the traditional Christian model and the normative negotiation of racial identity. Cleage and his movement endeavored to introduce new images and vocabulary into the Black public and specifically challenge the normative ideas and images associated with Afro-Christianity. He argued that the Black Christian Nationalist movement intended to "stay in the forefront of the black liberation struggle." Nevertheless, this chapter will argue that Cleage and King were both invested in finding and circulating language and ideas that would galvanize the Black public and create a broader range of opportunities to participate in the democratic process. Cleage's language, however, was deeply committed to merging African spiritualty and culture with a radical account of the African American Christian tradition. Specifically, Cleage argued that religious and economic self-determination were critical and that re-conceptualizing and sacralizing the Black body were integral to the achievement of those ideals. Therefore, the introduction of the Black Madonna was not just the interjection of a new signifier of or into Black Christian discourse, but it signaled a substantive restructuring of the role and import of the Black body.[9] Cleage wanted to circulate ideas that had been absent from Black religious and Christian discourse and challenge ideas and projects that rendered much of Black Christianity in opposition to the Black radical tradition.

# IN THE BEGINNING

The Shrine of the Black Madonna was an Afro-Christian movement that was started by Albert Cleage in 1966 in Detroit, Michigan. In a small storefront church on the corners of Linwood and Hogarth Avenues, Cleage after leaving the mainline Presbyterian church decided to start a church in the center of one of Detroit's hardest hit areas. In his resignation letter to the Midwest Presbyterian division, Cleage thanked the Presbyterian church for its support and its development of him as a leader and a pastor, but that he needed "to start a church that responded to the ills and miseries of being black in America."[10] He continued that "he could no longer endure the economic deprivation and privations that the American negro faced and that there were resources to save the black man."[11] He continued by arguing that these resources were not just symbolic or solely economic but that the spiritual resources available to Black men and women had the potential to reshape the streets of Detroit and the well-being of all who walk on them. Later that month, he purchased the first building and the adjacent storefront and those would become the Shrine of the Black Madonna. It was no accident that this first installation of Cleage's vision took the name of a Shrine. Cleage articulated in the *Detroit News* in the fall of 1962 that this was not just a symbol for Black Detroit, but for all to see the significance of Black contributions to the larger world in a way similar to the other Black Madonnas around the world.[12] The Shrine was explicitly designed to be a pilgrimage site (like the other shrines), a disruption of the local geography and urban blight of downtown Detroit, and a symbolic reordering of Christianity and religion's relationship to the Black body. Cleage was following a well-drawn pattern of cultural renaissance that was dependent on the shared resources of Black spirituality and Black economic mobilization. The Shrine and its attendant theology, Afro-Christian nationalism, always worked in the service of the local needs of the home community and its members as well as the larger concerns of Detroit and Black economic sustainability. The cultural renaissance that the Shrine supported was one that demanded a radical re-visioning of Black culture as well as the reorganizing of Black public spaces and democratic institutions in order to accommodate these revitalized Black bodies.

The Shrine and the building that housed it were a critique and correction to the city's disregard of its Black citizens, the religious communities' negotiation of the African legacy to Christianity, and an ongoing conversation with Detroit's activist community about the radical possibilities of Afro-Christianity and Afro-religions/spirituality. The Shrine, the image of the Black Madonna, Cleage's texts, and its model of community and economic development were the scriptures or the canonical texts, circulated, debated, and engaged in Detroit and around the country.[13] This chapter will address the ways that the Shrine and the movement's concomitant engagement with Black economic empowerment functioned as a lightning rod in the reconsideration of the relationship between Black economic solidarity/self-determination and the myth of Black middle-class identity in the middle of the twentieth century. The Black Madonna functioned as the demand for a renewed discussion on Black women/s bodies, the autonomy of Black religious communities, and the emergence of a new "politics of economic respectability or the economy of the black body" that centered on self-determination and communal sustainability as its primary components. The Shrine of the Black Madonna and its founding moment are critical because its genesis speaks to the debate over what constituted African American Christianity; however, it is the practice of self-determination via economic empowerment, cultural renewal, and electoral participation that will be emphasized in this account.[14] Cleage's departure from the Presbyterian church in Detroit was presented in the mainstream press as well as local conversations between Black Christian communities as primarily a theological disagreement, but this chapter will argue that it was more specifically a debate over the nature and role of African American religion. Cleage explicitly stated that normative Christianity, under the aegis of the Presbyterian and even autonomous Black churches, was no longer meeting the needs of the Black community and that Black religion, including the Black church, did not have a critical plan or mechanism for dealing with the Black body, Black political and economic sustainability, and their relationship to democracy.

Furthermore, Cleage couched his departure not only in the language of the failed or limited theological imagination of the Presbyterian church via its relationship to its Black members, but he highlighted the ways in which the denominational method, especially predominately Black churches within mainline traditions, functioned as a colonial arrangement. He particularly identified the absence of agency and ownership in many denominational configurations. Black churches and communities did not own land, did not have easy access to capital to expand its social and economic footprint, and there was constant surveillance of their activities by a structure/institution that did not share its ethical or political commitments. In a striking interview with the Detroit Free Press, Cleage likened the relationship of these types of churches with the economic model of sharecropping. Cleage says, "These churches are still beholden to ecclesial overseers."[15] Thus, it was not surprising that Cleage's initial move after the separation from the Presbyterian church was to gain ownership of a plot of land and to highlight the critically important role of economic self-determination and sustainability in the scriptural projects of alternative African American religions. For the remainder of this chapter, I will address the role that economic self-sufficiency and economic empowerment, especially among his female adherents, played in the sacred public that Cleage and his cohorts were trying to create. Furthermore, I will address the ways that the definition of Black economic sustainability and Black political engagement were debated and articulated within this community and the larger publics. Finally, this chapter will address the ways that the Shrine functioned not only as a symbol of Black pride and agency, but that the Shrine was a critical part of the economic model that Cleage created to support the mother church, the surrounding Detroit community, and other local communities around the United States. The Shrine was not only an example of a recovering and retelling of the Black community's narrative and introducing Afro-centered Christianity, but it was a rewriting of what constituted Black pilgrimage, radical political participation, and economic self-determination.

## THE SHRINE AND THE BLACK FEMALE BODY

The recovery of the Black female narrative of the Madonna and her historic African presence in the Bible and Christendom were just the beginning of the Shrine's agenda. In addition to telling the narrative of the Black Madonna, Cleage and the women who functioned as the primary caretakers of the Shrine presented the Madonna as not only a historic figure but as a modern reconfiguration of Black women and a re-envisioning of the Black women's role in the church and the public spaces of the Black community.[16] In Cleage's paper at the University of Michigan's Bentley Library, this portrait of the mural's model, Rose Waldon, is filed alongside the first newspaper article related to the commission. In the Detroit Free Press article, Dowdell highlights the relationship between the mural and his personal experiences, stating "[The Black Madonna mural] is me.... I can't divorce the Madonna from black women. I don't think that any of the experiences of the Madonna were more poignant or dramatic than those of any Negro Mother." Cleage recognized that a large percentage of the members of his church and other Black religious communities' adherents were African American women and rather than create spaces where their talents were limited or ignored, Cleage used the Shrine to center the logic of economic development around Black women, their strengths, and ultimately their leadership. At the very beginning of the Shrine, much of the curriculum and the preaching centered on the plight not only of the Black church or the Black community but specifically the Black woman and her ability to care for her family and community. Cleage was known for his radial critique of the northern Black churches and their failure to attain growth and transformation for Black communities. He argued, "the Negro church has prospered poorly in the North because it has been unable to relate the gospel of Jesus meaningfully to the everyday problems of an underprivileged people in urban areas."[17] While this argument was focused primarily at the economic devastation experienced by Black migrants to the urban North, it was also a reference to and recognition of the changing family structure and political pressures in the urban North context. The Shrine was clear that Black economic development and political participation should not only be the purview of Black men or normative Black male–led households.[18] Rather the Shrine, like other alternative religions in the first half of the twentieth century, opened up business and economic opportunities to anyone, and in the case of the Shrine, Cleage and his cohorts were very active in recruiting women and developing businesses that would meet the needs of Black women and their families.[19] At the opening sermon after the "Installation of the Shrine":

> We really don't need a sermon this morning. We could just sit here and look at the Black Madonna and marvel that we've come so far . . .; that we can conceive of the possibility of the son of God being born by a black woman.
>
> And that's a long way for us 'cause it wasn't so long ago when that would've been an impossible—an impossible—conception because our idea of ourselves was so distorted. We didn't believe that even God could use us for His purpose because we were so low, so despised, because we despised ourselves. We despised ourselves.
>
> And to have come to the place where we not only can conceive of the possibility, but to have come to the place where we are convinced, upon the basis of our knowledge, of our historic study, upon the basis of all the facts, that we are not only capable of conceiving of the idea, but we are convinced that Jesus was born to a black Mary; that Jesus, the Messiah, was a black man; [and] that the nation that he came to save was a black nation.[20]

It is important to note that while Albert Cleage or Jaromi Agymen, as he later become known, highlights the role of a Black nation and a Black messiah that his remarks are bookended by a focus on the Black mother in the form of the Black Madonna. Similarly, the church while focusing on economic and theological self-determination often approached these topics and a set of varied interests with a particular focus on the role of or impact on Black women. As it related to economics, politics, and aesthetics, the question of the role and import of Black women were often at the center of the discussion. While the church was decidedly Afro-centric and there was the evocation of Jesus as a Black messiah/man, the Black sacred community also engaged in a theological debate over the import of Mary and her relationship to the historic narrative of the Black Christian tradition. Therefore, the symbolic and theological discussion of the role of the Black Madonna led to supporters as well as critics to question the role of Black women in the movement and the status of Black women broadly. Cleage and the movement were eager to respond critically, theologically, and institutionally to the role of Black women, families, and the Black Madonna. While the Madonna began as an art installation, Cleage recognized that Black women as religious, political, and economic leaders had often been under-represented or not fully engaged. Cleage and the caretakers were eager to make sure that this was not the case at the Shrine of the Black Madonna.

As a result of this focus on the female migrants as well as the important role of the caretakers ministry, a majority of the Shrine's planning, schedules, and programming were dominated by issues and concerns that pertained to women. One specific example of this was the presence of female leaders and entrepreneurs throughout the Shrine enterprises. Women led the Shrine-developed Afro-centered schools but most impressively for that time period, Black female-run businesses and Black female writers were developed and supported by the Shrine and the emerging Shrine Bookstore and the press operations associated with it. In many ways, the second generation of Black female writers after the Harlem Renaissance began with smaller presses and community-based printers like the Shrine Bookstore.[21] This Shrine Bookstore was not the only organization that elevated Black female writers, but the Shrine Bookstore and its printing apparatus were known for the multiple sectors in which female writers were included. In many of the other presses, female writers were relegated to either fiction where women were the major protagonists or creating literature or self-help books that were dedicated to producing some form of the idealized Black woman. In the case of the Shrine Bookstore and its associated presses, the female authors who were featured and circulated were philosophers, academics, and activists who were actively involved in not only engaging an under-represented audience, Black females, but in engaging the larger Black public. Cleage was clear that he saw these writers as organic intellectuals and that they were critical not only to the economic success of the press but to the development and maintenance of the Black community.[22] For a brief moment, some academics and local universities, primarily in the region of the Mother Shrine, used the bookstore and the authors elevated by Cleage to produce scholarly texts with their audience not just being well-read African Americans but to a larger, more literate public. Thus, the diversity of the products and the audiences reached by the press highlight its goal to transform all areas of Black life and to provide a comprehensive curriculum for engaging the Black community's, including Black women, encounter with the modern moment. Central to this engagement of the modern moment was the emergence of new literatures that addressed alternatives for Black women, families, and economic participation. These authors wrote books that covered a wide range of categories, included texts on raising Afro-centric children to texts that explored the recovery of local textile and artistic practices. While the bookstore and its shepherding of local writers was relatively small, the range of topics embraced the wide variety of areas that Black community, including Black women, needed to embrace to foster the revolution that Cleage was proposing. As a result, Cleage was a key part of creating texts that helped to shape a new and alternative narrative around the modern Black women.

In addition to writers and cultural theorists who were featured in the bookstore, published by the press, and circulated within the Afro-Christian community, there was a significant amount of Black female leadership at the Shrine. While Cleage was the dominant prophetic figure and men tended to dominate the highest positions in the organization, he realized that Black female preachers, teachers, and cultural leaders/activists needed to be developed and given opportunities within the Shrine movement. Therefore, Cleage elevated a number of female preachers, activists, and teachers who played a major role in preaching at the Shrine, traveling with Cleage, and coordinating the cultural and economic life of the Shrine.[23] Additionally, when Cleage opened the Shrine Towers, a convalescence home, and a community center directly adjacent to the Mother Shrine, it was led by a woman and it had a particular focus on providing safe end-of-life housing and care for many of the aging female adherents of the movement as well as housing for single mothers with young children. While the home was a source of income for the movement, its programming was often run by women and geared to the needs of the majority female adherents. The Shrine House focused on supporting and nurturing young Black families and providing alternative models for integrating Afro-centric ideologies and practices into the family unit. Later in the history of the Shrine, there was the development of the Beulah Land and Farm Initiative. This was another Shrine initiative with African American women at the leadership forefront. The farm and its boarding school were initially constructed in order to provide communal school and parenting options for the women in the movement. Both the Shrine Towers and the Beulah Farm point to Cleage and the Shrine's focus on providing new and better alternatives for urban migrants, especially African American women. Importantly, these options were run and programmed primarily by the women who were serviced by them.

Finally, Cleage and the movement were also very active in developing political candidates and activists, and these often included Black women in Detroit and throughout the country. These Black candidates were often but not necessarily connected to the Shrine movement. Cleage was invested in finding activists and candidates who were philosophically connected to his vision of restoring and revitalizing urban communities around the country as well as rethinking the shape of democratic participation. Often, many of those identified came from different movements or were only tangentially related to the Shrine. Cleage was ecumenical, broad, and diverse, in the political and cultural communities that he was associated with, and thus he was deeply invested in engaging different methods and solutions to the problems of Black suffering. While he was actively involved in raising the profile of the Shrine of the Black Madonna and female leaders and thinkers associated with the movement, Cleage was first and foremost dedicated to developing and expanding the Black sacred public in Detroit and throughout the United States. He realized that Black women were central to the Black public and thus he created a model that actively engaged and developed African American women. His relationship with a wide variety of religious and emerging Africana religious movements as well as with women within these movements and within the Black radical political tradition highlights his desire to expand the shape and the narrative of the Black sacred sphere.

Therefore, it is not surprising that he elevated and engaged women from the Shrine movement as well as from other associated Christian and non-Christian movements, specifically, Cleage's work with Grace Lee Boggs with the Freedom Now Party and her work with the Correspondence Publishing Committee. He wanted to move away from the traditional norms, language, and symbols of the Black sacred space and that meant reinventing what constituted Christianity, what role Africa and Afro-centricity should play in the development of new African American religious traditions, and who would be seen as legible and integral contributors to this sacred sphere. He, therefore, elevated women who either held or combined characteristics that were central to his understanding of Black liberation and self-determination. Many of the women were attached to the Shrine and were known for the combination of Afro-Christianity and political resistance in their campaign or activist identities. While others were solely connected to the Cleage's newly developed political party and had limited commitment to Cleage's religious agenda, it was evident that Cleage was committed to getting women, specifically African American women, involved in political campaigns. Moreover, it was important to Cleage to accomplish liberation, including Black women's liberation, through all possible channels. That meant his network of radical activists, men and women, included a diverse group of people from a variety of religious and racial groups, and they were attacking the logic of liberation from a number of different perspectives.

## COMING TO THE SHRINE

Much has been written about the reasons that the Black Christian public was electrified and excited about the role of the Black Madonna.[24] The church's central narrative focused on the presence of this dark figure and how it constructed a counter-narrative for Black women, the Black body, and Black

Christianity. Furthermore, the Madonna was discussed as the means to bring a transnational politics of Black belonging to the Christian world and to center the experience of Africa and African-diasporic culture in the history of the African American church. The Black Madonna was understood as a figure of community-building amongst radical Black church movements in the United States and around the world. As a result, the first part of this section will focus on the aesthetics of the Black Madonna and the relationship of those aesthetics to a larger discourse on Black power, Black nationalism, and the Black diaspora. However, I will end this section by highlighting how coming to the Shrine has often been characterized in the language of new symbols and aesthetics, but that the Shrine was also an economic powerhouse and boon for Cleage, the community, and the idea of Black institutions as self-sustaining cultural institutions beyond the work done on Sunday.[25] More explicitly, the Shrine and its attendant discourse and institutions were a key component of Cleage's project of "culturally centered" economic self-determination that challenged many of the models of economic upward mobility and respectability.

Cleage and his movement were particularly popular because of the ways that it brought together multiple ideological streams and multiple sectors of the Black public that had not been in conversation with one another. The Shrine and Cleage brought together not only the Black Christian community, Black alternative religions, and radical political activist, but it ignited the Black arts and Black aesthetic world. There was an emerging consensus within the mainstream Black public that Black nationalism and Black religion were incompatible, especially Black Christianity and Black nationalism. Cleage saw the Shrine as a physical embodiment of not just the Black Madonna but the shrine was a physical embodiment of cultural development (or an emerging cultural renaissance) that included and was shaped by a newly emerging form of Afro-Christianity and new discourses on Black power and autonomy. He believed that Black nationalism and Black Christianity were not only compatible but were necessary conversation partners in the liberation of African Americans. His decision to have the Black Madonna commissioned was based upon his readings and understanding of Black cultural nationalism as well as Black radical religious thinkers. Cleage was as much a student of Thurman and King as he was an acolyte of Garvey and the Black Panthers.[26] This renaissance of Black culture, Cleage argued, was critical to the vital interests of Black populations and their eventual participation in public spaces. Black peoples and neighborhoods needed their own monuments and structures as a way of creating sacred spaces that did the work of orienting broken and bruised Black bodies to the possibilities of restoration (world-making). Furthermore, there is evidence that the Mother Shrine's commission of the mural in Detroit led to the creation of murals or a mural tradition throughout Afro-centric churches and the growing Pan-African Orthodox Christian community.[27] All the Shrines throughout the Detroit area and the United States included murals designed and produced by African American artists. Like Father Divine and Elijah Muhammad, the Black Madonna became the exemplar not of Christian theology or even maternal Marian devotion but rather an example of the fully actualized and venerated Black body.

Furthermore, the Black Madonna was central to the emerging Black Arts Movement and its circulation impacted a number of artists who began to address not only the Afro-centric dimensions of Christianity and religion but to engage the production and circulation of other Black Madonnas and the depiction of Africana women in the sacred sphere. The body needed to be a particular hue, a specific body type, and needed to elevate the particular role and work associated with Black motherhood. In this emerging tradition, there was a specific rejection of other Black maternal and Madonna figures that had been produced by artists and primarily populated museums in Europe. These African American "Black Madonnas" were not constructed as idealized Black women who conformed to traditional gender norms nor was she the reification of one particular stereotype or characteristic associated with Black women. The original committee tasked with the creation and installation of the Madonna at the Mother Shrine called for the artist to connect the Madonna to the everyday experience of suffering in America. Dowdell, the artist, argued that

> We have been told and shown through Italian Renaissance painters that Jesus was Aryan with blonde hair and blue eyes. We were also led to believe that Christianity called on black people to do nothing about oppression. . . . We reject these distorted teachings. Therefore, the Heritage Committee has embarked on the noble task of setting the record straight. That is showing the real meaning of our religion. Our first project was to commission a black artist to paint a picture of Mary, the mother of Jesus—our Black Madonna. We have also placed pictures of famous black heroes in the Fellowship Hall and Nursery.[28]

This critique of European Christianity and western culture alongside the elevation of Black women's experience became the hallmark of the Madonnas. There is evidence that these standards and concerns around what constituted an acceptable Afro-Christian Madonna were being negotiated. As much as the Madonna at the Mother Shrine was the standard for United States-based Afro-centered Madonnas, there was a great degree of variation within this emerging tradition. The Madonnas were essentially tasked with correcting the images of Blackness and Black motherhood within the Black sacred public as well as the larger public. It was clearly imagined as a sacred and political image simultaneously.

The original mural was to be African American and have echoes of the larger diaspora simultaneously (thus negotiating the diaspora). The aesthetics of the figure was to highlight the import of the Black family, Africana matriarchal relationships, and a deep connection with Africa and Afro-centric cultural rituals and systems. The image was disrupting the images of Black women at that time that identified them as domestic workers with little or no social and political capital and no connection to a cultural or ethnic foundation. The Black Madonna tradition was a counter-type to the domestic, the mammy, and the Black woman who was not ready to be fully integrated into democratic society. The Madonna was not just the presentation of the spiritualized Black woman, but she was the image of a Black women who is able to participate and who transcends the limitations of normative constructions of race, class, and gender. Other organizations and art movements were galvanized by the commissioning of the Shrine and began to create alternative images of and additional venues for representations of Black women; however, the Shrine was clearly engaged in creating one that represented the African, political, and Christian character of the African American community.

In the form of the Madonna or the biblical character Mary, this Black woman is simultaneously transcendent and human and this combination informs these communities' ability to move beyond the parochial and limiting context of U.S. democracy. Embodiment in this case was not just a valorization of the Black form, but it was the recognition of African Americans' right and imperative to participate in the modern word.[29] That is why unlike some other movements at that time, Cleage was not calling for an escape from or rejection of the public sphere or the responsibilities that came with democratic citizenship, rather he was calling for fundamentally different ways of thinking about Black participation in the democratic project and in some cases moving beyond it. This new form of participation is what Cleage and others in his cohort would identify as Black cultural restoration and culturally centered economic self-determination.[30] Cleage and his cohort were articulating a new way of understanding African Americans' participation in the democratic process and the economic marketplace, and he understood that as being deeply connected to Black women, their symbolic representation, as well as their role in the political sphere. When Cleage argued that the Black messiah came "to save a black nation,"[31] Cleage had a holistic understanding of who was included in this Black nation as well as expecting the restoration or revitalization experienced by the "Black nation" to have far-reaching consequences on the larger nation and the project of democracy.

The first step in the process of Black cultural restoration was the creation of self-sustaining communities with anchoring institutions like bookstores, religious organizations like the Shrine, archives, and artistic and musical installations were central to Cleage's vision of a Black cultural restoration. This model of holistic transformation and reordering of democratic society was borrowed from earlier Black nationalist communities and ideologies. Much of Cleage's encounters with the Panthers and early Black power/nationalist movements is instructive for the role of community transformation and the import of the body in this communal restricting. As a result, the Black Panther's creation of community centers, educational institutions, and even health clinics, where images of Black bodies and Black icons were dominant, was particularly attractive to Cleage as it represented the full range of their liberatory endeavors. Cleage wanted a religious system that fully embraced the nuanced and complicated lives of Black folks and the concerns of their Black bodies in the middle of the twentieth century. At the opening of the Shrine he states,

> Welcome to the Black Nation. Home of Black Christian Nationalism. . . . Our Creed—I believe that both my survival and my salvation depend upon my willingness to submerge my individualism in the Black Nation and so I commit my life to the Black Christian Nationalist Movement.[32]

Therefore, the Shrine was intentionally organized as a community center that played multiple and changing roles in the lives of the Black radical and everyday Detroit community.

The Shrine was at the center of a new model of resisting white racism and hegemony, and Cleage organized the Shrine so that it could stand apart from what he considered outdated or ineffective church models as well as outdated models of integration and economic dependence. While the Shrine functioned under the sign of Christianity, Cleage was an example of a Black pragmatic pluralist who believed that the means to Black liberation could not or should not be constrained or controlled by the limited imaginations or purview of white western religions or institutions or even the limited imaginations of progressive Black thinkers or Christianity.[33] It is therefore noteworthy that the image of the Madonna impacted not only a number of Black leaders and institutions throughout the Christian and religious world, but that this Black Madonna figure was seen as a critical intervention within the Black arts, Black economics, and even Black electoral political world. It was Amiri Baraka's address at the Mother Shrine and his iconic photograph in front of the mural that suggested that the Madonna's aesthetic significance was important for a number of different and often competing communities in the Black public. In his address on May 18, 1969, before 500 people at the Mother Shrine, Baraka engaged a number of his poems and addressed the issue of what constituted revolutionary action.[34] Baraka was presenting an argument that Black liberation and freedom could only be established via an anti-establishment agenda.

He challenged those activists and celebrities that used imperialism or the white establishment to create societal transformation. Baraka like Cleage was looking for Black-informed models and itineraries by which to shape the struggle. As a result, the methods and the language were necessarily extreme. As Baraka who called himself a "true missionary of blackness" and that is what the Shrine and its adherents desired to be.[35] While it shaped/informed these movements, the Shrine also borrowed and engaged Black religion, models of economic self-determination, and a broad range of political ideologies from a wide array of partners and interlocutors. Most specifically, Cleage borrowed from a number a Christian, Christian-adjacent (like the Nation of Islam), and Afro-diasporic traditions to create the scripture, circulate the canon, and develop a model for his Afro-Christian movement. However, it was the body and the attention to the body, including how other movements addressed and circulated the body, that became dominant for Cleage.

Caring for the body, attending to the psychic and physical traumas on the Black body, and providing alternative images and practices for the body were the central practices of the Shrine. Similar to the Panthers who focused on a new model of healthcare, this was not just an epidemiological response, but as Nelson argues, it was a radical attention to the physical deprivation and disregard for the Black body.[36] Therefore, the body was explicitly engaged in every area of the Shrine's holistic approach to Black liberation. In the school, the bookstore, and in the church liturgy, careful attention was paid to the body through its adornment and presentation as well as attending to the psychic and physical harms that it had endured. The Shrine's schools introduced yoga and Pu-Kau, which includes ancient practices of meditation and *tai-chi chaun* for the young adherents as well as all manner of self-defense classes. Additionally, the Shrine like the Panthers introduced a whole suite of health-based services for the body and the mind, with particular attention to the entire family. Furthermore, these interventions and attention given to the body were a part of a model to train and employ community members in practices and services that were integral to the Black body. As a result of the Shrine's attention to the body, a new generation of homeopathic doctors, clinical social workers, and counselors as well as kinesiologists and massage/body therapists emerged in Detroit as well as the areas around the other Shrines. The "business of the black body" moved from the purview of the cosmetologist and the mortician/funeral industry to a suite of services that were connected to attending to the physical Black body as well as the protection and extension of Black life.[37] In addition, Cleage was active in bolstering and supporting the mainstream medical system alongside creating these alternative practices of protecting and supporting the Black body. Therefore, the Shrine was very active in supporting the education and training of medical doctors and nurses as well as actively supporting Black doctors and their practices in the Detroit area as well as the others associated with the other Shrines. This attention to the Black body via medical and alternative medical practices was explicitly attached to developing Black businesses that were actively engaged in prioritizing the Black body. This body-centered model, however, was not just focused on the care and the creation of "body" workers or the development of income-generating businesses. Moreover, the affirmations of the body in the everyday rituals of the Shrine community as well as in the liturgy of the Sunday services were critical to maintaining the focus on the needs and concerns of the Black community. In the liturgy of the Shrine, the eleven sacraments were actively connected to Afro-centricity and the preservation of the Black body. The communion or the sacrament of healing actively connected adherents to a commitment to a relationship with the divine but specifically the divine's privileging and restoration of the body. Additionally, the sacraments of Renewal/Rebirth and Holy Unction were deeply connected to the restoration of the physical and the symbolic body. The Shrine saw this renewal and rebirth into a new model and vision of Christianity that rejected the individualism and exclusive logics of European Christianity and argued for a communal and inclusive notion of salvation as well as Christian community. In this regard, any sick body was seen as a failure of the project of emancipation and God's witness to the world.[38] The greatest sin was the sin of individualism and the rejection of the other, and thus care for any and every body was quintessential. The creation of community-based and easily accessible programs to anyone, regardless of faith, was an essential aspect of the body interventions offered by the church. The Shrine, therefore, was body-centered and an embodied model of Afro-Christianity that attempted to engage the body in all areas of its practice. In the liturgy of the Shrine and the life of the Shrine community, the body, specifically the Black body, was elevated and its care was seen as an integral part of Afro-Christianity as well as the pathway to the creation of business and practices that were integral to the sustainability of the Black community and Black body politic.

The body-centered nature of the Shrine and its programming were most actively seen in the construction of its communal venues. The Beulah Farm in South Carolina and its much larger and widespread model of the communal parenting that was practiced throughout the Shrine communities in the United States were notably connected to the care of the community, the protection of children's bodies and psyches, and freeing parents, specifically mothers, from the task of raising children and families in isolation. While the Mother Shrine operated much like a traditional church, as the movement developed, the idea that the Black body and Black community could survive and thrive within mainstream constraints was radically questioned. As a result, Cleage argued for the creation of communities within or adjacent to the cities with the Shrines that could operate as self-sustaining models of resistance and incubators for the creation of new ideas and models in responses to the failures of democracy and capitalism. The KUA (Swahili for becoming) communities and the Beulah Farm were two such responses that not only functioned as alternative responses, but they also had a high degree of an engagement with, analysis of, and ultimately the healing of the Black body. The KUA communities were organized around creating a communal model for childcare for the Shrine members as well providing extra-curricular cultural activities and training for the children involved in the movement. The KUA communities were also the space for training, community activities, and a Shrine-sanctioned engagement with the canonical texts. The Adult study groups were an essential part of the KUA communities, and this was the initial and primary space in which adult adherents were introduced to the canonical texts of the movement and the organizing doctrine of the larger denomination. The KUA spaces were designed for what the Shrine called "Reafrikanization" and revolutionary transformation. The communities were led by Shrine-educated leaders and were organized around curriculums that were intended to educate and politicize all the committed adherents, especially the Shrine children. These communities were designed to provide space for Shrine members to continue their educations and to become more actively involved in the work of the Shrine. Specifically, the KUA communities and later the Beulah Land Farm project were designed to provide childcare as well as economic opportunities for Shrine adherents and enable politically activated adherents to be more actively involved in the work of the Shrine and the larger project of African American liberation. KUA community members were able to travel freely and to be a part of the core membership that helped to plant new Shrine communities and develop economic and social projects that would ensure the long-term sustainability of the movement. It was the KUA community that actually organized and developed the plans for the Beulah Land Farm project.

Furthermore, Cleage states the Shrine was supposed to function as a utopic space for Black bodies, lives, and Black flourishing. He defined his Black Utopia as a "utopia in formation," because it was a space where Black bodies could freely engage their Afro-centered identity and enjoy a temporary respite from the assaults of white supremacy. Temporary utopias or respites, as Cleage theorized, were necessary for the psychic healing of Black minds and bodies, but it was necessarily temporary. This notion of a temporary or sabbatical came from Cleage's reading and reconceptualization of Thurman on Sabbath and his understanding of Utopia from Gramsci. However, the Black Utopia was not the end goal as it was in conversation with the larger and more systemic revolutionary praxis that would change the hegemonic system of white racism and oppression. It reflects plural, progressive forces in collective action, with the goal of recreating work and society and their relations to nature and the biosphere in a fruitful, forward looking, and socially just manner that is welcoming to the dispossessed, the refugees, and the outcasts of the planet. The concept is an attempt to capture new imaginaries, many from the creative ranks of indigenous peoples, landless workers, women's groups, concerned scientists, public workers, progressive trades unions, environmentalists, and peoples young and old seeking to forge new political alternatives, both real and imagined. Deeply embedded in this understanding of Utopia is the notion of new politics or a renewed engagement with the political world.[39] Cleage, therefore, understood Utopia as having two functions one is to be an incubator for an oppressed group that provides safety or protection but also an engine that opens up new models for moving forward.

He argued that this is the only method by which Black folks can thrive and survive while actively experiencing and participating in the modern democratic system. Cleage, therefore, while using the language of Utopia does not argue for the disestablishment of the modern project, but rather he wants to argue for its expansive and capacious possibilities, specifically for African Americans. It is, therefore, not surprising that the Shrine rejects any sort of disengagement from politics on the local, regional, or national levels. The Shrine is not only a pilgrimage site, but it functioned as a de facto university. It is meant to be a formative space that prepares and empowers the member to transform the larger society. Even the Beulah Farms and the housing units built adjacent to the Mother Shrine in Detroit all functioned as temporary respites but ultimately it was assumed that the church, its members, and the larger public of Black radicals would build models that would be sustainable and comprehensive enough to serve the broader Black public and all of democratic society. As a result of the formative nature of these places and their function as quasi-university or training ground, the guest list of the Shrine during its earliest years included politicians, leaders, religious gurus, and thinkers of every stripe. Cleage was trying to create a new canon or a new set of literatures or scriptures with which to engage the Black community and to provide them a mechanism to develop "new imaginaries" in order to transform the broader society. His desire for new knowledge projects and new models for his adherents was evidenced not only by the number of speakers but the ideological and political variety of those invited to the Shrine and the Shrine's associated venues.

While Cleage and the Shrine often operated as a de facto university or the free exchange of ideas and public opinion and at the center of this was the Shrine of the Black Madonna Cultural Center and Bookstore established in 1970, it was clear that there were certain concepts and ideas that Cleage wanted to insert and privilege in the Black sacred public. One of the key canonical ideas for Cleage outside of Black liberation and the bodily presence of the Black Madonna and Messiah was the reconfiguration of the Black family. Cleage found himself in a heated debated within both Black radical and sacred publics on what constituted the ideal configuration of the Black family and what was the essential role for the Black woman. Cleage, ever an iconoclast, was not wedded to normative models of gendered respectability or traditional gender roles as evidenced by the KUA system and the Beulah Farm's communal living arrangement, but he did recognize the Black family and Black community as the central units of liberation. Family, therefore, played a critical role in Cleage's reading and interpretation of Biblical scripture, his understanding of community and economic self-determination, and ultimately his method for Black liberation. Unlike Cleaver, Cleage argued that Black women must function as not just nurturers and bearers of the next generation of revolutionary leaders, but he maintained that Black women, specifically, must be street-level activists and a key component of the economic self-determination paradigm. Furthermore, Cleage understood that racism had systematically destroyed the psyche of Black men as well as Black women and had destroyed the connection between Black culture and African culture, where according to Cleage women were leaders, warriors, as well as mothers. The positioning of women throughout the leadership positions of the organization as well as developing these communal models of family rearing and economic sustainability provide opportunities for both men and women to participate in the building of the Shrine community unencumbered.

Central to the pedagogical and formative aspects of the shrine were the creation of an expansive library housed at the Shrine as well as the creation of Black publishing opportunities—the Shrine Bookstore, and the supporting of other local presses and bookstore. The rise of the independent Black publishing movement was a compelling and important turn that Cleage not only introduces but popularizes.[40] Cleage understood the publishing house, alternate presses, and even bookstores to be central to the protection, production, and circulation of alternative epistemologies as well as a model for cultural-based economic development. At that time, the thriving Black Arts Movement was developing presses, music, and cultural venues in the Detroit area.[41] Dudley Randall was one of the poets who was active in the development of an alternative press movement and used the press as a mechanism to circulate ideas and images in the late 1960s. Broadside Press was broad and expansive in its conception of Black culture and though Randall was the image and writer most attached to the press, it was known for its large collection of writers and thinkers.[42] Similarly, Cleage's nascent press was not only publishing the church's books or his own—so it did not function as a denominational or vanity press, rather the publishing house was deeply embedded in the production and circulation of Black radical and Black nationalist texts. So, while it did produce literature on the Black Madonna and some of Cleage's key texts on Black sacrality and Black sacred ideas, the Shrine Bookstore and press was also producing texts that were outside of the Black sacred public sphere that shaped the cultural renaissance of the late 1960s. The texts were broad from collections of poetry to philosophical treatises on the origins of man on the continent of Africa. Many have argued that the fields of Africology emerged as a result of early imprints published through the press. This is impressive because in many ways the press was recognized for its circulation of texts on a wide variety of topics from Black theology to meditation and pop culture. Therefore, Cleage and his elevation of Black presses played a significant role in shaping what was then known as Black Studies, but ultimately it was instructive in creating the interdisciplinary and more expansive field of Africana Studies. The Shrine saw its cohorts as other Black nationalist and Black cultural presses rather than the denominational presses that focused solely on internal organizational and theological conversations. Furthermore, this highlights Cleage's interest in and focus on creating an expansive public sphere through texts and the role that alternative Christian churches played in the creation, engagement, and distribution of these texts. Cleage's vision of a radical press was central to the creation of this public sphere and the development of sets of sacred texts that could be circulated within radical Christian and non-Christian Black communities, as Cleage felt that the Black public had to be in charge of not only the production but also the circulation, sale, and ultimately the economic benefits that emerged as a result of canonical texts and the ideas in them. Moreover, the production of texts through the press, the emergence of training centers, the creation of businesses on the body, and the production of economic models made the Shrine a destination not only for a new public of believers but it also implicated the Shrine on the debates about economic growth and critiques of certain forms of middle-class mobility and respectability.

## THE RISE OF AN ALTERNATIVE NEWSPAPER AND THE SHRINE OF THE BLACK MADONNA

While the Shrine of the Black Madonna was creating a newspaper, starting bookstores, and supporting local presses and accomplishing the goal of circulating both sacred and mainstream radical texts, there were a number of printing presses that emerged in the 1950s and 1960s. There was the Third World Press, Black Classic Press, Broadside Press, and a number of others that were actively involved in publishing new authors as well as bringing classic (read canonical) African American texts back into circulation.[43] The real innovation of the Shrine, through its bookstores, was in its connection of Black publishing not only to the circulation of new knowledges but the bookstores and the publications of key texts were emblematic of a conversation on

Black wealth and Black economic development. Cleage understood the press and Black publishing as an engine of economic change and a means to create a Black "sustainable" class that achieved full citizenship through a re-education of young Black minds and having resources to invest in and maintain its community. This re-education included economic, social, political, and religious foci with a particular focus on books that were connected to grass roots activism, business development, and social praxis. Cleage often challenged the secular presses as being too wedded to the university and certain constructions of Black middle-class bourgeoisie existence and that the church presses were often seen as too insular with a focus on narrow theological and ideological agendas. Similarly, Cleage was critical of mainstream Black periodicals and newspapers. He thought these papers and magazines often bought into a model of middle-class mobility that was either inaccessible to the vast majority of its readers or a version of political accommodation that was contrary to Black liberation.

Again, Cleage saw the periodicals, alongside with local presses, of Garvey and the Nation of Islam as exemplars for challenging both the mainstream white and Black presses. Additionally, these papers were clearly outlining a method and models of critical resistance to the failures of modern democracy. While Cleage did not always agree with specific ideological claims of these papers, he believed that their mission to galvanize the Black worker and Black urban areas were central to the reorienting of democracy. This focus on revolutionizing the reader were central to Cleage's *Black Periodicals* as well as the other texts and publications that he emphasized and circulated. Ultimately, the early demise of the *Black Periodicals* (after four years) was due to its inability to create a business model outside of the immediate Shrine community and using this organ to educate activists and a larger swath of the Black radical public. While certain issues during its four-year tenure had a substantial reach, the inability to create a model to sustain the business or to attract new readers ultimately left this as a local/regional paper with limited reach. Both the limited size of the movement and the marginal reach of the movement's ideological position left the *Black Periodicals* without the requisite resources to fully innervate the marketplace. While *Muhammad Speaks*, the newspaper of the Nation of Islam movement, was supported by a much larger network of adherents and the movement which had temples throughout the United States and supporters who rejected Christianity, *Black Periodicals* did not have a substantial base of support nor did it have the robust distribution network.[44] Part of the orientation and expectation of young male adherents in the Nation was not only the study of the Koran, the words of the Nation's founders, and engagement with the newspapers of the movement, but each young man was expected to be involved in the sale and distribution of this key information organ.

This dedicated and committed "sales force" helped to maintain the distribution and sustainability of this newspaper even as other organizational press organs either folded or became relatively insignificant. Cleage did not have the size or reach that Detroit's NOI chapter had. While that NOI chapter in the middle of the 1960s boasted of over 20,000 members, over 500 active participants in its food network, and a circulation of over 5000 readers of the NOI main organ in Detroit alone, the Shrine never had more than 5000 members at its height and did not have the reach to a younger, more physically able, "sales" force.

Cleage's press was deeply committed to the production of texts that could be used by a wide variety of audiences, specifically targeting those with limited or no formal education and those who had no religious or sacred leanings. In its initial form the texts were imagined as a tool to produce a comprehensive curriculum on Afro-American history and Black liberation. These texts would cover a wide variety of topics and it was expected that they would explore history broadly and not be constrained by any theological or epistemological imperative, other than the liberation of African Americans. As a result, the texts most widely touted by the Madonna Press were those that had or little or no connection to the Shrine. While the Shrine, its creation and support of local businesses, and the press functioned as a model of economic development and community empowerment, Cleage in no way saw his local community's format for development and growth to be normative or hegemonic. Actually, Cleage argued for the widest and most diverse responses to these models of community activation and growth. Cleage highlighted the need for the communities to develop solutions that were unique to their needs and represented the concerns of activists and local leaders. Cleage argued that culturally based economic development needed to be unique to the situation and organized by local leaders who were attentive to the local need and concerns. He often argued that central to most understandings of Black respectability and assimilation were either monological mandates and ideas from outside of the Black community or monological assumptions and imperatives from within. His desire was to expand the purview of Black experimentation on economic development and growth, and ultimately, he wanted to see the reproduction of these efforts throughout the Black diaspora. While the *Black Periodicals* was a limited success for Cleage and the Shrine, Cleage highlighted its potential and the desire for other communities to adopt its logic and to develop models that might better use a local or regional newspaper to share information and to radicalize communities. Furthermore, Cleage was quite cognizant that many of his economic models were limited in their transmission to other communities and that most of the models even had limited impacted in the Detroit community. He argued that the mandate was not for easy solutions but for communities to be involved in the practice of engaging unique and diverse models for economically and culturally revitalizing their communities.

## THE SHRINE AND THE PROJECT OF CULTURAL-BASED ECONOMIC REVITALIZATION

The Shrine included a number of economic ventures that positioned the Shrine as an economic as well as religious force in the late 1960s and throughout the 1970s. Critical to the economic programs that Cleage and the Shrine introduced were a critique of colonialist urban renewal alongside an interest in creating models of sustainability and economic self-determination. Particularly, Cleage was very critical of the federal 1967 Detroit Urban Renewal program and the colonialist impulses of this program. He argued that this idea of open occupancy was based upon the total erasure or denial of the Black community. Cleage argued, "All a person has to do is walk through any community which has been marked for 'open occupancy' and they can see what is happening."[45] He continued that the current apparatus of the democratically run government had the resources to change these conditions, but the current construction of democracy was built on the extension of the plight and the disregard and exclusion of the African American citizen. Cleage continued "the Board of Health, the Bureau of Building and Engineering, the City Planning Commission and other such bureaus have the machinery through which they can act to prevent the extension of this blight."[46] This signified not only Cleage's dismissal of the current city leadership and their plan for urban renewal, but it also signified his commitment to the levers of democracy. Cleage did not call for the outright destruction of these institutions, but he called for African American revitalization and ownership of the city and these boards.

He was committed to a vision of democracy that provided African Americans the sovereignty to control and shape the initiatives and institutions that impacted their well-being. This particular desire to rebuild Detroit was in response to the Detroit riots of 1963 and the overall gutting of the Paradise Valley and Black Bottom neighborhoods during the federal Urban Renewal programs. This process of removing and gutting Black neighborhoods was not unique to Detroit, and much of Cleage's discursive response was in line with the language and action of other Black-led movements and community-based economic responses around the country. Other Black-led movements like this included the Black Panthers, the National Liberationist Front, and the Black Communist Party, all of which identified the colonial logic that informed urban renewal and called for Black and poor communities to recognize this as an assault on their freedom and a direct violation of Black bodies and the Black body politic. Again, critical to Cleage's intervention was his focus on the alternative Afro-Christian response to these issues and his particular model of institution building. "We are calling together community leadership organizations and individuals to act in this matter of Urban Renewal," Cleage advised Mr. Dunmore. This meant that while Cleage was invested in the integration of tactics and paradigms from a number of Black radical movements, included but not limited to the aforementioned Nation of Islam and The Black Panthers, he diverged from these movements with his and the Shrine's commitment to a specific and nuanced account of African American Christianity. He did not see the call for labor rights, cultural revitalization, or even forms of violent protest as in violation of the ethical norms of his religious movement. For Cleage to be Black and Christian was to be the very ground for a radical politics and even in his discussion on electoral politics and economic self-determination the language of religion and Black theology were actively present. Economic and cultural revitalization depended on the critique of dominant institution as well as mechanisms to support and grow the new models. Resistance, even armed resistance, and economic revitalization were often connected for Cleage as he endeavored to create a self-sustaining model of businesses, political organizations, and educational models. The economic revitalization would require the physical and symbolic removal of language, institutions, and people that stood in the way of Black liberation.[47]

This remaking of the urban landscape required a comprehensive re-educating of all parties who were willing and interested in being involved. This model of training, vetting, and deploying a new vanguard of public servants was not unique to Cleage and his movement, but the quality of his interaction with the public domain often outstripped other alternative religions which suggested that insular- and ritual-based activities would better serve their interests and concerns. He called for the African American community to become "even more politically alert" and elect more "black people to public offices."[48]

In response to a wholesale reorganization of the Black public, in 1964 the MFNP ran a full slate of "Black" candidates for office, with Jaramogi Abebe (Cleage) as its gubernatorial candidate in Michigan. One primary example of the internalized or insular model of reform was the Nation of Islam movement which called for a nation within a nation. In the words of Elijah Muhammad, the United States and its institutions could never be amenable to Black freedom and flourishing, so the only option was to create a nation-state that was run and organized within the constraints or borders of western capitalism but that had qualitatively different rules, rights, and expectations for its primarily Black citizenry.[49] Cleage, however, was vocal that the Shrine's engagement with the Black public and the larger public should be explicit, extensive, and expansive. The larger goal was to re-invigorate and reposition African Americans in relationship to participatory democracy and using those resources to create newly imagined institutions, radically change existing institutions, and provide new mechanisms for cultural and economic growth. Cleage saw the Shrine, and ultimately the network of Shrines, as the first step to rethinking modern America and African American's relationship to it.[50] His language of nationalism was not dependent on exclusion or separatism but rather a call for a radical model of inclusion as well as a revitalizing of cultural, economic, and political systems. It was inclusive to the degree that everyone or anyone that pledged fealty to it and who understood the key and important role of Black bodies was considered an ally. Ultimately, the economic revitalization was dependent not solely on the success of any one of the individual businesses, but Cleage outlined that the economic revitalization must be accompanied by a wholesale transformation of the culture and the systems that surrounded African Americans and their communities. Therefore, the creation of a culture that valued Black history, elevated the Black radical as potential political leaders, and envisioned communal sustainability were key to the Shrine's economic plans. As a result, when the press and the newspaper failed to gain traction it was not seen as the end of the Shrine's economic engagement with Black public sphere, but it was just one aspect of the Shrine's interest in developing and empowering a Black public.

## CLEAGE AND THE BLACK CHURCH

If Cleage was actively involved with a number of interlocutors, ranging from politicians to Black Panthers, one relationship that was relatively fraught was his interaction with mainstream Black Christians. Cleage was actively trying to engage the broader Black public, which included the Black church, while simultaneously trying to dismantle its anchor institutions. As a result, the Black Christian mainstream bore the brunt of Cleage's dismissive or disruptive critiques. The leadership of the mainstream Black church as well as the structure and training of Black Christian leaders were questioned by Cleage and his movement. He argued in the manual for the BCN Training program in 1973, "The NAACP, The Urban League, SCLC, Jessie Jackson's Push, and the traditional Black Church offer Black people no alternative to powerlessness."[51] Furthermore, he argued that the task at hand not only required the restricting of these organizations and the seminaries that were training Black ministers, but that it was necessary "to restructure every aspect of [the] Black community through the building of church-centered Black counter institutions and the training of Black people."[52] It is the canonical story of Cleage's relationship with King that highlights Cleage's deep fissure with some aspects of the mainstream Southern civil rights movement and the Black Christian establishment. Prior to the famed March for Jobs and Freedom in Washington, DC, there was a freedom march organized by Cleage and Rev. C. L. Franklin and headlined by King in Detroit. The march was noted for its large numbers and for King using an earlier and longer version of his "I Have a Dream" speech. While King was complementary of the progress and the excitement of the Detroit participants, Cleage was critical of the conciliatory tone of King's speech, and he decried how the mainstream Black Christian establishment forced the march organizers to exclude a number of more radical local leaders and organizations.[53] Cleage, while not enamored with King's ideological position, argued that there was much to learn about resistance and transformation from the southern civil rights movement and often mentioned the extraordinary work of SNCC and its collaboration with the SCLC. These types of collaborations were essential to Cleage as he wanted to highlight the vibrancy and variety within the Black public sphere and the need for groups with different approaches to engage one another. He even was nominated in 1969 to be the chairperson of the National Council of Negro Churchmen, a mainstream Black church organization that was attempting to bring the Black church into conversation with the larger political and social changes taking place. While his candidacy was positioned as radical outsider and it was never considered as a viable option, this nomination and even his early relationship to this organization spoke to the ways that Cleage and the larger Black public and the Black church overlapped. Eventually, Cleage would break entirely from the National Council of Negro Churchmen, and he would argue that certain segments of the Black Christian public benefitted from silencing and excluding radical or alternative voices. As a result, Cleage felt that the potential transformation of Black Christianity was often muted or marginalized by these moderate and more inclusive (read assimilationist) movements.

Cleage often argued that the Black Christian community had defaulted on its responsibility to the Black community and bought into certain problematic models of respectability and that his only recourse was to rethink the whole of the African American Christian tradition. His Shrine not only departed in its rethinking of the economic and political legitimacy of Black development, but there were significant theological distinctions between Cleage and much of the mainstream Black Christian tradition. Cleage argued that the Christian encounter must seriously address the role of Africa in the Bible and for Cleage that meant not simply identifying and highlighting African locations in the Old and New Testaments or identifying noteworthy characters that had African genealogy or origins. Rather, Cleage wanted to suggest that African culture, practices, and religion were validated and engaged within the scriptural narrative. Cleage's reading and circulation of Afro-centric historians like Rabbi Hilu Paris, Dr. Yoself ben-Jochanan, and John G. Jackson deeply influenced the structure of the Shrine's liturgy and its implications for Black theological thought. These historians not only addressed the absence or suppression of African and thus African American history, but these theorists argued that all of modern civilization had its origin in Africa. For Cleage and these thinkers, this included Judaism and Christianity.[54] Furthermore, the Shrine movement suggested that the Christian tradition did not require a jettisoning of Afro-diasporic religious and cultural traditions. As a result, many Christian communities described the Shrine movement as a rejection of orthodoxy, but Cleage saw Black Christianity as a rejection of the European orthodoxy that was masquerading as Christianity and preventing more heterodox and culturally authentic presentations from gaining traction.

Therefore, Cleage establishes himself as one of the earliest and most explicit engagers of an Afro-centric Christian tradition. This meant that Cleage was heavily invested in identifying these African traditions, rituals, and practices and integrating them into the liturgical and cultural practices of the Shrine. Ultimately, Cleage's creation of the Black Nationalist Christian Movement and then the denomination that is still called the African Orthodox Church was invested in publicly engaging the theological and political role of African American religions. So, while he used the Christian text and emphasized the role of the Black Messiah and the Black Madonna, he was very interested in creating space for a variety of religious traditions. His conversations with Father Divine and his relationship with the Nation of Islam spoke clearly not only to a shared political or social critique but a desire to reimagine African American's relationship to religion. So, while the Shrine was a distinctively African American Christian intervention, there was a clear negotiation of the diaspora and particularly diasporic religious traditions. One specific example of this elevation of the African religious heritage were the images of the Yoruba gods on the walls of the Shrine, the libations to the ancestors that happened at each service, and the prioritization of Afro-religious texts within the bookstore, worship services, and Cleage's debates with the larger African American Christian Black sphere. Later in 1971 in a conversation with Wilfred X, Cleage again outlined the importance of not only accepting but integrating the variety of Black religious traditions. He was not tied to an exclusivist reading of Christianity, but he wanted to expand the shape and reach of the Black sacred sphere and who was bringing solutions and interventions to be considered by the broader Black public. Thus the rejection of the normative Black Christian church was not only a rejection of their methods and their historiography of Africa and Christianity, but it was a rejection of the refusal to include alternative voices in the projects for liberation. The Black Nationalist Christian Movement was at times more a Black nationalist organization than it was Christian and that specifically meant that it was not trapped by a narrow lens of what constituted Christianity and was far more invested in Black and African-diasporic liberation. It saw Afro-Christianity as a method by which to identify the liberatory possibilities within the broader context of Afro-religion and to look for ways to harness and engage these ideas within the broader community.

As a result, the canonical texts of the movement were not only the biblical text, but there was a new set of scriptures that included the Bible; as well as famous speeches by Garvey and Malcolm X; Cleage's books; the works of African and African American philosophers, Afro-Atlantic religious movements, activists and thinkers; and the works of thinkers in the field of Black theology, like James Cone. Furthermore, the canonical body of the Black Madonna and the symbolic and discursive work that the Madonna did for Cleage's community and the larger public were essential to his intervention. Cleage wanted sacred Black flesh or the importance of sacred Black bodies throughout the diaspora to not only be a part of African American's relationship to diasporic religions but also be a keen part of the African American Christian tradition. The body (the images of the body, the body of Jesus and Mary, and the bodies of the adherents) became a text (a sacred text) that was elevated within the spaces of worship, and Cleage and his movement identified and outlined different ways to incorporate the Black body into liturgy, ritual, and the everyday practice of African American Christian communities. As a result, the text or the idea that dominated Cleage's analysis and intervention was the body. The circulation of these new ideas and the construction of a new Black Christian identity were central to Cleage's larger project. For Cleage, Black scriptures and Black canonical texts could not be solely focused on otherworldly salvation, but Black Scriptures (canonical texts and institutions) must provide options to adequately account for the genesis, maintenance, and future of Black identity, including culture, politics, and economic self-determination. Therefore, Cleage identified texts, ideas, and projects that did this work and actively sought to circulate those texts to radically change the shape of the Black community. While he consumed texts and ideas from a number of religious movements and radical communities, he was very active in formalizing a set of canonical texts and attempting to introduce those texts both inside and outside of his Black Christian Nationalist movement. While his texts were critical to the development of the church and the creation of the Black sacred public in Detroit, Cleage was much more expansive in the texts and ideas that he circulated and popularized as he traveled the country.[55] The texts that he thought were essential for the Black sacred public were quite eclectic, but they all engaged Afro-centrism as a spiritual practice, the Black body as a site of sacred revelation, and the restoration or renewal of Black community and Black participation in democracy as central to freedom. Often this diverse and varied approach to Black religion meant that Cleage was often at odds with a Black church sector that wanted to highlight respectability, the Bible as the singular or most significant source of revelation, and was primarily interested in removing overt racial language from theology, liturgy, and political engagements rather than reconsidering the larger constraints for Black bodies embedded in Western Christianity.

## CLEAGE AND BLACK THEOLOGY

In many ways, Cleage functioned as one of the earliest progenitors, producers, and distributors of a method or set of texts that would eventually become Black theology.[56] He literally coined the term "Black theology" in the 1950s and he understood Black theology and his heterodox form of Black Christianity as being necessarily connected to the very needs of Black people. James Cone, the intellectual and systematic theologian most commonly associated with Black theology, found himself at the foot of Cleage as a teacher and intellectual provocateur. James traveled to the Shrine while a student at Eden Theological Seminary during the 1960s. In his initial text, *Black Theology and Black Power*, Cone introduces Cleage and the Shrine of the Black Madonna as one of the few authentic purveyors of Black theology.[57] In his dissertation he talks about Cleage as a progenitor and practitioner of what will later become Black theology. Cleage, unlike many of the other alternative religions in the middle of the twentieth century, had a particular relationship to Black theologians (which was very different from engaging with the Black church) and the Black academy and what might be labeled as the mainstream Black church (and should I say Black Christianity).[58] Early on Cleage was charter member of the National Committee of Black Churchmen and ultimately resigned because of his critique of their politics and overarching tendency to minimize its revolutionary impact and force. Cleage was not invested in creating Black theology as an academic discipline, but he wanted to create a new mechanism for thinking about Black self-determination as a political, economic, and religious possibility. Cleage's practical Black theology was a mechanism for using aspects of the Christian narrative to accomplish this, and it was also a key aspect of revolutionizing seminary education for Black pastors. Black theology was not as much as a disciplinary formation as it was a crucial part of transforming the mainstream seminary curriculum.[59] If colonizing the city to make it amenable to Black life and Black culture were central to Cleage's organizing model, decolonizing the seminary or the field of Black religion/Black church studies at that time was a secondary and necessary aspect of the movement. In addition to engaging activists and politicians, Cleage and the Shrine were known for their engagement with the Black theological thought leaders of that time. What constituted Black Christianity or the importance of Black religion in the modern world was something that Cleage and the Shrine wanted to specifically debate—therein creating a particular space upon which a Black sacred public could emerge and was not simply reduced to the political and social interventions of the Black church. The Black sacred public was one that took the entirety of African America's relationship to sacrality seriously and tried to create a space where these ideas and concepts were engaged. Cleage's vision for this public and who should be included was broad and the agenda for the Shrine represented that.

Important to this public were not only the appearance of denominational leaders or even theological provocateurs, but central to its vitality was the exchange of ideas, symbols, and language that constituted the public's concern with what constituted sacredness and what that meant for African Americans.[60] In this regard, Cleage and his cohorts moved from studying the burgeoning field of Black theology to thinking about the ways in which it could be distributed to cities and churches around the country. While the Shrine Press was one mechanism of distribution of these texts and ideas, the construction of theological centers (the Black Christian Nationalist Training Program) was another vision of Cleage and the Shrine.[61] While these "Afrocentric" programs and quasi-seminaries were not that successful, there were a couple that took off in Chicago, Atlanta, and Oakland. These schools or seminaries functioned as a training ground for activists and thinkers and often had a collection of adjunct faculty, theological thinkers, and religious leaders who provided classes, training, and mentorship. None of these centers ultimately provided any official degrees, but they did have a number of key participants who ultimately would become important writers and figures in the Black theological and African American religious movement. Most importantly, these training programs and quasi-seminaries were the pilots for new models and courses adopted by universities and extant seminaries.

In addition to these training programs for ministerial students or adjunct seminaries, Cleage was also heavily invested in shaping the emerging field of Black Studies. He wanted this field to actively reflect the Afro-centric character that was at the heart of the Shrine and his theological revolution, but he also wanted Black Studies and the emerging programs around the country to accurately reflect the broad religious and theological diversity of African Americans. Furthermore, he wanted Africana spirituality and wellness to be a constitutive component of these programs. The creation of the Black Studies program at Wayne State University was heavily influenced by Cleage and his religio-political revolution. Moreover, Cleage was an activist alongside students demanding the program at Wayne State be fully funded and staffed and was a speaker at the installation of the program. At that installation he argued and provided a cogent definition of the role of Black Studies and its role in the Shrine's holistic educational initiative. Transforming education and inserting

Black folks' relationship to religion was a part of all aspects of the Shrine program. From their primary and secondary schools in Detroit, adjunct seminaries and theological spaces, Black Studies program on university campuses, and a boarding school on the communal farm in South Carolina, the inclusion of Africana religious history was crucial and seen as a constitutive part of the curriculum. Black theology, in this sense, was not simply a theological or advance degree opportunity, but it was operative as the essential mechanism for the re-educating of Black children and the organizing of the Black sacred sphere. Cleage believed that the introduction of the methods and models of Black theology into the sacred public would radically shift the construction of religious institutions as well as models of social and political transformation.

One of the major critiques of these centers and the training programs was that they basically became a means for Cleage, his press, and particular bookstores to gain a stronger foothold in particular African American communities. The legitimacy of these institutions as robust training grounds was at question for folks within the Shrine community as well as other religious communities interacting with Cleage and the Shrine. Nevertheless, these centers created the model of counterinstitutions that created and circulated new knowledges, provided opportunities for public thinkers and activists, and provided audiences for texts and ideas that otherwise might have not made it to as broad an audience. However, the Black sacred public was not confined to these official or institutional spaces. While these spaces (the "seminaries" and ad-hoc seminars) highlighted that there was a robust intellectual discussion about what constituted African American religion and sacrality, Cleage and other leaders of alternative religious movements argued that the growth of their movements signaled a shift in how the larger African American community engaged religion and their desire to create a public debate or public conversation on how the sacred and Black freedom worked in relationship with one another. Cleage, in this regard, understood that his movement was a departure from the normative Black Christian tradition, and he wanted to create a space where new models for institution building and a new discourse in the form of a nascent Black theological project could be engaged by the broadest public possible. Therefore, some have argued that rather than seeing his denomination as an attempt codify or institutionalize the specifics of his tradition, that the denomination was the means to create a discourse on Black religion and Black freedom that would prove to be useful to a much larger segment of the Black public. This was most powerfully and clearly articulated in the ways that the debate about the Black messiah evolved and developed in the public. From articles in *Jet Magazine*, the *New York Times* article, and even in local newspapers around the country, it was clear that Cleage's discourse on Christianity and Black liberation had harnessed the Black public sphere.[62] Even the production of images that were bought and consumed by Black consumers and the introduction of this worldview into a series of large scale art installations, albums by well-known Black musicians, and even the emergence of the Black messiah in film and television. The mass dissemination and consumption of the Blackness of Christianity, specifically the Black messiah, led to opportunities for alternative religious formations as well as the radical restructuring of already existing ones.

While Cleage wanted to create new language for Black religious formation, he never abandoned the religious institution and its role as the basic unit for the creation and maintenance of Black freedom. He argued often that "When first class citizenship is achieved, I can go back to pastoring and working with young people."[63] Cleage was not inimical to the church but saw the re-envisioned church and the attendant discourse of Black theology as central to the Black public. His critique of mainstream Black Christian movements was that their theology and discourse functioned to ignore or evade the radical inequality or powerlessness present in political and ecclesial systems. Moreover, Cleage here uses the language of citizenship to suggest that African American belonging or full participation in the current moment was a critical part of his work and the role of religious institutions. His vision and version of Black theology had at its core the restructuring of not just theological claims and the church but the restructuring of citizenship and democracy. Cleage was insisting that democracy be responsive to the ideas and demands that were being formulated by these radical religio-political spaces. He therefore saw Black theology as a discursive framework to challenge Christianity as well as modernity.[64] As a result, he worked to create a Black theological method that provided the very parameters for a Black liberation agenda. His texts, therefore, alongside Cone and *Is God a White Racist* by Jones, not only developed key texts for the field of Black religious studies, but they become a central aspect of the curriculums of Afro-centric and politically radically Black churches. Additionally, Cleage is particularly nuanced and one of the earliest Black theological thinkers who argue for a return to Afro-centric and Black diasporic identities in order to create a more robust Christian narrative. Cleage's version of Christianity and Black theology is much more porous and amenable to a cultural narrative that is reconstituted based upon the needs of Afro-Americans and their relationship to the broader diaspora.

## THE END OF THE SHRINE AND THE SCRIPTURAL LEGACY

There is compelling evidence that while the Shrine and its local impact in Detroit began to decline by the end of the 1970s and that the larger impact of the Shrine on the Black public continues to have a relatively significant impact. On one level, the Shrine begat a number of other Shrines and installations of the Black body throughout the United States. Besides the Mother Shrine in Detroit, by the middle of the 1970s there were seven Shrines in the Detroit area, five to seven locally run Shrines in major cities around the country, and a growing network of churches that ascribed to the ideology and theological formation associated with Cleage's nascent denomination, the Pan-African Orthodox Christian Church (PAOCC). Additionally, many of the works developed by the press, especially Cleage's landmark texts, had become required reading for Black Studies and theological programs across the country. Cleage and his creation of Afro-Christianity with a focus on the "iconic" Black body had become a constitutive part of the Black sacred public and the development of community-centered churches throughout the country. While the physical Shrine and the original painting were no longer attracting the kind of attention that it had originally gained, the ideas and canon that Cleage had imagined were now more fully assimilated into the Black public, including the new formations within the Black church in the early 1980s. It is worth mentioning that the Shrines across the country did not only copy the deification of the Black female body and the integration of the idea of pilgrimage, but the Shrines included efforts to decolonize/colonize cities and to think about the viability of local bookstores and counter institutions. Examples of these efforts are visible in the still extant Shrine museum and bookstore in Atlanta and the work being done in Houston around engaging Afro-diasporic populations. The Atlanta Shrine and its associated institutions were renowned for its engagement of local activists, scholars, and the broader community. The bookstore associated with the Atlanta Shrine was and remains a key institution that is connected to the Black radical and progressive public in Atlanta. Similar to the original Shrine (Shrine #1), the Atlanta Shrine was and remains committed to rethinking the logic of Black economic revitalization and upward mobility amongst the Black middle class and sought to offer an alternative vision of Black community and Black economic empowerment and solidarity.

The Atlanta Shrine and its political activism challenged the mainstream Black community and normative Black respectability through its slate of progressive/radical African American candidates. It challenged the Black public sphere and status quo by suggesting that the race of the candidate alone did not qualify him or her to represent the interests of the Black community, especially the concerns of Black resistance. Similar to Detroit, the Atlanta Shrine attempted to challenge the mainstream project of urban renewal and to protect the interests of poor and working-class Blacks that were being displaced by this movement. One of the key moments in the life of the Atlanta Shrine was Cleage's visit to the Shrine in 1973 and his public debate with the city planner at that time. Cleage made a compelling argument in the city newspapers and in local venues that Atlanta was "masquerading" as a city concerned with Black lives and interests. He continued that true democracy and liberation required that Black nationalists and Black Christian nationalists be at the table and determine the terms of the agenda. In as much as the local Shrines were dedicated to developing a local and particular agenda, much of the press and attention of these local branches was connected to the attention brought by the Shrine's association with Cleage or the physical visits or interventions of Cleage to the Shrines or their agenda.

Cleage and the Shrines introduced a new means to do the Black church that enthusiastically and consistently combined a reverence for the Black body, a commitment to the Christian or religious worldview, and a desire to transform the political and cultural constraints of the democratic process. After Cleage, the claim to be Black and Christian was no longer the primary purview of the "the Black Church," but he extended the type of communities and narratives that were able and willing to join into this conversation. Black Christianity was more capacious and diverse as a result of the creation of this nascent language of Black theology and the return to the Black body that alternative Christianities, like Cleage's, revitalized within Black religious and Christian communities. So while the physical impact of the Shrine was limited during the second half of the twentieth century, the philosophical and symbolic reach of the movement was experienced quite broadly. The creation of an Afro-centric church that critically rejected the language of respectability and integration, developed radical alternatives to democracy, and re-imagined cultural and economic self-determination as a model that was deeply connected to Africana aesthetics, religions, and practices. There was a desire to challenge the notion that middle-class mobility and Black integration were the mechanisms to transforming society or even a ticket to full participation. Both Cleage and his cohort of Afro-centric Christian movements as well as the mainline Black churches were looking for new ways to do Christianity in light of the limited success of the Civil Rights Movement, the continuing decay of urban America and its citizens of color, and the desire to create sustainable economic and social interventions. As a result, there was the emergence of a new respectability and a new canon that was centered on the elevation and sacrality of the Black body and the body's full participation in Christendom and democracy. Furthermore, the respectability that was centered in these counter traditions was not the adoption of white, western normative standards, but what might be called an African-centered self-determination that included a certain demand that Black folks control their institutions and local communities.

Finally, while the Shrine constituted and was a part of an emerging alternative Black public in the United States, it was also a part of a nascent internationalist public. The structure of the Shrine and its model of pilgrimage sites connected the Shrine to a growing number of Black pilgrimage sites around the world. In the foundational moments of the Shrine, Cleage was always clear to highlight the deep tradition of Black Madonnas that existed around the world. The Shrine, he argued, was one of many that highlighted the non-European, non-Western character of Christianity. Ultimately, Cleage was interested in rethinking the relationship of the Black public to the broader diaspora and how to revitalize all these areas of Black diasporic culture. While the transnational component of Cleage's work was hindered by access to capital and his resources and connections in these far-flung diasporic cities, he like Father Divine and Mason all recognized that the transforming of the Black public in the United States inherently needed and had repercussions for a transatlantic Black public.[65]

## CONCLUSION

The Shrine still stands today and is still visited by thousands of tourists. The PAOCC is still a fledgling denomination attempting to bring together disparate corners of Black radicalism and post-Black Christianity.[66] Neither the church nor the denomination, however, has the same impact on the Black sacred public as it did fifty years ago. In a crumbling church on an underdeveloped street and struggling section of Detroit, the shrine stands as a reminder of the desire to revitalize the Black sacred public and to save the city of Detroit. Sixty years later, African American schools in this neighborhood have been taken over by the state, the deaths of young Black and brown men are higher than they have ever been in the last fifty years, and the vast majority of the housing and business properties are being brought by developers hoping for a white renaissance of downtown Detroit. The vision of a new form of Black respectability or economic self-determination that was deeply intertwined with a renewed vision of economic development, social and educational autonomy, and the colonizing of a city for Black well-being ultimately fell short. Many of the people who remain as caretakers of the Shrine are a cohort of African American women who travel in from far-flung suburbs or were members of the satellite Shrines having moved away from the vision that Cleage had for the Shrine, Black respectability, and economic development. They are now "docents" of a tourist site and the maintainers of an institution that endeavored to bring development and attention to Black Detroit and now provides very little for the economy or infrastructure of downtown Detroit.[67] The Shrine now stands as a memory of an earlier movement, a nascent attempt to sacralize the Black body, and a vision for re-imagining the twentieth century modern project in a way that the world serves the needs and interests of the Black community.

While the Shrine of the Black Madonna and its network of shrines and local bookstores no longer exist, or exist as a shadow of their former selves, the turn to the body, a reinvention of the project of Black and religious self-determination, and the demand for Afro-centric Christianity and methods for Black economic development reverberated and still have traction throughout the Black sacred public. In Andrea Abram's work on an Afro-centric church in Atlanta, the two forebears mentioned by the leaders of these churches were the Trinity United Church of Christ in Chicago and the Cleage's Shrine of the Black Madonna.[68] This church and a series of contemporary churches like them signal the importance of the Black body, the inclusion of Afro-diaspora rituals, the supporting of the Black arts, and a new model of economic respectability. From the adoption of African dress to the reincorporation of community banking and new diet regimes, there is a re-imagining of Black middle-class identity and alongside that there is an alternative vision of Black self-determination. This attention to Cleage (and Cone) and his vision of Afro-centric radical Christianity has opened up the possibility of Black sacred spaces and a much wider set of rituals and ideas. In addition to setting the ground for a vision of Afro-centric churches, the Cleage model also set up the logic of community-based (or community responsible) economic development that was organized around economic sustainability for the local community rather than just the sustainability of a single institution. This model of deliberate and organic wealth creation for the community rather than simply accepting the dominant model of integrating into the capitalist infrastructure was a unique feature of Cleage. Cleage's holistic and alternative approach (should we call it Black alternative capitalism) is one that has spawned a number of imitators and his model and the Black Madonna remain canonical for Afro-Christian religious movements. At the center of most of these movements are not only direct references to the Shrine of the Black Madonna, but there are the installations of sacred Black bodies, the insistence on Black self-determination, and the desire to provide alternative solutions to the democratic state. While Cleage's intervention clearly led to brown and Black "Jesuses" as well as Black Madonnas filling the pulpits and walls of a number of African American sanctuaries, it also led to the reconsideration of the everyday Black body, the needs for Black communal sustainability, and a new set of texts and ideas that became canonical in the Black public sphere. It is Cleage's shift to the body and his work in expanding the Black sacred sphere that provided the new vocabulary for thinking and creating not only diverse Black religious spaces but critiques and responses to the system of democracy. While the Madonna herself may not have persisted in the vocabulary and iconography of the Black church or even alternative Black religious systems, a call for a renewed attention to the Black body and Black body politic have.

## NOTES

1. Cleage and the planning committee actively engaged and researched the history of Black Madonnas around the world. While Cleage argued that the presence of black Madonnas throughout Europe and the Middle East reflected a long-held understanding of the African genealogy of the Madonna and its significance for a variety of communities, the Shrine of the Black Madonna in Detroit, however, would represent the first installation of a Black Madonna in the United States by an African American church.
2. The Shrine Archives, "Why We Exist," 1967.
3. Lawrence, "The Black Madonna."
4. The African Methodist Episcopalian Church under the leadership of and the Garveyite movement was known for celebrating Africa as well as the relationship between African Americans and the African symbols and communal models. See "Black Power and the Garvey Movement."
5. See the Albert B. Cleage, *The Black Messiah* (New York, NY: Sheed and Ward, 1968).
6. Repeated in articles in the *Detroit Free Press* and the *Michigan Chronicle*. The *Michigan Chronicle* was the most widely distributed African American newspaper in Detroit during the first half of the twentieth century.
7. The Shrine Archives, 1968, "Speech on the Opening of the Church."
8. *Detroit Free Press*, January 1963.
9. Long, *Significations*.
10. The Shrine Archives, 1966, "Letter of Resignation to the Presbyterian Church."
11. Ibid.
12. One of the key aspects of Cleage's introduction of the Black Madonna was to highlight its unique and radical importance for the African American Protestant Movement in the United States. However, Cleage also wanted to highlight that the Black Madonna was not a modern or African American invention. The Black Madonna and shrines to this dark figure were found in myriad places around the world, and therefore Cleage and his Shrines were making historical, theological, and culture claims. He was specifically engaging what it meant for African Americans to reclaim the legacy of the Black Madonna in the middle of the twentieth century and connect this figure to a struggle for autonomy and liberation.
13. The terms "scripture" or "canonical text" both represent ideas, symbols, conversations, or actual written texts that were acknowledged and circulated in the Black public. In this text, I lean toward the use of canonical text, because I am arguing that the text was not just circulated as an option for the Black public sphere, but it became a dominant and influential force in how Black religious and Black political communities were assessed.

14. In particular, the Shrine and Cleage's writings commenced a discussion on what constituted Afro-centric Christianity and what was the relationship between Afro-centric Christianity and more normative and mainline movements. Cleage's was not the first, but what this chapter argues is that his movement was central in organizing and distributing texts, ideas, and conversations about the values of an Afro-centric Christianity in the Black sacred sphere.

15. Detroit Free Press, "Cleage and the Presbyterian Church" 1970.

16. This particular group of women was entitled the "Women of the Shrine," and they were primarily tasked with the upkeep of the Shrine and the coordination of Cleage's schedule. Alongside Cleage's coordinating secretary, this committee was instrumental in maintaining the physical plant and creating and maintaining the Shrine's calendar of events.

17. Archives of the Shrine.

18. While Cleage included and often highlighted the needs of Black women, there was still the presence of the masculinist language that shaped much of the nationalist and radical discourse of Black religious and political movements at the late 1960s. Black women were an essential component of the Shrine's programs and practices, but often its forward-facing language included traditional language that bolstered or centered the concerns of Black men.

19. A great deal of work has been done on the Divine and the washer women that his movement supported and the role that he played in shattering the image of the Black domestic and Black washer woman and transforming that into a model of economic development for Black female entrepreneurs. See Weisenfeld, *New World a-Coming*; R. Marie Griffith, *Born Again Bodies: Flesh and Spirit in American Christianity*, California Studies in Food and Culture (Berkeley, CA: University of California Press, 2004). Additionally, there is important work that has been done on the role that Black women played in the UNIA, especially as entrepreneurs and economic and political activists.

20. Jaramogi Agyeman (also known as Albert Cleage), "Easter Sunday Sermon," 26 March 1967, www.shrineoftheblackmadonna10.org.

21. Kahan, "The Other Harlem Renaissance."

22. Cleage was an explicit fan of the Gramscian notion of organic intellectuals. He believed that knowledge should be produced by citizens who had a clear relationship with the community and that knowledges should be elevated that are critically connected to the well-being of the local community.

23. Velma Thomas in the Jawanza Clark Volume, Jawanza Eric Clark, Albert Cleage Jr., and the Black Madonna and Child, http://search.ebscohost.com/login.aspx?direct=true&scope=site&db=nlebk&db=nlabk&AN=1353243.

24. There have been a number of debates on the popularity and the reach of the mother Shrine. While the Shrine archives highlight the growth of the church, especially through the creation of "satellite" Shrines throughout Michigan and the United States, other newspapers have measured the reach of the Shrine through the amount of funds collected or the number of members on its rolls. However, Cleage makes a compelling argument that its reach could not and should not be limited to people, institutions, or even funds associated with the Shrine, but rather Cleage wants to

engage the ways that it impacted other movements, churches, and cultural institutions and their method of liberation and economic empowerment.

25. It is important to note that the Shrine functioned as a comprehensive community development initiative with housing units, a bookstore, and activities six or seven days a week during the height of the Shrine movement. This section is particularly interested in the ways that Cleage's understanding of economic development was deeply invested in producing a religious movement that met the political, economic, and educational needs of its adherents in a holistic fashion that deviated from the traditional black church model at that time. I used the language of "between Sundays" to highlight the ways that Cleage was invested in "decolonizing" all aspects of his adherents' practices and beliefs. See Marla Frederick's use of this phrase in Frederick, *Between Sundays*.

26. Cleage's readings of Thurman are particularly instructive here for his sermons and writings on Thurman highlight that Cleage primarily agreed with Thurman's argument in *Jesus and the Disinherited*. See Howard Thurman, *Jesus and the Disinherited* (Richmond, IN: Friends United Press, 1981).

27. The mural tradition speaks to the idea that this practice was being adopted in a number of traditions. There is the important distinction between an artistic tradition that was being developed and refined by artists and a new set of practices that made this type of artwork available in commercial settings.

28. *Detroit Free Press*, 1967.

29. The discussion of the embodiment of the divine was a crucial aspect of Thurman's *Jesus and the Disinherited*, and this focus on embodiment is a critical part of James Cone and Delores Williams as they developed the projects of Black Theology and Womanist Theology and Ethics. Embodiment, however, was a critical component of the alternative religious movements at that time as well as the mainstream Christian public sphere. The body or the disregard of the body was a central part of civil discourse at that time and religious movements had to explicitly respond to the body in order to be rendered legible to the African American public. See Evans, *The Burden of Black Religion*.

30. Black Cultural Restoration as defined by this project sought to restore images of Africa, African Americans, and its relationship to social, cultural, and religious rituals.

31. The Shrine of the Black Madonna Archives, 1968.

32. The Shrine of the Black Madonna Archives, 1971.

33. The most well-known pragmatist traditions of the twentieth century in this regard would be Booker T. Washington's adoption of the early forms of American industrialism and Martin Luther King as a pragmatic adopter of Western democracy during the early stages of his public career. Many would argue that both King and Washington and most in the African American pragmatist camp argue for moral suasion and "incrementalism" as methods for the advancement of the race. See Dawson, *Black Visions*.

34. FBI Files, 1969, Speaking Appearance of Le Roi Jones at the Shrine of the Black Madonna, Detroit, MI.

35. This is a quote by John Webster, Chairman of the Forum Committee at the Mother Shrine in the FBI Files, Speaking Appearance of Le Roi Jones at the Shrine of the Black Madonna, 1969.

36. See Alondra Nelson, *Body and Soul: The Black Panther Party and the Fight against Medical Discrimination* (Minneapolis, MN and London: University of Minnesota Press, 2011).

37. The term the "business of the body" is a term that is used by Karla Holloway to describe the significant role that Black churches, morticians, and funeral homes played in dealing with the often and premature deaths of African Americans throughout the twentieth century. See Holloway, *Passed On*. This idea could further be extended to the idea of "necropolitics" and the way that it shapes Africana existence throughout the world. The politics of dying and the role of dying in the practices and cultures of marginalized people impact the way that oppressed groups resist as well as the way that dominant groups sustain systems of oppression. See J. A. Mbembé, *On the Postcolony*, Studies on the History of Society and Culture (Berkeley, CA: University of California Press, 2001).

38. See Pinn, Finley, and Alexander, *African American Religious Cultures*.

39. See Cleage, *The Black Messiah*. It is important to note that Cleage engages the concept of Utopia in this text and begins to unpack the relationship between Utopia, collective action, and African Orthodox tradition. In Cleage's analysis, Utopia is not a rejection of the modern but the creation of sustainable practices and models for African-derived peoples.

40. The rise of Black press, specifically newspapers and magazines, has been chronicled in a number of texts. See Gardner, *Black Print Unbound*. While Gardner is central to understanding the development and circulation of Black newspapers and periodicals, he only hints at the independent Black presses of the nineteenth and early twentieth centuries. Cleage and the Shrine Press are the continuation of what Gardner calls the "Black Literate Public" in that these presses circulate new ideas, studies, and theories and provide the capital infrastructure for the books and authors to be engaged in the public sphere.

41. Julius Eric Thompson, *Dudley Randall, Broadside Press, and the Black Arts Movement in Detroit, 1960–1995* (Jefferson, NC: McFarland, 1999).

42. Melba Joyce Boyd, *Wrestling with the Muse: Dudley Randall and the Broadside Press* (New York, NY: Columbia University Press, 2003).

43. See Gardner, *Black Print Unbound*. Also see Thompson, *Dudley Randall, Broadside Press*.

44. See Edward E. Curtis, *Black Muslim Religion in the Nation of Islam, 1960–1975* (Chapel Hill, NC: University of North Carolina Press, 2006), https://BZ6FJ9F L8E.search.serialssolutions.com/ejp/?libHash=BZ6FJ9FL8E#/search/?searchCont rol=title&searchType=title_code&criteria=TC0000112872, https://KG6EK7CQ2B .search.serialssolutions.com/ejp/?libHash=KG6EK7CQ2B#/search/?searchControl =title&searchType=title_code&criteria=TC0000112872, https://MN3KU4AR6Y.s earch.serialssolutions.com/ejp/?libHash=MN3KU4AR6Y#/search/?searchControl.

45. The Shrine Archives, University of Michigan Bentley Library, Box 105.

46. Ibid.

47. Albert B. Cleage and George Bell, *Black Christian Nationalism: New Directions for the Black Church* (Detroit, MI: Luxor, 1987).

48. See *Detroit News*, May 1963.

49. See Edward E. Curtis, *Islam in Black America: Identity, Liberation, and Difference in African-American Islamic Thought* (Albany, NY: State University of New York Press, 2002).

50. Cleage had a vision of a network of Shrines that was never fully achieved, but this vision of fully sustainable communities anchored by a Shrine, neighborhood elders, and Afro-inspired institutions was a critical part of Cleage's broader vision for urban revitalization throughout the United States.

51. *Black World*, January 1974.

52. Ibid.

53. Particularly, CL Franklin and the SCLC mandated that the Nation of Islam not be involved in the planning or allowed to participate in the actual activities on the day of the event. This exclusion was not only for the Nation's political and racial radical ideologies, but Cleage felt that this highlighted the continued hegemony of certain forms of Black Christianity and Black religion.

54. Christian history needed to be explicitly connected to African history. See Cleage, *The Black Messiah*.

55. See Valerie Lee, *The Prentice Hall Anthology of African American Women's Literature* (Upper Saddle River, NJ: Pearson Prentice Hall, 2006). See Cleage, *The Black Messiah*.

56. This genealogy of Black theology and the Black sacred public that created the scriptures of Black theology is one of the central tasks of this work. I argue that while Black theology as an academic method is relatively new and most clearly identified with James Cone and William Jones as its progenitors, there are a number of earlier texts and movements that gesture in the direction of the Black theological method. Furthermore, this text argues that alternative movements, like Cleage's and Divine's, in providing competition for the mainline Christian traditions, both expedited and shaped the terms for what would become Black theology. In Cleage's case, his attention to the diaspora and Afro-diasporic religious traditions were central features of Black theology and theorists that engaged this method.

57. James H. Cone, *Black Theology and Black Power*, An Original Seabury Paperback, Sp 59 (New York, NY: Seabury Press, 1969).

58. It is very important to distinguish between Cleage and the Shrine's relationship with mainline African American institutions and leaders and his engagement and overlap with the burgeoning field of Black theology. Cleage sees Black theology as creating the possibility for disrupting the hegemony of mainline Black churches and really responding to the crisis of Black suffering and oppression.

59. Cleage's "Black theological project" was in this sense a political project, whereas Cone's was deeply situated within a disciplinary debate and what constituted systematic theology.

60. This notion of the Black sacred public obviously takes it cues from the Black public and the number of theorists that have done work on the shape, expansion, and contraction of that public. See Higginbotham, *Righteous Discontent*. See Frederick, *Between Sundays*. However, the Black sacred public highlights a particular subset of the Black public that is animated by discussions on what constitutes sacredness and why sacredness is central to the African American's relationship to the modern

moment. Moreover, this definition of the Black sacred is attempting to highlight the ways that this public was and is shaped by a variety of voices and movements and that while Christianity was dominant it was not always normative.

61. Cleage's theological centers or what might be better framed as "Afro-centric" seminaries were quite different from the seminaries or libraries that many of the other movements created. The libraries and the seminaries of the other movements, like COGIC, were often narrow in their scope and had as their primary goal to maintain the archives of the movement and to create future leaders for the movement. Cleage's Afro-centric seminaries, on the other hand, were committed to producing expansive knowledge and ideas that could be used in the spiritual development and growth of Black communities, regardless of denomination or even faith commitment.

62. It is important to note that this discussion had also harnessed mainstream seminaries and the larger Christian public. *The Christian Century* devoted an issue to Cleage in a manner that was similar to the coverage of Malcolm X and the Nation of Islam. Cleage was identified as the creator of a nascent movement that had the potential to disrupt the normative historiography of Jesus and Christianity. The title, "Will We All Have to Worship a Black Jesus," of the article aptly highlights the anxiety that Cleage created within all of American Christendom.

63. Shrine of the Black Madonna Archives, 1968.

64. In this sense, Black Christianity was a decidedly modern formation that sought to engage and reshape the public sphere as much as did the liturgy and language of believers.

65. This highlights the ways that all of these movements had some hopes for international audiences and outposts. However, there is a distinction between having members or even churches in spaces outside of the United States and having a thoughtful engagement of the Black diaspora. Cleage, unlike Mason and Divine, had a clear articulation of the importance of the diaspora and the need to think about the economic and political liberation of Black folks throughout the diaspora.

66. See *The Detroit Times*, June 2011 article "The Anniversary of Cleage and the PAOCC."

67. I particularly use the language of "docent" as many of the women who provide tours for the Shrine are far removed from the both the historical and radical message of Cleage and the Shrine. The Shrine is seen as an artifact of an early age or moment of Black economic development, and thus the Shrine is now a historical marker or a museum rather than a site of cultural and political activation.

68. Abrams, *God and Blackness*.

*Chapter 5*

# Toward Embodied Freedom
## *Crisis and Collaborations on the Margins of the Black Church Tradition*

This particular reading of African American religion, specifically Black Christianity, requires that we read alternative Christian movements, their leaders, and their engagement with the Black body with a particular attention to their transgressions of normative Blackness, Christianity, and the project of democracy. To read their canon formation, exegesis of the biblical text, and formation of the Black public as outside of or only tangential to modernity is to eliminate the possibility that their interaction with Christianity, democracy, and race had any impact on institutional, structural, and disciplinary realities. This disregard for their theological and political sophistication is an attempt to leave biblical studies, democracy, and Christianity free from the gaze and insight of the other, particularly the insights of African Americans. Wimbush and his call to read the Bible darkly, and by extension communities that engage the Bible, will not allow for the hegemony of Western biblical or theological scholarship. His proposal for reading darkly is that "African American experience, or what African American experience can come to represent, be placed at the center of serious study of the Bible, including academic study of the Bible."[1] This representation of African Americanity he further defines as those who are "exiled, homely, and uncomely."[2] This centering of darkness or this centering of the outside means that there will be a more consistent and intense and critical focus on the modern world; more consistent and intense focus on the phenomenology of social-cultural formation and the creation and uses of sacred texts; and more critical focus on the Bible as script/manifesto that defines and embraces darkness.[3] Wimbush pushes us to engage not only the African American experience and public from the perspective of its contemporary experience but to use its situation and all of its complexity to re-engage the Bible, the discipline, and religion more broadly. He continues that this is not only done for practical theological purposes but that the centering of their experience must become the methodological tool adopted by scholars of religion. His theorization of darkness is a useful method for the thinking of the broad Black church tradition or the "other Black church," its alternative/hidden approaches to modernity, its new methods for excavating these hidden epistemologies, and its resonance for people and groups seeking new ways of belonging. Reading darkly and reading with attention to Black bodies privileges an attention not only to scholarly engagement with African Americans but the rupture of a singular or unitary Black vision for freedom. These practices in his later works are more explicitly theorized as signifying or playing. He argues that this type of endeavor "includes the practices discovered among peoples off the stage, away from the center—in the dark" which often "bring into focus the power relations and dynamics involved in but often masked in communication and interpretation."[4] This reading of darkness pursues not what "scriptures" or texts mean (as the other reading of darkness attempts to reify Africa and Africans) but rather how scriptures and reading practices are used to inform the lived realities and practices of people and impact the trajectory of institutions that we consider normative. Therefore, we are not just reading Christianity through a dark lens, but we are reading the broad Black church tradition, its multiple iterations, and its relationship to democracy through this lens. This book has argued that this signifying and creating new canons on and around Black bodies is what is at the core of alternative Black Christianities and the broad Black church tradition in the twentieth century.

One particular model of reading darkly is what this book has done as it has examined alternative Christianities that engage the body and racialization in the middle of the twentieth centuries. While some have misread the movements examined in this text as an evacuation or outside of critical reason and modernity, I argue that they function as a dark or alternative reading of modernity. In light of the failure of modern projects to fully and adequately include Black subjects as a part of the settler-based democracy of the United States, these movements use the practices of scriptural restructuring, canon formation, and the privileging of the Black body in order to imagine alternatives to the state, capital, and the logics of respectability. These prophet-based alternative Christianities functioned on the borders of Christianity, cultural nationalism, and political Utopia. These movements must not be simply read as a rejection of race or Christianity or even certain structures of the state, but as creating the logic for alternate worlds not fully circumscribed by the market, racial hegemony, or the dominant scriptural reading of the Bible. The movements set into action the symbolic and discursive possibility for the creation of new world subjects or what Bogues terms "a counter symbolic world and order."[5] They, alongside other movements throughout the long duree of Black presence in the Atlantic, set into play the possibility of counteracting colonial "darkness" and engaging the robust histories of African and African American subjects. These movements argue that the formally colonized/ enslaved body is a body worth repairing and that the economic and political ground is worth participating in. These movements not only attempt to repair the history of African American participation and the African American body but to insert in oppressive and circumscribed economies the possibility for enchantment and participation. Divine, Mason, and Cleage were faced with the difficult task of re-inscribing subjectivity in the midst of multiple crises and increasingly complex logics of death and exclusion or what Mbembe so aptly describes as "necropolitics."[6]

These movements' attention to the local or the specific bodies of migrants, Black women, and the urban requires that we return to the space, the people, the prophets, and texts that are excavated by these movements' rich account of subjugation and resistance to subjugation. The salience of Mbembe's analysis of the politics of death and Wimbush's account of reading darkness is that they take seriously the politics of death and disease that is often essentialized in racial categories or erased by normative methods but never fully engaged by theorists of these movements. Mbembe critically looks at the ways in which the negation of Africa and the African American subject, both in popular and scholarly sites, have prevented an engaged look at the trajectories of subjectivities and modernities in the diaspora and the United States. His method forces us to take a second look at the politics of death and its associated death-worlds and to faithfully engage the creation of alternate modernities or life worlds that attempt to acknowledge African American subjectivity. Wimbush and Mbembe alongside the Delores Williams and Kelly Brown Douglas provide us the analytical tools to think about different forms of thinking, subject formation, and intellectual production. Their attention to the derogated archives of Black religions and Black prophets pointed us to alternative Christianities and the broad Black church tradition that are theorizing and thinking across boundaries. This book has taken seriously Mbembe's call to wrestle with the long duree of the African/American subject in the colonial/postcolonial world and Williams's and Douglas's call to address the body. The book has argued that one particularly poignant site to do this is alternative Christian movements and their prophetic leaders. These prophetic movements or alternative Christianities provide historical clarification as well as provide an opportunity to discuss the African American subject, the failure of settler-colonial democracy, and the development of a practice (scripture) and logic (Black theology of liberation) as the central tenants of the Black religious public sphere in the twentieth century.

These movements help us to understand the construction of alternative Christian communities and their construction of critiques of the nation-state, democracy, the body, and the Christian canon. More specifically these analyses have suggested that Christianities are not solely defined by their unique and innovative constructions of a text or existent theology, but this examination highlights the importance of interrogating their strategies and the resulting transformation caused by inter-textuality, hybridity, and miscegenation. These movements are examples of collaborations on the margins of fugitivity.[7] They represent a new impulse and method to describe and name the Black public's relationship to freedom and democracy. These new movements challenge the idea that the supposed closed text of colonial mission Christianity, normative Western Christianity, or even the traditional Black church are the repository of truth and holds a monopoly on the characterization of the divine, Jesus, and human participation. These prophet figures in the Black Christian public function as a critique of not only normative Christianity and the construction of the Black racial identity, but they also disrupt the idea that modernity and Christianity function as "a code form for the search for white male identity."[8] The hybridity of the prophetic figures and the border crossing that they theologically and politically engage in point to their willingness to claim and engage in the performance of a renewed vision of the divine, state, and modern racial project. These movements in their critique of the political system, evocation of a Black Jesus, and the erection of Divine as the godhead physically highlight the tensions between the public and the prophetic, inside and out, human and divine, egalitarian and hierarchical, and conformist and radical. It is not just the inherent tension between these categories, but the genius of these movements' is their abilitiy to fuse these categories to form categories, institutions, and models that are new, imaginative, and unruly for the Black public.

These categories or tensions between the public and the prophetic are what Wimbush would call the "homely" and "unrefined," and it is exactly their resistance to order, modernity, and colonial hegemony that make them useful for the popular imagination. The new symbols, ethical categories and standards, and new canons transported and invested in by these alternative traditions are what make them essential to reading the Black public and its relationship to the twentieth century. They do as Marcia Riggs suggests in her groundbreaking womanist ethics treatise, *Awake, Arise, and Act*, to fully engage the possibility of something new emerging. She urges, "expect kairos experiences wherein the Spirit breaks into our midst and reclaims us so that we can renounce the privilege of domination; so that we can commit ourselves to discovering untried ways"[9] Delores Williams and Kelly Brown Douglas continue this work in the womanist tradition by looking at "untried ways" by recovering the stories of particular characters and communities as well as returning to the multiple resources used to address the Black body.[10] The voices of Mason, Divine, and Cleage suggest that this tension of public and prophetic is a ripe space to think and engage the contours of the modern moment and more specifically the contours of modern theological imagination.

Riggs like Wimbush continues by arguing that what is needed is responsiveness to the humanity and creativity of all members on the margin or those who experience the hybrid realities of being Black, Christian, and embodied in the modern era. Riggs calls for a communal consciousness within the marginalized group that seeks for mediation rather than a competitive one that demonizes and co-opts uncritically the project of empire. Often the presupposition of monolithic social, religious, and class demographic compromises this idea of communal consciousness. As womanist ethicists, Riggs and Douglas recognize that social stratification within marginalized communities is a derivative factor of colonial oppression and white supremacy.[11] Riggs unlike many race theorists spends time to discuss the impact of assimilation (not negotiation and hybridity) in the psyche and lived reality of African and subaltern identity. She profoundly rejects the notion that class stratification within the colonial/postcolonial complex is an autonomous phenomenon.[12] She rejects this assumption, because it fails to acknowledge the way that individuals and communities interact to inform and determine systems and ideologies. Riggs and Douglas are aware of that and thus provide a clear analysis of what they call integration and what I refer to as negotiation in the colonial/postcolonial complex and how it functions to deny hybrid or authentically embodied performances.[13] In looking at the roots of integration and acceptance of normative white culture as being a factor of oppression, Riggs requires that a greater number of systems be challenged and examined in light of womanist ethics. She reminds the members of the colonial/postcolonial complex throughout the Africana diaspora that the stench of white oppression does not evaporate when whiteness disappears but that the impact of white oppression has limited marginalized groups' vision for a liberative future informed by a communal consciousness.[14]

However, calls for a liberative community consciousness often fall short or fail because they are so tethered to an understanding of Christianity, modernity, or race that renders it relatively inflexible or unable to account for the unique needs and concerns of Black embodied existence. The embodied vision for a liberative future must not retreat to a truncated or foreclosed vision of Christianity, the modern moment, or the modes of citizenship but must see their community consciousness and thus their community being constitutive of the white oppressors and their problematic ideologies. In the separate spaces of imagining reserved for African Americans, they must radically address the functioning of hybridity in the lives of the margin and be decisive about what performances of hybridity and difference should be valued, circulated, and canonized. It cannot however attempt to privilege or essentialize African American identity or to narrow the possibilities of other alternative performances and responses to the modern encounter. It is this tension that we see in Father Divine's negotiation not only of Black Christianity, but also socialism, American exceptionalism, and the larger questions of race. Riggs's mediating ethic and Douglas's attention to the multiple sources (like the blues) that address the centrality of the Black body are of particular importance because it is through the continued engagement of democracy, Christianity, and what constitutes Blackness that power, hybridity, and intertextuality are brought to the fore and are not allowed to be disregarded as an insignificant factor in the creation of the alternative hybrid space.

The new construction of Pentecostal citizenship that emerges from the reading of the Church of God in Christ and the new understanding of nonracialized commune in the Divine movement as seen through the lens of Wimbush and Riggs is essential. They both foreground not the suffering bodies of their adherents but the prioritization of the new logics and concerns of the oppressed, who are attentive to hybridity and willing to engage in the public domain. Again, these movements are hybrid because they attend to both their embodied political and embodied theological commitments. Riggs's mediating ethic in conversation with Wimbush's insistence on starting with the "unhomely" character of African Americans, especially the migrants and disenfranchised of the first half of the twentieth century, suggests that because of human mutuality there can be a prophetic figure or what might be termed a racial or religious "trespasser" that negotiates between the disparate and often antagonistic parts of community. This attention to trespassers or hybridity demands that sheer intellectual, material, and social proximity and dexterity of competing groups must be engaged. This respectable prophet in the Church of God in Christ, the Afro-centric Madonna in Cleage, and the new-thought inflected Christianity of Divine rejects the idea that Christianity or Christian expression is not determined by community, interaction, and context.

The conscientious objection of Mason or the nonracialized Divine community as gleaned from the public engagement of Divine and Mason do not erase or ignore suffering, but suffering understood as political, social, and economic misery can no longer function as the height of spiritual piety and belief. Suffering, therefore, does not give a group greater access to the truth or closeness with God. Suffering, moreover, is now read as the absence of movement, negotiation, and contestation. Suffering is being totally submerged in a monolithic and univocal community. It is the inability to perform hybridity or to engage the culturally other that makes one incapable of encountering the fullness of God. It is the inability to perform the varieties of Blackness and Black Christianity that these movements highlight. The idea that suffering, specifically embodied suffering or negation of the body, is assigned to one group or is validated as a sign of this group's closeness to God is understood as preposterous.[15] COGIC, Cleage, and Divine, like womanists, assess a much broader purview and identify systems and institutions that fail to provide Black bodies full citizenship. These movements refuse to see their suffering as a sign of divine proximity, but rather see the multilayered interactions between groups as a site of possible transformation. It is clear that Cleage sees the prioritization of Blackness and cultural specificity as an important response and remedy to cultural imperialism. It is cultural interaction that Cleage and Divine identify as the height of knowledge and thus suffering is not allowed to ossify helplessness and hopeless (or even racial and political identities), but suffering is a created to remind people to reject the hegemony of others and their marginalization. Suffering is caused to galvanize people to resist, think creatively, and engage the stranger. It is caused to remind that neither tense hate nor isolated poverty is an acceptable state of being. Suffering is the product of social sin and separation and therefore is allowed to force people to reclaim the possibility of something better and hybrid as a result of community.[16]

Like womanists Delores Williams and Kelly Brown Douglas, the vision for the future is a future without suffering. This is exactly where the logics of Black Lives Matter cohere with the visions and concerns of the broader Black church tradition. While the broad Black church tradition, including the movements in this book, demystifies the cross and refuses to subject Jesus and Christian movements to a valorization of suffering, unfulfilled dreams, and rejection of the body, Black Lives Matter also refuses to valorize or normalize the suffering or destruction of the Black body.[17] The vision is one that challenges silence that emerges as a result of the hegemony of the oppressive models within the colonial/postcolonial complex. The future is one that is fraught with uncertainty as the value of establishing stable rules, and even social mores is de-emphasized. Mason and Cleage are surprisingly in line with one another as they prophesy that the twentieth century is the century of spiritual reinvigoration, Cleage and his re-engagement with African ancestors and Mason with his rearticulating of the Pentecost as it relates to Black Christian suffering.[18] Their understanding of spirit is that it cannot be contained, controlled, or over-determined by Western hegemony, Christian provincialism, the dictates of normative Blackness, or the mandates of settler-colonial imperialism. The spirit operates outside of the boundaries of Western reason and logic, and thus creates dissonance and hybrid dis-equilibrium as its foundational characteristic.

These alternatives Christianities and their attention to scriptural variety and resistance to imperial scriptural imperatives demand for the presence, persistence, and prioritization of dissonance. They effectively challenge what has heretofore been understood as religious, Christian, or even normative Blackness and imagine as a result of disparate theoretical and experiential resources something beyond the normative Western post-Enlightenment Christianity. Furthermore, the valuing of dissonance and hybridity found in the alternative Christian movements demand a reinterpretation of biblical exegesis, Christian theology, Africana experience, and the dissonance that is part and parcel of the Western Christian movements that have achieved canonical status. The demand to own up to and boldly proclaim the constituent parts of the myriad Christianities that have been operating as pure and unified is the enduring contribution that dissonance, hybridity, and darkness bring to the field of Christian ethics and religious studies.

## READING HYBRID PUBLICS, READING THE OTHER BLACK CHURCH

The value of re-engaging Mason, Cleage, and Father Divine's movements is that it centers reading both the desires and the repulsions of religious movements. These movements clearly affirm the role of contested space and the creation of Black publics and Black Christian publics with attention to bodily needs and concerns, specifically the bodily needs and concerns of those most marginalized within the community. Wimbush and Crawley remind us that those whose experiences are characterized by darkness are often problematically associated with terms with impurity, hybridity, and discontinuity. The acceptance or prioritization of an unqualified or "pure" identity continues to give ownership of the "un-hyphenated" types or categories to the West. Darkness or the "logic of Pentecost" must be employed to rethink race, the West, and a universal Christianity and not simply as a new problematic location to begin the interpretation. Darkness must be the renegotiation or reformulation that Wimbush speaks of when he suggests that this can only take place when people are able to effectively challenge the genocidal conditions in which they live.[19] However, this primary genocidal condition for people in this mixed and intermingled globe is the assumption of race and religion and its denigrated status in relation to mythic whiteness and Christianity. Reading hybridity vis-à-vis these alternative Christian traditions, therefore, is reading in light of one's miscegenated and hybrid status and reading for an affirmation of this unstable identity in equal relation to other hybrid and unstable beings. In many ways, the racially negotiated spaces of Divine and the Church of God in Christ movement are central to the growth of a new racial imaginary in the twentieth and twenty-first centuries, and they ultimately provide language and the logic for the broad religious practices around the Black body, including Black atheism and the Black Lives Matter movement. Both Divine and the Church of God in Christ are engaging the precarious spaces of race, modernity, and Christianity. Thus, these alternative religious movements are an important corrective to the ways in which Black theology and critical race thinking in religion has failed to take seriously these movements and others like them.

## ALTERNATIVE MODERNITIES, CONSTRUCTED THEOLOGIES

Furthermore, Wimbush reminds that reading darkly is seeing the "Bible as that which both reflects and draws unto itself and engages and problematizes a certain complex order of existence associated with marginality, liminality, exile, pain, and trauma."[20] Hybridity demands that we engage how the Bible also provides a foundation for the opposing complex associated with democracy, capital, and citizenship. However, notwithstanding difficulty and failure, scholars and nonscholars alike must resist the sterile and pure categories of African American (or Black) and Christian and must begin to look for the new and creative possibilities that exist in different, marginal, and even dark spaces. The incongruence of searching for "peace in a strange land" and what many might consider a strange text is what is at the core of reading darkness as well as hybridity. This is what is at the core of Riggs's mediating ethic, Kelly Brown Douglas's attention to the blues tradition in African American culture, and the engagements of Mason, Cleage, and Father Divine. Reading hybridity and alterity is often reading for the unexpected overlaps and resonance. It means that as much as the renewed analysis opens us to the affirmation of darkness it also provides us greater insight into the defamation of darkness. These readings allow us to more clearly name and recognize the misreading or misalignments of the modern moment. Cleage's critique of urban revitalization or Divine's critique of racialism is an example of seeing the structure of negating certain bodies. Reading darkness and hybridity remind that the desire for legitimacy amongst alternative Christianities is as much about self-determination as it is a call for renewed attention to the relationship between Black bodies and democracy.

## THE FUTURE OF AFRICAN AMERICAN RELIGION, THE BLACK CHURCH, AND BLACK THEOLOGY

Using alternative African American Christianities as the center of African American religious studies and Black theological analysis not only helps us to rethink the nature of the biblical narrative and biblical scholarship but also the so-called mainstream and mainline traditions that have been traditionally studied by Black theologians and thinkers of African American religious studies. The history of alternative African American Christianties is often written to suggest that influence only operated in one direction. Robert Young argues otherwise:

> Culture never stands alone but always participates in a conflictual economy acting out the tension between sameness and difference, comparison and differentiation, unity and diversity, cohesion and dispersion.[21]

While it is clear that the construction of Christianity from extant normative imperial sources plays an extremely important role in the production of alternative Christianities, the purpose of this reading is to include the ways in which a largely disaffected Black Christian public began to explore the limits of European, American, and even Black American discursive hegemony. The creation of discourses and practices that were configured within the crucible of the Black Atlantic not only created the very possibilities for Africana Christianities but also radically re-organized the way that the normative modalities adapted and produced Christianities. The postcolony and the modern metropolis were the places where the master and the margin significantly overlapped and became the site of "rhizomatic" possibilities for a reorganizing of Christian practices.[22] The creation of a counter-public for all groups becomes more accessible because of the work of African American Christianities to rethink and explore the boundaries of the nation-state, race, and belonging as citizens. The very language of liberation and racial reconstruction are expanded to not simply include this new class of African American migrants, but it enlarges the critical and practical capacities for the Christian witness to account for the varieties of existence or deprivation that are often obscured if not ignored by normative methodologies. African American Christianities, therefore, in many ways return to the constitutive insight of Black theology that is often overlooked by critical theorists and readers of Black thought. Black theology and the critical questions that it engaged make possible not simply an-other or another rendering of Black Christian witness but it opens up the very possibility for thinking the parameters of settler-colonialism and Black existence in a much larger frame.[23] It is essential and exploratory in that it shows one particular instantiation of a much larger, more robust critique of epistemology, theology, and the modern project that cements racism, hegemony, and the supremacy of particular universalizing projects. It is, therefore, important to note that while Black theology purports to give Black Christians access to Christendom within the guise of Black subjects, it should also be noted that it provides a more robust account of variability and mutability of the Christian project.[24] Therefore, Divine, Mason, and Cleage remind that the modern moment was not the end of enchantment or the Black church, but it is more broadly a recognition that enchantment as constructed within the narrow confines of a post-enlightenment modernity no longer exists. This notion of spirituality or enchantment has not receded, but rather it has multiplied and taken on previously unrecognizable or irreconcilable forms.

## SCRIPTURALIZING, BLACK THEOLOGY, AND AFRICAN AMERICAN PUBLICS

Finally, what the readings of Divine, Cleage, and Mason have exposed is the process of establishing new canons or creating or reshaping sacred scriptures within the African American Christian public. This attention to the Black body as canonical and essential to alternative African American Christian publics is one practice that attempts to create a discourse for existence, resistance to suffering, and flourishing that often travels within an unexpected trajectory and between seemingly unconnected discourses. Thus, while the practice of exegesis and imperial epistemological projects of biblical studies, theology, and political theorizing have attempted to narrow the very possibilities of certain modes of Christian discourse, canon, and scripture formation, this book attempts to de-center these normative texts and to create a much wider berth for theological possibilities by mandating a renewed way of thinking about those peculiar or estranged from modernity. This wider berth recognizes texts and discourses that are of import to an African American religious identity and to take seriously those discourses and practices that move in this Black Christian public. Furthermore, this wider berth makes room for organizations and new practices that helps us better understand Black Lives Matter as not a reactive project to the concerns of police brutality, mass incarceration, and the continued economic vagaries of late capital, but it places the Black Lives Matter movement within this long history of theorizing and engaging the sacred Black body.

The normative Black church and this broad Christian tradition, therefore, have always been in conversation about the contested nature of imperial and alternative epistemologies. Specifically, the role of the extra-canonical prophetic figure, who is often not constrained by nation-state politics or regimes, is central to a method that wants to take seriously a people's experience with the divine and the creation of "texts, textures, and gestures" to account for this renewed understanding. The leaders of Black Lives Matter fit perfectly in the categorization of an extra-canonical figure who is not constrained by normative Blackness, historical African American organizations aligned with respectability or upward mobility, or the logics and limitations of Black Christian reading and ethical strategies. Just like the extra-canonical figures engaged in this book, the trans, lesbian, and non-gender binary leaders of the

Black Lives Matter movement faced attempts to be nullified or erased by the mainstream Black public and what has been held up as the normative Black church. The impulse to expunge these voices from certain forms of Black theologizing, political organizing, or simply the Black public is to render the Black theological enterprise as one that is comfortable with a depiction of Black Christianity or Blackness that is not attentive to the margins, variety, and those influences from beyond or within the borders of the nation-state. The Black church has never fully expunged the alternative, but this is a narrative of how these alternative movements and Black Lives Matter's focus on the body, or what is different type of text, becomes the very ground for the Black church and the Black theological project of the second half of the twentieth century. Wimbush reminds with this shift from normative texts and disciplines that, "the primary focus should be placed not upon texts per se but upon textures, gestures, and power . . . associated with the phenomenon of the phenomenon of the invention and engagement of scriptures."[25] In this regard, Wimbush and Moten provide us a mechanism to return to the African American embodied experience. In this book, we have looked at the margins through a renewed reading of Divine, Mason, and Cleage and have identified multiple spaces where the varieties of religion, sacrality, racial identity, and resistance can be engaged more fully. The return to the archive of the alternative and their invocation of different texts lead to a broader engagement of what constitutes a text and the notion of sacrality within the Black Christian tradition.

This intervention of engaging and building new canons within the frame of citizenship and the creation of alternative publics enables those interested in African American Christianities, the varieties of God talk amongst dark and marooned bodies, to see and account for the production of discourses that are rendered invisible or relatively insignificant by modern accounts of Black theology and Black resistance to the modern nation-state. The return to the body and canon formation, therefore, is an extension of the Black theological project that enables us to not only see the constructive projects of competing Christianities like Father Divine and the Church of God in Christ movements but to also read the popular and the pedestrian in new and exciting ways. Thus, alternative Black religions open not only the very possibility for variety and dissonance but using this method allow us to see the ways in which democracy, Christianity, and Blackness identities were being shaped and restructured to imagine Black thriving and survival in the modern world. This method or way of thinking about Black religious formation forces us to attend not only to the sources and discourses that are made visible by theology but also those sources and discourses that are often seen as insignificant to western and Black theologies' organizing projects. In many ways, a renewed attention to resistance to state and state-authorized racialization and the practices of canon formation encourages us to rethink Black theology's foundational moments and to offer a space for scriptural projects that imagine liberation and Christianity in a variety of ways. The outcome of this work, therefore, is to re-engage the variety of scriptural/canon projects within the Black Christian public and to read how these projects shape and reframe the possibility of alternative modernities. Thus, the new attention to alternative African American Christianities gives us resources to see a variety of responses to state-organized democracy, the limits of capital, and the quest for Black flourishing and liberation. It also argues that in order to understand the quest for Black liberation and the long civil rights movement in the twentieth century that careful attention must be given to alternative Christian movements and their scriptural and canon projects regarding the Black body. This focus on alterity, hybridity, and the body is ultimately a way to think about the broad Black church tradition or those spaces that affirm and protect Black bodies as connected to alternative vision for Black belonging and citizenship.

## WHAT IS THE FUTURE OF THE BLACK CHURCH?

The future of the Black church is the other Black churches and the continued engagement with the broad Black church tradition. A central aspect of this book's argument is that the concerns of the Black body and Black public ideas and practices were engaged and unpacked during conversations between a broad range of Black religious figures in the middle of the twentieth century. Cleage, Divine, and Mason clearly understood these Black prophetic thinkers, amongst others, as offering African Americans not simply alternative religious identities and practices but a reframing of the modern project. Cleage like Father Divine argued that African Americans' safety and flourishing within the modern democratic state not only depended on civic and economic protections but a revisiting of normative racialized understandings and practices. While Divine argued for the jettisoning of normative racial identity markers and others like Elijah Muhammad called for a racialized enclave that protected Black bodies from the demonic and debilitating threat of white supremacy, Cleage argued for a renewed attention to connections with the continent of Africa and the diaspora as well as a connection to the lived practices and interventions of everyday Black folks. He wanted to share with the broader world, especially within the U.S. democratic public, the interventions of African American communities and the individual and collective genius that emerged from these places.[26]

It is particularly noteworthy that at that time when Christian leaders' conversations with the Nation of Islam were either shunned or heavily surveilled, Cleage and Divine were clear in wanting to learn from others, including the

Nation of Islam, inviting Elijah Muhammad, Malcolm X, Wilfred X, and other leaders from the original Nation of Islam temple in Detroit to the Shrine. Specifically, Cleage's dissatisfaction with the Detroit March for Freedom and the later development of the Northern Christian Leadership Conference was as a result of the group's unwillingness to include other religious voices, specifically the Nation of Islam. Additionally, Cleage seemed to be interested not only in their form of activism or their vision for cultural renewal, but their particular deployment of Black religion. Moreover, Cleage as an exemplar of Black religious futures was interested in their engagement and deployment of the Black body. In all of these movements, there was not just an attention to the Black body and its engagement with economic and social pressures of the twentieth century, rather there was specific and discrete attention to the divine being a Black or brown body. Divine and Muhammed were not simply prophetic leaders and teachers, but they functioned as physical examples of the canonical sacred body. While Cleage, Mason, and many in contemporary religious communities did not have a contemporary/extant sacred body to race or to create, they have elevated the image of the Christian Messiah, the Virgin Mary, or the working-class Black subject as examples of the long history of Black sacrality. For Cleage and other alternative Christian movements, the notion of the Black sacred therefore did not have to be the purview of alternative religious movements or non-Christian movements, but in Christian-adjacent movements like his there was room and space for an engagement with the sacred Black body. Therefore, this notion of the Black divine or the sacred Black body was canonical for all of these movements even as their understanding of the divine and the engagement with race had explicit differences.

On one level, Cleage, Divine, and Mason, through the invocation of the Black sacred body or the sacred nature of Black participation in creating alternatives for democracy, were making a case for the absolute humanity of Black bodies and their fitness for participation in the larger public. Black Americans were modern, were creating modern configurations of African-inspired religions, and were demanding visibility in the modern political and economic spheres. Since African Americans exhibited genius and grit, they should be afforded the opportunity to participate in the larger political public spaces. Cleage and these prophets of modernity, however, offered that there was something intrinsically problematic with models of modernity and the current construction of the political public that rendered African Americans and African American contributions as unrecognizable or of little value. They were and are especially critical of those publics that excluded certain expressions of Black radicalism or religion. Thus, they were calling for a radical reordering not simply of segregated spaces or even the creation of utopic spaces where race and ethnicity were absent, rather they argued for the restructuring of the modern public to include the images and examples of Black genius for the benefit of all democracy. For example, when Cleage opened the Shrine he heralded it as a unique space for Black Christians or Black pilgrims; furthermore, Cleage was specific to highlight its importance for Christendom, democracy, and all the world. Cleage as a result often challenged and chided Father Divine and Muhammad in this area and their tendency to be absent from conversations with the larger public. Cleage envisioned a world where African Americans would be a constitutive part of the economic and democratic systems and actually functioning as a vanguard for the broader public. Cleage was critical that Divine, Mason, and others often forsook the broader public and were not actively involved in responding to or remedying their everyday problems. Cleage was by design public facing, and he imagined the Black public and the larger Black church tradition that he was trying to reach as quite broad.

If the Black church tradition is the negation of Black suffering, the elevation of the multiplicity and variety of Black performances, and the promotion of new responses to modernity and neoliberal capital, then the study of Black religion was and remains the study of the Black body and its relationship to reframing the logic and limits of modern democracy. The other traditions studied in this text have not just addressed the body, but they have allotted significant theological, political, aesthetic, and theoretical resources to the study and engagement of the body. The future, therefore, is to think critically and creatively what constitutes a sacred Black body or what type of Black body is worth saving and protecting. This study suggests that just like these movements provided and protected marginalized and often "unremarkable" bodies, that the future of the Black church and the broader tradition will be forced to remark upon bodies and embodied realities that have been ignored or misrepresented. It will be forced to address the suffering body as not just one that suffers under the racialist or imperialist language of modernity, but it must also address bodies that are transgressive due to gender status, desire, mobility, and performance. We must look at new movements and their attention to the body as not simply resources for this broader, embodied Black church tradition, but we must see movements like Black Lives Matter, Black labor organizing, Black gay, lesbian, and trans movements, and Black humanist movements as central to this broad tradition and critical to creating space and language for Black liberation and flourishing.

The future of the Black church is imagining new vistas for Blackness and new ideas for belonging. The Black church is wherever Black publics are challenging the logics of colonial and state-driven practices that deny the participation and thriving of non-normative bodies. It is to be a signifier of another possibility, a possibility that is not wedded to modernity or democracy. The Black church, in this sense, is not a place or a prescribed set of theological commitments, but it is a signifier of a transgressive imaginary that we must continue to assess and engage in light of Black visions of liberation.

## NOTES

1. Vincent Wimbush, ed., *African Americans and the Bible: Sacred Texts and Social Textures* (New York, NY: Continuum Publishing Group, 2000), 12.
2. Wimbush and Rodman, *African Americans and the Bible*, 15.
3. Ibid.
4. Vincent Wimbush, "Textures, Gestures, and Power: Orientation to Radical Evcavation," Paper Presented at the American Academy of Religion, San Antonio, TX, 2004, 14–17.
5. Bogues, *Black Heretics, Black Prophets*, 34.
6. Mbembé, *On the Postcolony*. Also see Bantum, *Redeeming Mulatto*.
7. See Moten, *Stolen Life*. Vincent L. Wimbush, *Theorizing Scriptures: New Critical Orientations to a Cultural Phenomenon* (New Brunswick, NJ: Rutgers University Press, 2008).
8. Laura E. Donaldson and Pui-lan Kwok, *Postcolonialism, Feminism and Religious Discourse* (New York, NY: Routledge, 2002), 178.
9. Marcia Riggs, *Awake, Arise, & Act: a Womanist Call for Black Liberation* (Cleveland, OH: Pilgrim Press, 1994), 100; Marcia Riggs and Sallie Bingham Center for Women's History and Culture, *Awake, Arise, & Act: A Womanist Call for Black Liberation* (Cleveland, OH: Pilgrim Press, 1994), 17.
10. See Kelly Brown Douglas, *What's Faith Got to Do with It?: Black Bodies/Christian Souls* (Maryknoll, NY: Orbis Books, 2005); Douglas, *Black Bodies and the Black Church*; Williams, *Sisters in the Wilderness*.
11. Riggs and Sallie Bingham Center for Women's History and Culture, *Awake, Arise, & Act*, 12.
12. Ibid., 14.
13. See Douglas, *Black Bodies and the Black Church*.
14. Riggs, *Awake, Arise, & Act*, 85.
15. Emilie Townes, ed., *Troubling in my Soul: Womanist Perspectives on Evil and Suffering* (Maryknoll, NY: Orbis Books, 1993), 2; Emilie Maureen Townes, *A Troubling in My Soul: Womanist Perspectives on Evil and Suffering*, The Bishop Henry Mcneal Turner Studies in North American Black Religion (Mayknoll, NY: Orbis Books, 1993), 13–17.
16. Ibid., 4.
17. Cone, *The Cross and the Lynching Tree*.
18. Mbon, *Brotherhood*, 42.
19. Wimbush, *Theorizing Scriptures*.
20. Wimbush and Rodman, *African Americans and the Bible*, 17.
21. Robert Young, *Colonial Desire: Hybridity in Theory, Culture, and Race* (London and New York, NY: Routledge, 1995), 53.

22. Ibid. Also see Gilles Deleuze and FelixGuattari, Anti-Oedipus: Capitalism and Schizophrenia (1972) and their theorization of the rhizome as a space of cultural hybridity and engagement.

23. Long, *Significations*, 23.

24. Pinn, *Varieties of African American Religious Experience*, 36.

25. Vincent Wimbush, "Textures, Gestures, and Power: Orientation to Radical Excavation," Paper Presented at the American Academy of Religion, San Antonio, TX, 2004, 5.

26. Cleage's focus on Black genius and sharing that genius with local Black communities as well as the larger Black public aligns Cleage and his vision with both Marcus Garvey and W. E. B. Du Bois. See W. E. B. Du Bois, David W. Blight, and Robert Gooding-Williams, *The Souls of Black Folk*, The Bedford Series in History and Culture (Boston, MA: Bedford Books, 1997).

# Bibliography

Abrams, Andrea C. *God and Blackness: Race, Gender, and Identity in a Middle Class Afrocentric Church*. New York, NY: New York University Press, 2014. Print.

Agamben, Giorgio. *Homo Sacer: Sovereign Power and Bare Life*. Meridian. Stanford, CA: Stanford University Press, 1998. Print.

Alexander, Estrelda. *Black Fire: One Hundred Years of African American Pentecostalism*. Downers Grove, IL: IVP Academic, 2011. Print.

Althaus-Reid, Marcella. *Indecent Theology: Theological Perversions in Sex, Gender and Politics*. London and New York, NY: Routledge, 2000. Print.

———. *Liberation Theology and Sexuality*. Aldershot, England and Burlington, VT: Ashgate, 2006. Print.

Althaus-Reid, Marcella, and Lisa Isherwood. *Controversies in Body Theology*. Controversies in Contextual Theology Series. London: SCM Press, 2008. Print.

———. *Controversies in Feminist Theology*. Controversies in Contextual Theology Series. London: SCM, 2007. Print.

American Colonization Society [from old catalog], and Edward Wilmot Blyden. *The American Colonization Society*. Washington, DC, 1890. Print.

Amoah, Elizabeth, and Circle of Concerned African Women Theologians. *Divine Empowerment of Women in Africa's Complex Realities: Papers from the Circle of the Concerned African Women Theologians*. Accra-North, Ghana: For the Circle of Concerned Women Theologians by Sam-Woode Ltd., 2001. Print.

Anderson, Allan. *An Introduction to Pentecostalism: Global Charismatic Christianity*. Cambridge, U.K. and New York, NY: Cambridge University Press, 2004. Print.

Anderson, Benedict R. O'G. *Imagined Communities: Reflections on the Origin and Spread of Nationalism*. Rev. and extended ed. London and New York, NY: Verso, 1991. Print.

———. *Under Three Flags: Anarchism and the Anti-Colonial Imagination*. London and New York, NY: Verso, 2005. Print.

Anderson, Victor. *Beyond Ontological Blackness: An Essay on African American Religious and Cultural Criticism*. New York, NY: Continuum, 1995. Print.

———. *Creative Exchange: A Constructive Theology of African American Religious Experience*. Innovations. Minneapolis, MN: Fortress Press, 2008. Print.

Appadurai, Arjun. *Globalization*. Durham, NC: Duke University Press, 2001. Print.

———. *Modernity at Large: Cultural Dimensions of Globalization*. Public Worlds. Minneapolis, MN: University of Minnesota Press, 1996. Print.

Bantum, Brian. *Redeeming Mulatto: A Theology of Race and Christian Hybridity*. Waco, TX: Baylor University Press, 2010. Print.

———. *The Death of Race: Building a New Christianity in a Racial World*, 2016. https://login.revproxy.brown.edu/login?url=http://www.jstor.org/stable/10.2307/j.ctt1c84g1t. View online version.

Benson, Bruce Ellis, and Peter Heltzel. *Evangelicals and Empire: Christian Alternatives to the Political Status Quo*. Grand Rapids, MI: Brazos Press, 2008. Print.

Blyden, Edward Wilmot. *A Chapter in the History of Liberia: A Lecture Delivered in the Baptist Church at Edina, Grand Bassa County, Liberia, October 26, 1891*. Liberia: S.N., 1892. Print.

———. *The Problems before Liberia. A Lecture Delivered in the Senate Chamber at Monrovia, January 18, 1909*. London: C. M. Phillips, Printer, 1909. Print.

———. *West Africa before Europe, and Other Addresses, Delivered in England in 1901 and 1903*. London: C. M. Phillips, 1905. Print.

Blyden, Edward Wilmot, and Hollis Ralph Lynch. *Black Spokesman: Selected Published Writings of Edward Wilmot Blyden*. London: Cass, 1971. Print.

Bogues, Anthony. *Black Heretics, Black Prophets: Radical Political Intellectuals*. Africana Thought Series. New York, NY: Routledge, 2003. Print.

Bowler, Kate. *Blessed: A History of the American Prosperity Gospel*. New York, NY: Oxford University Press, 2013. Print.

Boyd, Melba Joyce. *Wrestling with the Muse: Dudley Randall and the Broadside Press*. New York, NY: Columbia University Press, 2003. Print.

Brown, Karen McCarthy. *Mama Lola: A Vodou Priestess in Brooklyn*. Comparative Studies in Religion and Society. Berkeley, CA: University of California Press, 1991. Print.

———. *Mama Lola: A Vodou Priestess in Brooklyn*. Comparative Studies in Religion and Society, Rev. and expanded ed. Berkeley, CA: University of California Press, 2001. Print.

Burkett, Randall K., and Richard Newman. *Black Apostles: Afro-American Clergy Confront the Twentieth Century*. Boston, MA: G. K. Hall, 1978. Print.

Burnham, Kenneth E. *God Comes to America: Father Divine and the Peace Mission Movement*. Boston, MA: Lambeth Press, 1979. Print.

Burroughs, Todd Steven. *Warrior Princess: A People's Biography of Ida B. Wells*. Brooklyn, NY: Diasporic Africa Press, 2017. Print.

Butler, Anthea D. *Women in the Church of God in Christ: Making a Sanctified World*. Chapel Hill, NC: University of North Carolina Press, 2007. Print.

Butler, Judith. *Gender Trouble: Feminism and the Subversion of Identity*. New York, NY: Routledge, 1999. Print.

———. *Precarious Life: The Powers of Mourning and Violence*. London and New York, NY: Verso, 2004. Print.

———. *Subjects of Desire: Hegelian Reflections in Twentieth-Century France*. New York, NY: Columbia University Press, 1987. Print.

———. *Undoing Gender*. New York, NY: Routledge, 2004. Print.

Butler, Judith, Eduardo Mendieta, and Jonathan VanAntwerpen. *The Power of Religion in the Public Sphere*. A Columbia/SSRC Book. New York, NY: Columbia University Press, 2011. Print.

Cannon, Katie G. *Black Womanist Ethics*. American Academy of Religion Academy Series. Atlanta, GA: Scholars Press, 1988. Print.

———. *Katie's Canon: Womanism and the Soul of the Black Community*. New York, NY: Continuum, 1995. Print.

Carbado, Devon W. *Black Men on Race, Gender, and Sexuality: A Critical Reader*. Critical America, 1999. http://getitatduke.library.duke.edu/?sid=sersol&SS_jc=T C0000112869&title=Black%20men%20on%20race%2C%20gender%2C%20and %20sexuality%20%3A%20a%20critical%20reader.

Carter, J. Kameron. *Race: A Theological Account*. Oxford and New York, NY: Oxford University Press, 2008. Print.

Chakrabarty, Dipesh. *Habitations of Modernity: Essays in the Wake of Subaltern Studies*. Chicago, IL: University of Chicago Press, 2002. Print.

———. *Provincializing Europe: Postcolonial Thought and Historical Difference*. Princeton Studies in Culture/Power/History. Princeton, NJ: Princeton University Press, 2000. http://getitatduke.library.duke.edu/?sid=sersol&SS_jc=TC000008470 9&title=Provincializing%20Europe%20%3A%20postcolonial%20thought%2 0and%20historical%20difference.

Chamoiseau, Patrick, Rose-Myriam Réjouis, and Val Vinokur. *Texaco*, 1st Vintage International ed. New York, NY: Vintage International, 1998. Print.

The Church Mission Society. *The Archives of the Church Mission Society, Western Africa*. London, England: CMS Publications, 1865–1948. Print.

Church of God in Christ, and John Hope Franklin Research Center for African and African American History and Culture. *From the Beginning of Bishop C.H. Mason and the Early Pioneers of the Church of God in Christ*. Memphis, TN: Church of God in Christ, 1991. Print.

Clark, Jawanza Eric. *Albert Cleage Jr. and the Black Madonna and Child*. Black Religion/Womanist Thought/Social Justice. http://search.ebscohost.com/login.a spx?direct=true&scope=site&db=nlebk&db=nlabk&AN=1353243.

Cleage, Albert B. *Black Christian Nationalism: New Directions for the Black Church*. New York, NY: Morrow Quill Paperbacks, 1980. Print.

———. *Black Christian Nationalism: New Directions for the Black Church*. New York, NY: W. Morrow, 1972. Print.

———. *The Black Messiah*, 1st AWP ed. Trenton, NJ: Africa World Press, 1989. Print.

———. *The Black Messiah*. New York, NY: Sheed and Ward, 1968. Print.

Cleage, Albert B., and George Bell. *Black Christian Nationalism: New Directions for the Black Church*. Detroit, MI: Luxor, 1987. Print.

Clemmons, Ithiel C. *Bishop C.H. Mason and the Roots of the Church of God in Christ*. Centennial ed. Bakersfield, CA: Pneuma Life Pub., 1996. Print.

Coleman, Monica A. *Ain't I a Womanist, Too?: Third-Wave Womanist Religious Thought*, 2013. http://www.duke.eblib.com/EBLWeb/patron/?target=patron&extendedid=P_1168096_.
———. *Making a Way out of No Way: A Womanist Theology*. Innovations. Minneapolis, MN: Fortress Press, 2008. Print.
Collins, Suzanne. *Mockingjay*. Hunger Games, 1st ed. New York, NY: Scholastic Press, 2010. Print.
Cone, James H. *A Black Theology of Liberation*, 20th Anniversary ed. Maryknoll, NY: Orbis Books, 1990. Print.
———. *A Black Theology of Liberation*, 40th Anniversary ed. Maryknoll, NY: Orbis Books, 2010. Print.
———. *Black Theology and Black Power*. An Original Seabury Paperback, Sp 59. New York, NY: Seabury Press, 1969. Print.
———. *Black Theology and Black Power*. Maryknoll, NY: Orbis, 1997. Print.
———. *God of the Oppressed*, Rev. ed. Maryknoll, NY: Orbis Books, 1997. Print.
———. *Martin & Malcolm & America: A Dream or a Nightmare*. Maryknoll, NY: Orbis Books, 1991. Print.
———. *The Cross and the Lynching Tree*. Maryknoll, NY: Orbis Books, 2011. Print.
———. *The Spirituals and the Blues: An Interpretation*. Maryknoll, NY: Orbis Books, 1991. Print.
———. *The Spirituals and the Blues: An Interpretation*. A Seabury Paperback. New York, NY: Seabury Press, 1972. Print.
Cone, James H., and Gayraud S. Wilmore. *Black Theology: A Documentary History*, 2nd ed., 2 vols. Maryknoll, NY: Orbis Books, 1993. Print.
Cooper, Brittney C. *Beyond Respectability: The Intellectual Thought of Race Women*. Women, Gender, and Sexuality in American History. Champaign, IL: University of Illinois Press, 2017. Print.
Costa, Emília Viotti da. *Crowns of Glory, Tears of Blood: The Demerara Slave Rebellion of 1823*. New York, NY: Oxford University Press, 1994. Print.
Crawley, Ashon T. *Blackpentecostal Breath: The Aesthetics of Possibility*. Commonalities, 1st ed. New York, NY: Fordham University Press, 2017. Print.
Crenshaw, Kimberlé. *Critical Race Theory: The Key Writings That Formed the Movement*. New York, NY: New Press, 1995. Print.
Curtis IV, Edward. *Black Muslim Religion in the Nation of Islam, 1960–1975*, New edition. Chapel Hill: University of North Carolina Press, 2006. https://ebookcentral-proquest-com.proxy.ulib.uits.iu.edu/lib/iupui-ebooks/detail.action?docID=427138.
———. *Islam in Black America: Identity, Liberation, and Difference in African-American Islamic Thought*. Albany, NY: State University of New York Press, 2002. Print. http://search.ebscohost.com/login.aspx?direct=true&scope=site&db=nlebk&db=nlabk&AN=98719.
———. *The Columbia Sourcebook of Muslims in the United States*. New York, NY: Columbia University Press, 2008. Print.
Curtis, Edward E., and Danielle Brune Sigler. *The New Black Gods: Arthur Huff Fauset and the Study of African American Religions*. Religion in North America. Bloomington, IN: Indiana University Press, 2009. Print.

Curtis, Finbarr. *The Production of American Religious Freedom*. North American Religions. New York, NY: New York University Press, 2016. Print.
Cusac, Anne-Marie. *Cruel and Unusual: The Culture of Punishment in America*. New Haven, CT: Yale University Press, 2009. Print.
Daniel, Yvonne. *Dancing Wisdom: Embodied Knowledge in Haitian Vodou, Cuban Yoruba, and Bahian Candomblé*. Urbana, IL: University of Illinois Press, 2005. Print.
Davis, Angela Y. *Are Prisons Obsolete?* Open Media Book. New York, NY: Seven Stories Press, 2003. Print.
———. *Blues Legacies and Black Feminism: Gertrude "Ma" Rainey, Bessie Smith, and Billie Holiday*. New York, NY: Pantheon Books, 1998. Print.
———. *Lectures on Liberation*. New York, NY: N.Y. Committee to Free Angela Davis, 1971. Print.
———. *Women, Race & Class*, 1st Vintage Books ed. New York, NY: Vintage Books, 1983. Print.
Davis, Angela Y., and Joy James. *The Angela Y. Davis Reader*. Blackwell Readers. Malden, MA: Blackwell, 1998. Print.
Day, Keri. *Unfinished Business: Black Women, the Black Church, and the Struggle to Thrive in America*. Maryknoll, NY: Orbis Books, 2012. Print.
Deleuze, Gilles and Felix Guattari. *Anti-Oedipus: Capitalism and Schizophrenia*. New York, NY: Penguin Books, 2009. Print.
Deloria, Vine. *Custer Died for Your Sins; an Indian Manifesto*. London: Macmillan, 1969. Print.
———. *God Is Red*. New York, NY: Grosset & Dunlap, 1973. Print.
———. *God Is Red: A Native View of Religion: The Classic Work Updated*, 2nd ed. Golden, CO: Fulcrum Publishing, 1994. Print.
Dillard, Angela D. *Faith in the City: Preaching Radical Social Change in Detroit*. Ann Arbor, MI: University of Michigan Press, 2007. Print.
Donaldson, Laura E., and Pui-lan Kwok. *Postcolonialism, Feminism and Religious Discourse*. New York, NY: Routledge, 2002. Print.
Douglas, Kelly Brown. *Black Bodies and the Black Church: A Blues Slant*. Black Religion/Womanist Thought/Social Justice. New York, NY: Palgrave Macmillan, 2012. Print.
———. *Sexuality and the Black Church: A Womanist Perspective*. Maryknoll, NY: Orbis Books, 1999. Print.
———. *The Black Christ*. The Bishop Henry Mcneal Turner Studies in North American Black Religion. Maryknoll, NY: Orbis, 1994. Print.
———. *What's Faith Got to Do with It?: Black Bodies/Christian Souls*. Maryknoll, NY: Orbis Books, 2005. Print.
Earl, Riggins Renal. *Toward a Black Christian Ethic: A Study of Alexander Crummell and Albert Cleage*. Thesis, Vanderbilt University, 1978. Print.
Edwards, Brent Hayes. *The Practice of Diaspora: Literature, Translation, and the Rise of Black Internationalism*. Cambridge, MA: Harvard University Press, 2003. Print.

Erickson, Keith V. "Black Messiah: The Father Divine Peace Mission Movement." *Quarterly Journal of Speech* 63, no. 4 (1977): 428. Print.

Erskine, Noel Leo. *From Garvey to Marley: Rastafari Theology*. Gainesville, FL: University Press of Florida, 2005. Print.

Farmer, Ashley D. *Remaking Black Power: How Black Women Transformed an Era*. Justice, Power, and Politics. Chapel Hill, NC: The University of North Carolina Press, 2017. Print.

Father, Divine. *The New Day*. Philadelphia, PA: New Day Pub. Co. v., 1973. Print.

Fauset, Arthur Huff. *Black Gods of the Metropolis: Negro Religious Cults of the Urban North*. Philadelphia, PA: University of Pennsylvania Press, 1971. Print.

The Federal Government of Nigeria. *The Archives of the Nigerian State*. Ibadan, Nigeria, 1905–1945. Print.

Floyd-Thomas, Stacey M. *Deeper Shades of Purple: Womanism in Religion and Society*. Religion, Race, and Ethnicity. New York, NY: New York University Press, 2006. Print.

———. *Mining the Motherlode: Methods in Womanist Ethics*. Cleveland, OH: Pilgrim Press, 2006. Print.

Foucault, Michel. *Discipline and Punish: The Birth of the Prison*, 2nd Vintage Books ed. New York, NY: Vintage Books, 1995. Print.

———. *Language, Counter-Memory, Practice: Selected Essays and Interviews*. Cornell Paperbacks. Ithaca, NY: Cornell University Press, 1992. Print.

Frances Cress Welsing, and John Hope Franklin Research Center for African and African American History and Culture. *The Isis (Yssis) Papers*, 1st ed. Chicago, IL: Third World Press, 1991. Print.

Frances Cress Welsing, Nailah Banks, and National Visionary Leadership Project. *Frances Cress Welsing Oral History, 2005: National Visionary Leadership Project*.

Frazier, Edward Franklin. *Black Bourgeoisie*. Glencoe, IL: Free Press, 1957. Print.

———. *The Negro Church in America*. New York, NY: Schocken Books, 1964. Print.

———. *The Negro Family in Bahia, Brazil*. n.p., 1942. Print.

Frederick, Marla Faye. *Between Sundays: Black Women and Everyday Struggles of Faith*. Berkeley, CA: University of California Press, 2003. Print.

Freedom Behind Bars Productions, and Bullfrog Films. *The Dhamma Brothers*. Videorecording. Bullfrog Films, Oley, PA, 2007.

Fulkerson, Mary McClintock. *Changing the Subject: Women's Discourses and Feminist Theology*. Minneapolis, MN: Fortress Press, 1994. Print.

———. *Places of Redemption: Theology for a Worldly Church*. Oxford and New York, NY: Oxford University Press, 2007. Print.

Gafney, Wilda. *Womanist Midrash: A Reintroduction to the Women of the Torah and the Throne*, 1st ed. Louisville, KY: Westminster John Knox Press, 2017. Print.

Gilroy, Paul. *Against Race: Imagining Political Culture Beyond the Color Line*. Cambridge, MA: Belknap Press of Harvard University Press, 2000. Print.

———. *Darker Than Blue: On the Moral Economies of Black Atlantic Culture*. W. E. B. Du Bois Lectures. Cambridge, MA: Harvard University Press, 2010. Print.

———. *Postcolonial Melancholia*. The Wellek Lectures. New York, NY: Columbia University Press, 2005. Print.

———. *The Black Atlantic: Modernity and Double Consciousness*. Cambridge, MA: Harvard University Press, 1993. Print.

———. *There Ain't No Black in the Union Jack: The Cultural Politics of Race and Nation*. Routledge Classics. London and New York, NY: Routledge, 2002. Print.

Glaude, Eddie S. *Exodus!: Religion, Race, and Nation in Early Nineteenth-Century Black America*. Chicago, IL: University of Chicago Press, 2000. Print.

"God," He's Just a Natural Man. New York, NY: Printed by Gailliard Press, 1937. Print.

Gordon, Lewis R. *An Introduction to Africana Philosophy*. Cambridge Introductions to Philosophy. Cambridge, UK and New York, NY: Cambridge University Press, 2008. Print.

———. *Bad Faith and Antiblack Racism*. Atlantic Highlands, NJ: Humanities Press, 1995. Print.

———. *Existence in Black: An Anthology of Black Existential Philosophy*. New York, NY: Routledge, 1997. Print.

———. *Fanon and the Crisis of European Man: An Essay on Philosophy and the Human Sciences*. New York, NY: Routledge, 1995. Print.

———. *Her Majesty's Other Children Sketches of Racism from a Neocolonial Age*, 1997. http://getitatduke.library.duke.edu/?sid=sersol&SS_jc=TC0000170360&title=Her%20Majesty%27s%20other%20children%20%3A%20sketches%20of%20racism%20from%20a%20neocolonial%20age.

Gordon, Lewis R., and Jane Anna Gordon. *A Companion to African-American Studies*. Blackwell Companions in Cultural Studies. Malden, MA: Blackwell Pub., 2006. Print.

———. *Not Only the Master's Tools: African-American Studies in Theory and Practice*. Cultural Politics & the Promise of Democracy. Boulder, CO: Paradigm, 2006. Print.

Greenberg, Cheryl. "God and Man in Harlem." *Journal of Urban History* 21, no. 4 (1995): 518. Print.

Griffith, R. Marie. "Body Salvation: New Thought, Father Divine, and the Feast of Material Pleasures." *Religion & American Culture* 11, no. 2 (2001): 120. Print.

———. "Body Salvation: New Thought, Father Divine, and the Feast of Material Pleasures." *Religion & American Culture* 11, no. 2 (2001): 120. Print.

Gutiérrez, Gustavo. *A Theology of Liberation: History, Politics, and Salvation*. Maryknoll, NY: Orbis Books, 1973. Print.

Hall, Stuart. *Culture, Media, Language: Working Papers in Cultural Studies, 1972–79*. London, Birmingham, West Midlands: Hutchinson and Centre for Contemporary Cultural Studies, University of Birmingham, 1980. Print.

Hardt, Michael, and Antonio Negri. *Empire*. Cambridge, MA: Harvard University Press, 2000. Print.

———. *Multitude: War and Democracy in the Age of Empire*. New York, NY: Penguin Press, 2004. Print.

Hardy III, Clarence E. "'No Mystery God': Black Religions of the Flesh in Pre-War Urban America." *Church History* 77, no. 1 (2008): 128–150. Print.

Harney, Stefano, and Fred Moten. *The Undercommons: Fugitive Planning & Black Study*. Minor Compositions, 2016. Print.

Harris, Melanie L. *Gifts of Virtue, Alice Walker, and Womanist Ethics*. Black Religion/Womanist Thought/Social Justice, 1st ed. New York, NY: Palgrave Macmillan, 2010. Print.

Harris, Sara. *Father Divine, Holy Husband*, 1st ed. Garden City, NY: Doubleday, 1953. Print.

Harris, Sara, and Harriet Crittenden. *Father Divine*, Newly rev. and expanded ed. New York, NY: Collier Books, 1971. Print.

Harvey, David. *The Condition of Postmodernity: An Enquiry into the Origins of Cultural Change*. Oxford, England and New York, NY, USA: Blackwell, 1990. Print.

Herring, Cedric, Verna Keith, and Hayward Derrick Horton. *Skin Deep: How Race and Complexion Matter in The "Color-Blind" Era*. Urbana, IL: University of Illinois Press: Institute for Research on Race and Public Policy, University of Illinois at Chicago, 2004. Print.

———. *Skin Deep: How Race and Complexion Matter in The "Color-Blind" Era*. Urbana, IL: University of Illinois Press: Institute for Research on Race and Public Policy, University of Illinois at Chicago, 2004. Print.

Holloway, Karla F. C. *Passed On: African American Mourning Stories: A Memorial*. Durham, NC: Duke University Press, 2002. Print.

Hopkins, Dwight N., and Anthony B. Pinn. *Loving the Body: Black Religious Studies and the Erotic*. Black Religion, Womanist Thought, Social Justice, 1st ed. New York, NY: Palgrave Macmillan, 2004. Print.

Horsley, Richard A. *Hidden Transcripts and the Arts of Resistance: Applying the Work of James C. Scott to Jesus and Paul*. Semeia Studies. Atlanta, GA: Society of Biblical Literature, 2004. Print.

Hoshor, John. *God in a Rolls Royce: The Rise of Father Divine: Madman, Menace, or Messiah*. The Black Heritage Library Collection. Freeport, NY: Books for Libraries Press, 1971. Print.

Jackson, John L. *Thin Description: Ethnography and the African Hebrew Israelites of Jerusalem*. Cambridge, MA: Harvard University Press, 2013. Print.

Jennings, Willie James. *The Christian Imagination: Theology and the Origins of Race*. New Haven, CT: Yale University Press, 2010. Print.

Johnson, Sylvester A. *African American Religions, 1500–2000: Colonialism, Democracy, and Freedom*. New York, NY: Cambridge University Press, 2015. Print.

———. *The Myth of Ham in Nineteenth-Century American Christianity: Race, Heathens, and the People of God*. Black Religion, Womanist Thought, Social Justice, 1st ed. New York, NY: Palgrave Macmillan, 2004. Print.

Jones, Angela. *The Modern African American Political Thought Reader: From David Walker to Barack Obama*. New York, NY: Routledge, 2013. Print.

Kahan, Benjamin. "The Other Harlem Renaissance: Father Divine, Celibate Economics, and the Making of Black Sexuality." *Arizona Quarterly: A Journal of American Literature, Culture, and Theory* 65 (2009): 37–61. Print.

Knight, Henry H. *From Aldersgate to Azusa Street: Wesleyan, Holiness, and Pentecostal Visions of the New Creation*. Eugene, OR: Pickwick Publications, 2010. Print.

Kwok, Pui-lan. *Postcolonial Imagination and Feminist Theology*, 1st ed. Louisville, KY: Westminster John Knox Press, 2005. Print.

Lawrence, Bruce B., Aisha Karim, and ebrary Inc. *On Violence a Reader*, 2007. http://www.loc.gov/catdir/toc/ecip0717/2007019209.html, http://site.ebrary.com/lib/dukelibraries/Doc?id=10236491.

Le Blanc, Paul. *Black Liberation and the American Dream: The Struggle for Racial and Economic Justice: Analysis, Strategy, Readings*. Revolutionary Studies. Amherst, NY: Humanity Books, 2003. Print.

Lee, Valerie. *The Prentice Hall Anthology of African American Women's Literature*. Upper Saddle River, NJ: Pearson Prentice Hall, 2006. Print.

Lewis, Gordon K., and Anthony P. Maingot. *Gordon K. Lewis on Race, Class, and Ideology in the Caribbean*. Kingston and Miami, FL: Ian Randle Publishers, 2010. Print.

Lincoln, Bruce. *Holy Terrors: Thinking About Religion after September 11*, 2nd ed. Chicago, IL: University of Chicago Press, 2006. Print.

———. *Religion, Rebellion, Revolution: An Inter-Disciplinary and Cross-Cultural Collection of Essays*. New York, NY: St. Martin's Press, 1985. Print.

Lincoln, C. Eric, and Lawrence H. Mamiya. "Daddy Jones and Father Divine: The Cult as Political Religion." *Religion in Life* 49, no. 1 (1980): 6–23. Print.

Long, Charles H. *Significations: Signs, Symbols, and Images in the Interpretation of Religion*. Series in Philosophical and Cultural Studies in Religion. Aurora, CO: Davies Group, 1999. Print.

Madhubuti, Haki R. *Black Pride: Poems*, 1st ed. Detroit, MI: Broadside Press, 1968. Print.

Mahmood, Saba. *Politics of Piety: The Islamic Revival and the Feminist Subject*. Princeton, NJ: Princeton University Press, 2005. Print.

Mangin, Charlotte, et al. *America by the Numbers: The New Deciders*. Print.

Marable, Manning, and Hisham Aidi. *Black Routes to Islam*. The Critical Black Studies Series, 1st ed. New York, NY: Palgrave Macmillan, 2009. Print.

Mbembe, Achille, and Laurent Dubois. *Critique of Black Reason*. Durham, NC: Duke University Press, 2017. Print.

Mbembé, J. A. *On Private Indirect Government*. State of Literature Series. Dakar, Senegal: Council for the Development of Social Science Research in Africa, 2000. Print.

McBride, James. *The Color of Water: A Black Man's Tribute to His White Mother*, 1st Riverhead trade pbk, 10th Anniversary ed. New York, NY: Riverhead Books, 2006. Print.

McKay, Claude. "The Story of Father Divine and His Angels." *Nation* 140, no. 3631 (1935): 151–153. Print.

Meeks, Brian, and Stuart Hall. *Culture, Politics, Race and Diaspora: The Thought of Stuart Hall*. Kingston, Miami, FL, and London: I. Randle Publishers and Lawrence & Wishart, 2007. Print.

Mignolo, Walter. *Local Histories/Global Designs: Coloniality, Subaltern Knowledges, and Border Thinking*. Princeton Studies in Culture/Power/History. Princeton, NJ: Princeton University Press, 2000. Print.

———. *The Darker Side of the Renaissance: Literacy, Territoriality, and Colonization*. Ann Arbor, MI: University of Michigan Press, 1995. Print.

Morris, William Wesley. *Strategies for Liberation: A Critical Comparison of Martin Luther King, Jr. And Albert B. Cleage, Jr*. Thesis, Vanderbilt University, 1973. Print.

Morrison, Toni. *Beloved: A Novel*, 1st Vintage International ed. New York, NY: Vintage International, 2004. Print.

———. *The Dancing Mind Speech Upon Acceptance of the National Book Foundation Medal for Distinguished Contribution to American Letters on the Sixth of November, Nineteen Hundred and Ninety-Six*, 1996. http://getitatduke.library.duke.edu/?sid=sersol&SS_jc=TC_004208689&title=Dancing%20mind%20%3A%20speech%20upon%20acceptance%20of%20the%20National%20Book%20Foundation%20Medal%20for%20Distinguished%20Contribution%20to%20American%20Letters%20on%20the%20sixth%20of%20November%2C%20Nineteen%20hundred%20and%20ninety-six.

Moten, Fred. *In the Break: The Aesthetics of the Black Radical Tradition*, 2003. https://getitatduke.library.duke.edu/?sid=sersol&SS_jc=TC0000177842&title=In%20the%20break%20%3A%20the%20aesthetics%20of%20the%20Black%20radical%20tradition.

———. *In the Break: The Aesthetics of the Black Radical Tradition*. Minneapolis, MN: University of Minnesota Press, 2003. Print.

———. *Stolen Life. Consent Not to Be a Single Being v 2*. doi:10.1215/9780822372028.

Mother, Divine. *The Peace Mission Movement: Founded by M.J. Divine, Better Known as Father Divine*. Philadelphia, PA: Imperial Press, 1982. Print.

Mudimbe, V. Y. *The Idea of Africa*. African Systems of Thought. Bloomington, IN and London: Indiana University Press and J. Currey, 1994. Print.

———. *The Invention of Africa: Gnosis, Philosophy, and the Order of Knowledge*. African Systems of Thought. Bloomington, IN: Indiana University Press, 1988. Print.

Naylor, Gloria. *The Women of Brewster Place*. Penguin Contemporary American Fiction Series. New York, NY: Penguin Books, 1983. Print.

Ndungu, Nahashon W., and Philomena Mwaura. *Challenges and Prospects for the Church in Africa: Theological Reflections for the 21st Century*. Ecumenical Symposium of Eastern Africa Theologians (Eseat). Nairobi: Paulines Publications Africa, 2005. Print.

Neal, Mark Anthony. *Looking for Leroy: Illegible Black Masculinities*. Postmillennial Pop. New York, NY: New York University Press, 2013. Print.

———. *New Black Man*. New York, NY: Routledge, 2005. Print.

Nelson, Alondra. *Body and Soul: The Black Panther Party and the Fight against Medical Discrimination*. Minneapolis, MN and London: University of Minnesota Press, 2011. Print.

Nwankwo, Ifeoma Kiddoe. *Black Cosmopolitanism: Racial Consciousness and Transnational Identity in the Nineteenth-Century Americas*. Rethinking the Americas. Philadelphia, PA: University of Pennsylvania Press, 2005. Print.

Person-Lynn, Kwaku. *First Word: Black Scholars, Artists, Warriors: Knowledge, Wisdom, Mental Liberation*, 2nd edition. Chicago, IL: Third World Press, 2015. Print.

Pinn, Anthony B. *African American Humanist Principles: Living and Thinking Like the Children of Nimrod*. Black Religion, Womanist Thought, Social Justice, 1st ed. New York, NY: Palgrave Macmillan, 2004. Print.

———. *Black Religion and Aesthetics: Religious Thought and Life in Africa and the African Diaspora*, 1st ed. New York, NY: Palgrave Macmillan, 2009. Print.

———. *Embodiment and the New Shape of Black Theological Thought*. Religion, Race, and Ethnicity Series. New York, NY: New York University Press, 2010. Print.

———. *Noise and Spirit: The Religious and Spiritual Sensibilities of Rap Music*. New York, NY: New York University Press, 2003. Print.

———. *The End of God-Talk: An African American Humanist Theology*. Oxford and New York, NY: Oxford University Press, 2012. Print.

———. *Varieties of African American Religious Experience*. Minneapolis, MN: Fortress Press, 1998. Print.

———. *What Is Humanism, and Why Does It Matter?* Studies in Humanist Thought and Praxis. Durham, NC: Acumen, 2013. Print.

Pinn, Anthony B., Stephen C. Finley, and Torin Alexander. *African American Religious Cultures*. American Religious Cultures Series. Santa Barbara, CA: ABC-CLIO, 2009. Print.

Piot, Charles. *Remotely Global: Village Modernity in West Africa*. Chicago, IL: University of Chicago Press, 1999. Print.

Primiano, Leonard Norman. "'Bringing Perfection in These Different Places': Father Divine's Vernacular Architecture of Intention." *Folklore* 115, no. 1 (2004): 3–26. Print.

Randall, Dudley. *Broadside Memories: Poets I Have Known*. Detroit, MI: Broadside Press, 1975. Print.

Randall, Dudley, and Margaret Taylor Burroughs. *For Malcolm; Poems on the Life and the Death of Malcolm X*. Broadside Poets, 2nd ed. Detroit, MI: Broadside Press, 1969. Print.

Roberts, Neil. *Freedom as Marronage*. http://chicago.universitypressscholarship.com/view/10.7208/chicago/9780226201184.001.0001/upso-9780226127460.

Satter, Beryl. "Marcus Garvey, Father Divine and the Gender Politics Of." *American Quarterly* 48, no. 1 (1996): 43. Print.

Savage, Barbara Dianne. *Your Spirits Walk Beside Us: The Politics of Black Religion*. Cambridge, MA: Belknap Press of Harvard University Press, 2008. Print.

Scott, James C. *Domination and the Arts of Resistance: Hidden Transcripts*. New Haven, CT: Yale University Press, 1990. Print.

Semmes, Clovis E. *Roots of Afrocentric Thought: A Reference Guide to Negro Digest/Black World, 1961–1976*. Bibliographies and Indexes in Afro-American and African Studies. Westport, CT: Greenwood Press, 1998. Print.

Shange, Ntozake. *For Colored Girls Who Have Considered Suicide When the Rainbow Is Enuf: A Choreopoem*, 1st Collier Books ed. New York, NY: Collier Books, 1989. Print.

Simmons, Martha J., and Frank A. Thomas. *Preaching with Sacred Fire: An Anthology of African American Sermons, 1750 to the Present*, 1st ed. New York, NY: W.W. Norton, 2010. Print.

Singh, Nikhil Pal. *Black Is a Country: Race and the Unfinished Struggle for Democracy*. Cambridge, MA: Harvard University Press, 2004. Print.

Skocpol, Theda, Ariane Liazos, and Marshall Ganz. *What a Mighty Power We Can Be: African American Fraternal Groups and the Struggle for Racial Equality*. Princeton Studies in American Politics. Princeton, NJ: Princeton University Press, 2006. Print.

Smith, Mitzi J. *I Found God in Me: A Womanist Biblical Hermeneutics Reader*. Cascade Books, 2015. Print.

Smith, Theophus Harold. *Conjuring Culture: Biblical Formations of Black America*. Religion in America Series. New York, NY: Oxford University Press, 1994. Print.

*Spoken Word* 1935. Print.

Stewart, Dianne M. *Three Eyes for the Journey: African Dimensions of the Jamaican Religious Experience*. New York, NY: Oxford University Press, 2005. Print.

Stewart, Jeffrey C. *The New Negro: The Life of Alain Locke*. New York, NY: Oxford University Press, 2018. Print.

Sullivan, Winnifred Fallers. *Prison Religion: Faith-Based Reform and the Constitution*. Princeton, NJ: Princeton University Press, 2009. Print.

Thomas, Dominic Richard David. *Black France: Colonialism, Immigration, and Transnationalism*. African Expressive Cultures. Bloomington, IN: Indiana University Press, 2007. Print.

———. *Not on Any Map: Essays on Postcoloniality and Cultural Nationalism*. Exeter Studies in American and Commonwealth Arts. Exeter, Devon, UK: University of Exeter Press, 1997. Print.

Thompson, Julius Eric. *Dudley Randall, Broadside Press, and the Black Arts Movement in Detroit, 1960–1995*. Jefferson, NC: McFarland, 1999. Print.

Thurman, Howard. *Deep Is the Hunger; Meditations for Apostles of Sensitiveness*. Richmond, IN: Friends United Press, 1973. Print.

———. *The Creative Encounter; an Interpretation of Religion and the Social Witness*, 1st ed. New York, NY: Harper, 1954. Print.

Thurman, Howard, Walter E. Fluker, and Catherine Tumber. *A Strange Freedom: The Best of Howard Thurman on Religious Experience and Public Life*. Boston, MA: Beacon Press, 1998. Print.

Townes, Emilie Maureen. *Womanist Ethics and the Cultural Production of Evil*. Black Religion, Womanist Thought, Social Justice. New York, NY: Palgrave Macmillan, 2006. Print.

Turman, Eboni Marshall. *Toward a Womanist Ethic of Incarnation: Black Bodies, the Black Church, and the Council of Chalcedon*. Black Religion, Womanist Thought, Social Justice, 1st ed. London: Palgrave Macmillan, 2013. Print.

Tweed, Thomas A. *Crossing and Dwelling: A Theory of Religion*. Cambridge, MA: Harvard University Press, 2006. Print.

———. *Our Lady of the Exile: Diasporic Religion at a Cuban Catholic Shrine in Miami*. Religion in America Series. New York, NY: Oxford University Press, 1997. Print.

Wacker, Grant. *America's Pastor: Billy Graham and the Shaping of a Nation*. Cambridge, MA: The Belknap Press of Harvard University Press, 2014. Print.

———. *Heaven Below: Early Pentecostals and American Culture*. Cambridge, MA: Harvard University Press, 2001. Print.

Walker, Alice. *In Search of Our Mothers' Gardens: Womanist Prose*. San Diego, CA: Harcourt Brace Jovanovich, 1983. Print.

———. *The Temple of My Familiar*. San Diego, CA: Harcourt Brace Jovanovich, 1989. Print.

Walker, Alice, and George Washington Flowers Collection of Southern Americana. *The Color Purple: A Novel*. New York, NY: Harcourt Brace Jovanovich, 1982. Print.

Wallerstein, Immanuel Maurice. *Geopolitics and Geoculture: Essays on the Changing World-System*. Cambridge, England, New York, NY and Paris: Cambridge University Press and Editions de la Maison des Sciences de l'Homme, 1991. Print.

———. *World-Systems Analysis: An Introduction*. Durham, NC: Duke University Press, 2004. Print.

Walton, Jonathan L. *Watch This!: The Ethics and Aesthetics of Black Televangelism*. Religion, Race, and Ethnicity. New York, NY: New York University Press, 2009. Print.

Warnock, Raphael G. *The Divided Mind of the Black Church: Theology, Piety, and Public Witness*. Religion, Race, and Ethnicity. New York, NY: NYU Press, 2014. Print.

Warrior, Robert Allen. *Tribal Secrets: Recovering American Indian Intellectual Traditions*. Minneapolis, MN: University of Minnesota Press, 1995. Print.

Waters, Kristin, and Carol B. Conaway. *Black Women's Intellectual Traditions: Speaking Their Minds*. Burlington, VT and Hanover: University of Vermont Press and Published by University Press of New England, 2007. Print.

Watts, Jill. *God, Harlem U.S.A.: The Father Divine Story*. Berkeley, CA: University of California Press, 1992. Print.

———. "'This Was the Way': Father Divine's Peace Mission Movement in Los Angeles During the Great Depression." *Pacific Historical Review* 60, no. 4 (1991): 475. Print.

Weems, Renita J. *Just a Sister Away: A Womanist Vision of Women's Relationships in the Bible*. San Diego, CA: LuraMedia, 1988. Print.
Weisbrot, Robert. *Father Divine and the Struggle for Racial Equality*. Blacks in the New World. Urbana, IL: University of Illinois Press, 1983. Print.
Weisenfeld, Judith. *African American Women and Christian Activism: New York's Black YWCA, 1905–1945*. Cambridge, MA: Harvard University Press, 1997. Print.
———. *New World a-Coming: Black Religion and Racial Identity During the Great Migration*. New York, NY: New York University Press, 2016. Print.
Wells-Barnett, Ida B., and Jacqueline Jones Royster. *Southern Horrors and Other Writings: The Anti-Lynching Campaign of Ida B. Wells, 1892–1900*. The Bedford Series in History and Culture, 2nd ed. Boston, MA: Bedford/St. Martins, Macmillan Learning, 2016. Print.
West, Cornel. *Prophesy Deliverance!: An Afro-American Revolutionary Christianity*, 1st ed. Philadelphia, PA: Westminster Press, 1982. Print.
———. *Prophetic Fragments*. Grand Rapids, MI and Trenton, NJ: Eerdmans and Africa World Press, 1988. Print.
———. *Race Matters*, 1st Vintage Books ed. New York, NY: Vintage Books, 1994. Print.
———. *The American Evasion of Philosophy: A Genealogy of Pragmatism*. The Wisconsin Project on American Writers. Madison, WI: University of Wisconsin Press, 1989. Print.
———. *The Cornel West Reader*, 1st ed. New York, NY: Basic Civitas Books, 1999. Print.
Williams, Delores S. *Sisters in the Wilderness: The Challenge of Womanist God-Talk*. Maryknoll, NY: Orbis Books, 1993. Print.
Wimbush, Vincent L. *Theorizing Scriptures: New Critical Orientations to a Cultural Phenomenon*. Signifying (on) Scriptures. New Brunswick, NJ: Rutgers University Press, 2008. Print.
———. *White Men's Magic: Scripturalization as Slavery*. New York, NY: Oxford University Press, 2012. Print.
Wimbush, Vincent L., and Rosamond C. Rodman. *African Americans and the Bible: Sacred Texts and Social Textures*. New York, NY: Continuum, 2000. Print.
Yelvington, Kevin A. *Afro-Atlantic Dialogues: Anthropology in the Diaspora*. School of American Research Advanced Seminar Series, 1st ed. Santa Fe, NM and Oxford: School of American Research Press and James Currey, 2006. Print.

# Index

Abram, Andrea, 136
acquisitive capitalism: critique of, 57
Africa, 62–64
African: communalism, 102; cultures, 62, 77n28; spirituality, 102
Africana: Christian bodies, 80; Christianities, 152; diaspora, 64; prophets, 79; studies, 86
African American, 89, 94, 108, 113, 130, 132, 143–45, 147, 156; Christian, 10 (Black sphere, 127; communities, 128; tradition, 63, 103, 126, 128); Christianity, 8, 12, 18, 24, 28, 33, 78n46, 102, 105, 124, 151–52, 154–55; church, 111; communities, 15, 17, 18, 33, 124, 131; culture, 6, 39, 151; denominations, 8; economic empowerment, 6; liberation, 28; migrants, 89, 152; political resistance, 6; religions, 8, 16, 23–26, 30–32, 34, 36, 38, 40, 105, 143, 151–53 (alternative, 37–40; Black theology, 26–28; and New Religious Movements, 28–29); religious gatherings, 7; religious movements, 35, 130; scriptural readings, 54; studies, 86; suffering, 5, 64; women, 106, 110, 135; working-class, 72, 89 (citizenship, 16, 55)
African-centered Christianity, 102, 103
African-centered self-determination, 134
Africology, 120
Afro-American. *See* African American
Afro-centric character, 130
Afro-centric Christianity, 106, 136, 138n14
Afro-centric Christian tradition, 127
Afro-centric church, 112, 134
Afro-centrism, 128
Afro-Christian: Madonna, 112; movement, 104, 115, 136; nationalism, 104
Afro-Christianity, 103, 104, 109, 116, 128, 133
Afro-diasporic religious impulse, 10
Afro-diasporic traditions, 115
Afro-divinities, 38
Afro-religions/spirituality, 104
Afro-religious texts, 127
Agyeman, Jaramogi Abebe (Albert B. Cleage), 5, 107, 145, 146, 148–57; Afro-centric Christianity, 138n14; Afro-centric seminaries, 142n61;

Black and Christian, 124; and Black Church, 101, 125–29; Black-informed models and itineraries, 115; Black Madonna, 137n1, 137n12; Black messiah, 101–3, 113, 127, 131, 132, 140n39; *Black Periodicals,* 121, 122; Black public, 133; Black radical and sacred publics, 119; Black theological project, 141n59; and Black theology, 129–31; Black Utopia, 117; and caretakers, 108; Christian movements, 103; Detroit Urban Renewal program, 123; functions of Utopia, 118; with Grace Lee Boggs, 110; Presbyterian Church, 105; press and Black publishing, 121; Shrine of the Black Madonna, 136; and Shrines, 104, 106, 107, 109, 111, 118, 134; vision of a Black cultural restoration, 114; vision of radical press, 120

Ali, Muhammad, 48, 63, 75n9

alterity, 151, 155

alternative African American Christianities, 151–52

alternative Black publics, 37–40, 82–85

alternative Black religions, 9

alternative Christianities, 6, 15, 18

alternative Christian movements, 36, 38; in Black public sphere, 5–10; and other Black church, 10–11

alternative modernities, 151

alternative publics, 32, 36, 37–40, 154

alternative religions, 9, 15, 24–26, 28, 33–35, 38, 124

alternative religious movements, 156

American: citizenship, 80; democracy, 81; exceptionalism, 97

*an American Slave* (Douglass), 75n12

anthropology, 28

anti-racialist, 85

*Appeal to the Colored Citizens of the United States* (Walker), 75n12

Assemblies of God movement, 53

Atlanta Shrine, 133

Baby Suggs Holy, 36

Back-to-Africa Utopia, 87

Baker, George A Jr. *See* Father, Divine

Bantum, Brian, 35

Baraka, Amiri, 114–15

Barber, William, 2

BCN Training program, 125

beloved community, 57

ben-Jochanan, Yoself , 126

Beulah Farm in South Carolina, 116, 117, 119

Beulah Land and Farm Initiative, 109

Bible, 10, 13, 30, 42n22, 50, 143, 144

Biblical texts, 2, 13, 27, 30, 45, 47, 128, 143

Black: and African-diasporic liberation, 128; autonomy, 74n3; Baptists movements, 65; canonicity, problems and promise, 32–37; Christianities, 61–64; Christian movements, 81; Christology, 35; citizenship, 9–10, 37, 40, 47, 70, 98; communists, 57; community, 106, 118; consumers, 132; cosmopolitanism, 77n29; economic mobilization, 104; exceptionalism, 83, 85; flourishing, 34, 40; freedom, 5, 9, 15, 17–18, 28, 33, 37, 62, 74n3; genocide, 36; gentrification, 36; identity, 30, 32, 72; liberation, 4; Methodists, 71; middle-aged women, 90; middle class/critique of capital, 93–94; mourning, 36; nationalism, 80, 111; nationalist movements, 86, 87; nationalist organization, 127; nationalist projects, 83; nationalists, 134; organizations, 54, 94; Pentecostal beliefs, 67; Pentecostalism, 62, 73; Pentecostals, 69, 72, 73; pilgrims, 157; press, 140n40; press power, Mason, Charles Harrison and, 67–69; public sphere, 2–4, 87, 111 (alternative Christian movements in, 5–7; role of, 7–10; critical role,

25; margins of, 14–15); racial identities, 14, 38; radical movements, 124; radical participation, 49, 61, 73; relationship, 80; religion, 6, 9, 14–16, 24, 27–29, 32, 37, 71, 111; religiosity, 63; religious freedom, denial of, 34; religious identity, 35; religious movements, 63, 67; religious protest, 45–48; religious public, 63; respectability/protest, 55, 56, 58–59, 76n23; sacrality, 4, 40; sacred body, 71; sacred public, 3–4, 6, 9, 10, 13, 15, 25, 34, 55, 59, 62, 141n56 (defined, 24); spirituality, 104; subjectivity, 55, 67; suffering, 63, 71, 110, 157; theology, 24, 29, 31, 34–36, 40, 57, 58, 65, 67–68, 80, 129–31, 141n58, 151–55 (foundation of, 27 28; genealogy of, 141n56); women, 28, 31, 65, 90–93, 101 (auxiliary's critique, 61; dehumanization, 31; multiple identities, 32, 36; normative spaces, 32; role in COGIC church, 60; truancy, 31); working-class, 16–17, 46, 51, 53, 54, 60, 71, 72, 133, 156. *See also* African American

Black Americans, 83, 86, 91, 98; relationship to Christianity, 27

Black Arts Movement, 119

Black Atlantic, 152

Black Baptists, 71

*Black Bodies and the Black Church* (Douglas), 7, 41n10

Black body(ies), 83–84, 88, 95, 98, 143, 155; attacks on, 35, 88; canonization, 6, 10, 15, 18, 34, 39–40 (problems and promise, 32–37); encounters and representation, 36; physicality, 35; religious encounter, 35, 36; role of, 25; sacrality, 28, 35; sacralization, 25–26

Black Christian, 157; communities, 105, 111, 125; movements, 83; nationalists, 134; public sphere, 82, 85, 110, 152 (rearticulation of, 81–82); suffering, 149; tradition, 3, 4, 107, 154

Black Christianity(ies), 10, 13, 27, 37, 47, 61–64, 73, 74, 82, 129, 134, 143, 144; construction of, 46; Father, Divine and, 80–81; flexibility, 59

Black Christian Nationalist movement, 103, 114, 128

Black Church, 8, 35, 106, 125–29, 134, 151–58; blackness, 12–15; category of, 11, 12; declining, 3; deradicalization of, 99n5; hegemony of, 28; history of, 4–5, 7, 13; and institutions/organizations, 4; Mason, Charles Harrison and, 64–67; movement, 82, 85, 89, 98; physicality, 20n23; spirituality, 13, 14; tradition, 1–2, 4–5, 9, 11

Black Classic Press, 120

Black Communist Party, 123

"Black Gods," 81, 86

*Black Gods of the Metropolis* (Fauset), 80

Black Harlem, 91

Black international public, Father, Divine and, 85–89

Black Liberation movement, 101, 103

"Black Lives Matter and the Long Humanist Tradition" (Pinn), 19n6

Black Lives Matter (BLM) Movement, 1–2, 4, 36, 149, 150, 153–54, 157; sacrality, 5; sacred traditions, 3

Black Madonna, 101–3, 105–8, 110, 111, 113, 118, 119, 127, 128, 137n1, 137n12

*Black Man* (Garvey), 87

Black Memphis economy, 68

Black Messiah, 101, 102, 118, 127

*The Black Messiah* (Cleage), 103, 140n39

Black Nationalist Christian Movement, 127

blackness, 24, 37, 46; Black church, 7, 12–15; normative, 60–61; roles, 14

Black Panthers, 114, 123–25
*Black Periodicals* (Cleage), 121, 122
*Black Print Unbound* (Gardner), 67, 140n40
Black Prophet, 81
*Black Religion and Black Radicalism: An Interpretation of the Religious History of Afro-American People* (Wilmore), 99n5
Black Studies, 120, 130–31
Black theology: Cleage, Albert B., 129–31
*Black Theology and Black Power* (Cone), 129
Black Utopia, 117
*Black Visions* (Dawson), 41n11
Bland, Sandra, 1
BLM Movement. *See* Black Lives Matter (BLM) Movement
Blood is blood, Spirit is Spirit, Mind is Mind!, 87
blues women, 36
Blyden, Edward Wilmot, 83
Boggs, Grace Lee, 110
Bogues, Henry, 10, 19n10
Brazilian religious practices, 31
broad Christian tradition, 5–7, 11, 15
Broadside Press, 119, 120
Brown, Michael, 1
*Brown v. Board of Education* decision, 70
business of the body, 140n37
Butler, Anthea D., 60, 70, 77n23; *Women in the Church of God in Christ*, 65, 77n27

Camp, Stephanie M. H., 31–32, 43n29
Cannon, Katie G., 33
canonical texts, 6, 10, 33–34, 42n22, 137n13; idea creation and, 36; white supremacy, 30, 42n22
canonicity, 32–37
canonization: of Black body, 6, 10, 15, 18, 34, 39–40; Christian scripture, 6, 10
Caribbean, 62–64; cultures, 62, 77n28

Carter, J. Cameron, 35
Cassius Clay. *See* Ali, Muhammed
"charlatan," 79
Christian: discourse, 84; institutions, 60; modalities, 86; movement, 54, 79; projects, 82; provincialism, 149; scripture, 82 (limitations of, 31); theology, 150
Christian-adjacent movements, 24, 156
Christianity(ies), 8–9, 14, 27, 28, 46–48, 71; African Americans, 12, 24, 33, 78n46, 105, 124, 152, 154–55; alternative African American, 6, 15, 18, 151–52; Black, 10, 13, 27, 37, 47, 61–64, 73, 74, 82, 129, 134, 143, 144 (construction of, 46; Father, Divine and, 80–81; flexibility, 59); colonial mission, 146; conversation with, 28; flexibility, 59; normative, 8, 9, 13, 14, 30, 146, 150
Christian Messiah, 156
Church of God in Christ (COGIC) movement, 16, 45, 46–48, 52–54, 57, 59–62, 64–68, 70–71, 75n6, 77n28; archival features, 67; democracy and, 45
citizenship, 6, 13, 59; American, 80; Black, 9–10, 37, 40, 47, 70, 98; Pentecostal, 148
civil rights, 97–98
Civil Rights Movement, 134
Cleage, Albert B. (Jaramogi Abebe Agyeman), 5, 145, 146, 148–57; Afro-centric Christianity, 138n14; Afro-centric seminaries, 142n61; Black and Christian, 124; and Black Church, 101, 125–29; Black-informed models and itineraries, 115; Black Madonna, 137n1, 137n12; Black messiah, 101–3, 113, 127, 131, 132, 140n39; *Black Periodicals*, 121, 122; Black public, 133; Black radical and sacred publics, 119; Black theological project, 141n59; and Black theology, 129–31; Black

Utopia, 117; and caretakers, 108; Christian movements, 103; Detroit Urban Renewal program, 123; functions of Utopia, 118; with Grace Lee Boggs, 110; Presbyterian Church, 105; press and Black publishing, 121; Shrine of the Black Madonna, 136; and Shrines, 104, 106, 107, 109, 111, 118, 134; vision of a Black cultural restoration, 114; vision of radical press, 120
COGIC movement. *See* Church of God in Christ (COGIC) movement
colonial mission Christianity, 146
Communist ideology, 89
Cone, James H., 28, 128, 129, 132; *The Cross and the Lynching Tree*, 35
conscientious objection, 54–60
constant surveillance, 79
constructed theologies, 151
Cooper, Brittney C., 44n46, 58
Crawley, Ashon T., 150
*The Cross and the Lynching Tree* (Cone), 35
Crow, Jim, 52
Crunk Feminism, 44n46
Cullors, Patrisse, 1, 3
cultural anthropology, 28
cultural-based economic revitalization, 123–25
cultural movements: social and, 8
cultural renaissance, 104
cultural revolution, 5–7
cultural theory, 9

Dancing of God, 60
darkness, 150
Dawson, Michael C., 74; *Black Visions*, 41n11
Day, Keri: analysis of church's struggle, 19n9
democracy, 6, 14, 15, 17, 29, 46, 48, 54–57, 62, 65, 66, 73, 75n12; Black Christianity and, 63; critique of, 60–61; racialized, 97–98; U.S., 113, 155

denominationalism, 70, 72
Depression era, 84
Detroit community, 104, 106, 114, 122
*Detroit News* (Cleage), 104
Detroit Urban Renewal program, 123
dissonance, 9, 27, 149, 150, 154
*The Divided Mind of the Black Church* (Warnock), 20n22
Douglas, Kelley Brown, 4, 7, 12, 26, 28, 35, 36, 59, 145–49, 151; *Black Bodies and the Black Church*, 7, 41n10
Douglass, Frederick: *an American Slave* (Douglass), 75n12; *My Bondage and My Freedom*, 75n12; *The Narrative Life of Frederick Douglass*, 75n12
Dowell, Glanton V., 101
Du Bois, W. E. B., 47–48, 91; *The Philadelphia Negro*, 47, 64; *The Philadelphia Negro a Social Study*, 75n7

early Pentecostals, 39
Eaton, Isabel: *The Philadelphia Negro a Social Study*, 75n7
economic communalism, 89
Edwards, Brent Hayes, 10
embodiment of divine, 139n29
*The End of God-Talk* (Pinn), 21n30
epistemological hegemony, 33
Equiano, Olaudah, 30–31, 35, 42nn24–25; *The Interesting Narrative Life of Olaudah Equiano, or Gustavus Vassa, The African*, 30; narrative, 30–31; theorization of, 37
ethnic identities: Pan-African, 87
Euro-American culture and value, 59
European Christianity, 112, 116
"evangelical" standards, 93
Evans, Curtis J., 7, 8

Father, Divine, 5, 9, 16–17, 34–37, 46, 57, 62, 77n30, 79–80, 112, 145–50, 152–55, 157; and alternative Black publics, 82–85; Black

body, 35; and Black Christianity, 80–81; Black Christian public, rearticulation of, 81–82; and Black international public, 85–89; Black middle class/critique of capital, 93–94; movement, 99n17; racialized democracy and civil rights, 97–98; Righteous Government and lynching, 94–96; and working-class scripture, 89–90
Father Divine's movement, 9, 16, 34, 76n16
FBI files, 48, 54, 55, 70
federal Urban Renewal programs, 123
Fluker, Walter E.: *The Ground Has Shifted*, 21n30
Franklin, C. L., 126
fugitive Blacks, 14
fugitive discourse, 13
full citizenship, 55

Gardner, Eric: *Black Print Unbound*, 67, 140n40
Garveyite movement, 83, 88, 102
Garvey, Marcus, 5, 80, 81, 83, 86–88, 128; and Nation of Islam, 121
Gates, Henry Louis, 42n24
Glaude, Eddie S., 2; fugitive discourse, 13
global politics, 64
glossalia, 74n1, 74n12
*God in a Rolls Royce* (Horshor), 80
"God's laws," 96
Gordon, Lewis K., 33
Gramsci, Antonio, 117; organic intellectuals, 66, 138n22
Gray, Freddie, 1
Griffith, R. Marie, 83–84
*The Ground Has Shifted* (Fluker), 21n30

Harlem Renaissance, 5, 85, 86, 108
Hebrew Israelites, 82
Heritage Committee, 112
Higginbotham, 58, 76n23

Holiness, 70
holiness movements, 54
Holloway, Karla F. C., 36
Hot Springs Convention, 53
hybridity, 146–48, 150–51

"iconic" Black body, 133
"Installation of the Shrine," 107
*The Interesting Narrative Life of Olaudah Equiano, or Gustavus Vassa, The African (Equiano)*, 30
internationalist discourse, 86
International Peace Mission Movement, 34
*In White Men's Magic* (Wimbush), 30, 42n22
*Is God a White Racist* (Jones), 132

Jackson, John L., 24, 29, 126; *Thin Description*, 44n49
Jamaican spirituality, 31Jennings, Willie James, 35
*Jesus and the Disinherited* (Thurman), 139n29
Johnson, James, 66
Johnson, Sylvester A., 7; African American religion, 23
Jones, Charles P., 53, 58; Pentecostal movement, 54
Jones, William R.: *Is God a White Racist*, 132
Judeo-Christian tradition, 2

Kaiser, 61; Mason's critique of, 56, 62, 63; war with Romans, 56
"The Kaiser in the Light of the Scriptures" (Mason), 56
*Katie's Canon* (Cannon), 21n31, 44n38
King, Martin Luther, 63, 66
"kingdom" language, 57
Kingdom of God, 56, 57
KUA (Swahili for becoming) communities, 117, 119

Lawrence, Harold G., 101–2
*Liberator* newspaper, 92
Lincoln, C. Eric., 84
Lindsey, Treva B., 44n46, 58
"logic of Pentecost," 150
Long, Charles, 27, 30
lynching, 94–96

mainstream Black Christian movements, 6, 132
Malcolm X, 48, 75n9, 128; Black respectability, 55, 58–59; "War and the Ballot Box," 63
Mamiya, Lawrence H., 84
marginal Christian communities, 4
Mason, Charles Harrison, 5, 9, 16, 55, 60, 73–74, 74nn3–4, 145, 146, 148–55, 157; acquisitive capitalism, critique of, 57; alternative Black publics and, 69–70; Black Christianity, and alterity, 61–64; and Black Church, 64–67; blackness, 55; Black protest, 56; Black respectability/protest, 45–48; citizenship, 59; COGIC movement, 45, 46–48, 52–54, 57, 59–62, 64–68, 70, 71, 77n28; critique of failed democracy, 60–61; critique of the Kaiser, 56, 62, 63; debates with other religious leaders, 70–72; evocation of kingdom, 57; Father's Divine Movement, 5, 9, 16–17; glossalia, 74n1; imprisonment, 47; interaction with the Black public, 69–70; interrogation of democracy, 55; Pentecostal movement, 45, 52–54, 58, 59, 71; and power of press, 67–69; problem of white man's scripture, 52–53; radical egalitarianism, 64; radical forms of democracy, 70; Randolph, A. Philip and, 69–71; reading of scripture, 66; religious self-determination, 76n16; righteous resistance, 54, 76n21; testimony, 50, 75n9; "The Kaiser in the Light of the Scriptures," 56; Theological Seminary in Memphis, 68–69; *The Truth*, 57–58; version of democracy, 72
Mbembe, J. A., 145
McKay, Claude, 86
Mekesson, DeRay, 1
Memphis Labor Rights Commission, 70
menace: language of, 75n5
Methodists movements, 65
methodological hegemony, 33
Mignolo, Walter, 32
modern Christianity, 84
modern metropolis, 152
modern racism, 97–98
Moten, Fred, 154; fugitive discourse, 13
Mother Shrine, 116
Muhammad, Elijah, 48, 112, 124, 155
multiple identities, 32, 36
*My Bondage and My Freedom* (Douglass), 75n12

NAACP. *See* National Association for the Advancement of Colored Peoples (NAACP)
*The Narrative Life of Frederick Douglass* (Douglass), 75n12
narrative of civility, 4
National Association for the Advancement of Colored Peoples (NAACP), 47, 55, 71, 81, 87, 96
National Baptist Convention (NBC), 47, 55
National Committee of Black Churchmen, 126, 129
National Liberationist Front, 123
Nation of Islam, 34, 76n16, 87, 102, 121, 124, 156
nation-state, 24; U.S., 62–63
NBC. *See* National Baptist Convention (NBC)
necropolitics, 140n37, 145
"Negro," 82, 83, 91

Negro church, 106
Nelson, Alondra, 115
new religions, 28–29, 32–34. *See also* alternative religions
new religious movements, 34; African American religions and, 28–29; limits, 28–29
new world order, 70–72
*New York Times,* 79
non-Christian: Black communities, 120; movements, 110, 156
nonracial Utopia: Father, Divine, 87
normative Black Christian tradition, 4, 8, 131
normative blackness, 60–61
normative Christianity, 8, 9, 13, 14, 30, 146, 150
normative whiteness, 29
Northern Christian Leadership Conference, 156

organic intellectuals: Gramsci, Antonio, 66, 138n22
orthodox Christianity, 81
orthodox denominations, 82
"other Black church," 3, 5–6, 13, 144, 150–51; alternative Christian movements and, 10–11; reason for need of, 11–12
other "Blacks," 13–14
other churches, 13, 14, 106

Pan-African: ethnic and racial identities, 87; movement, 62
Pan-African Orthodox Christian Church (PAOCC), 133, 135
Pan-African Orthodox Christian community, 112
PAOCC. *See* Pan-African Orthodox Christian Church (PAOCC)
Paris, Rabbi Hilu, 126
Peace Houses, 80
Peace Mission, 92, 96–98
Peace Movement, 80–84, 88–90

Pentecostal citizenship, 148
Pentecostal institutions: Black women in, 60
Pentecostalism, 53, 59, 70, 71, 73
Pentecostal movement, 45, 52–54, 58–59, 64, 71, 82
Pentecostal revival: and practice, 74n1; white, 71
Pentecostals: God and religious experience of, 73
Pentecostal scripture, 74
People Improving Communities through Organizing (PICO), 2
periodical culture, 67
*The Philadelphia Negro* (Du Bois), 47, 64
*The Philadelphia Negro a Social Study* (Du Bois and Eaton), 75n7
PICO. *See* People Improving Communities through Organizing (PICO)
Pinn, Anthony B., 27; "Black Lives Matter and the Long Humanist Tradition," 19n6; *The End of God-Talk,* 21n30; *Varieties,* 27
political theory, 9
Presbyterian Church, 105

"rabble rouser," 79
Raboteau, Albert, 12
race: colonialist/imperialist construction of, 81
racial identities: Black, 14, 38; Pan-African, 87
racism, 16, 35, 94, 95; Divine's critique of, 81, 98, 151
racialized democracy, 97–98
"racial-religio" identity, 23
racism, 52, 53, 119; white, 114, 117
radical egalitarianism, 64
radical politics: defined, 20n20
Randall, Dudley, 119
Randolph, A. Philip: Mason, Charles Harrison and, 69–71
"Reafrikanization," 117

religion(s), 41n15; African Americans, 8, 16, 23–26, 30–32, 34, 36, 38, 40, 105, 143, 151–53 (alternative, 37–40; Black theology, 26–28; and New Religious Movements, 28–29); Black, 6, 9, 14–16, 24, 27–29, 32, 37, 71, 111; role, 27
religious freedom, 16, 55, 72, 73, 76n16
religious identity, 32
religious practices: pastiche of, 78n46
religious self-determination, 57, 74n3, 76n16
respectability/protest, 60–61, 73, 77n23, 78n46; Black, 55, 56, 58–59, 76n23
Riggs, Marcia, 146–48, 151
Righteous Government, 88, 96–97; and lynching, 94–96
righteous resistance, 54, 76n21
rituals: pastiche of, 78n46
rival geographies, 32
Roosevelt, Franklin D., 95

sacrality, 3, 5, 24, 28, 35, 38, 40
sacralization, 34; Black body, 25–26
sacred Black body, 25, 28, 32, 34–36, 38, 72
sacred publics, 37; signifying as disruption of, 30–32
sacred whiteness, 30
Scottsboro Boys trial, 95
scriptural texts, 30, 63, 80
scripture, 30, 31, 66, 137n13; communities of conscientious objection, 54–60; for Divine, 89; Pentecostal readings, 71; white man's, 52–53
Shrine and Black female body, 106–10
Shrine Bookstore, 108
Shrine communities, 116, 131; in the United States, 116
Shrine House, 109
Shrine of the Black Madonna, 9, 17, 101, 102, 104, 105, 108, 110, 120–23; and project of cultural-based economic revitalization, 123–25; and scriptural legacy, 132–35
Shrine Press, 130
Shrine Towers, 109
Shug Avery, 36
signifying, 24–26, 32; as disruption of sacred publics, 30–32
*Sisters in the Wilderness* (Williams), 27, 31
slave narratives, 42n24
spirituality, 13, 14
Statute of the State of North Carolina, 7
Stewart, Dianne M., 28, 31
suffering, 148–49; African American, 5, 64; Black, 63, 71, 110, 157

Tamar, 31, 36, 37
"That the Black Church Is Dead," 2
Theological Seminary in Memphis, 68–69
theology, 16; Black, 24, 29, 31, 34–36, 40, 57, 58, 65, 67–68, 80, 129–31, 141n58, 151–55 (Cleage, Albert B., 129–31; foundation of, 27–28; genealogy of, 141n56); scholarship, 143; theorizing, 80
*Thin Description* (Jackson), 44n49
Third World Press, 120
Thurman, Howard, 49, 66, 111, 117; Cleage's readings of, 139n26; *Jesus and the Disinherited*, 139n29; "kingdom" language, 57; *A Way of Life That Is Worth Living*, 63
Townes, Emilie Maureen, 10, 27, 28, 31, 33
traditional Black church: model, 84, 90; movements, 89
traditional theological scholarship, 9
transnational politics, 64
"truancy" of Black women, 31
"true missionary of blackness" (Baraka), 115

*The Truth* (Mason), 57–58
Tweed, Tom, 41n15

United Negro Improvement Association (UNIA), 81, 87
United States-based Afro-centered Madonnas, 112
university system: critique of, 33
Urban League, 96
U.S.: democracy, 113, 155 (critique of, 55); nation-state, 62–63

Van Der Zee, James, 86
*Varieties* (Pinn), 27
Virgin Mary, 156

Waldon, Rose, 106
Walker, Alice, definition of womanism, 43n31
Walker, David: *Appeal to the Colored Citizens of the United States,* 75n12
"War and the Ballot Box" (Malcolm X), 63
war industrial complex, 62, 63, 66, 75n9
Warnock, Raphael G.: *The Divided Mind of the Black Church,* 20n22
Washington, Booker T., 66
*A Way of Life That Is Worth Living* (Thurman), 63
Weisenfeld, Judith, 23, 24, 29, 38
Wells-Barnett, Ida B., 48
Western Christianity, 129
western culture: critique of, 112
Western hegemony, 149
white: Pentecostal denomination, 52; Pentecostal revival, 71; racism, 114, 117; scripture, problem of, 52–53; supremacy, 30, 33, 53 (disruption of, 43n32). *See also* African American
white ministers, 52, 53
whiteness, 53
Williams, Delores S., 16, 26, 27, 31–33, 37, 145, 146, 149; critique of Black theology, 27; *Sisters in the Wilderness,* 27, 31
Wilmore, Gayraud S.: *Black Religion and Black Radicalism: An Interpretation of the Religious History of Afro-American People,* 99n5
Wilson, Thomas Woodrow, 47
Wimbush, Vincent L., 10–11, 16, 23–24, 30, 33, 35–37, 143, 145–47, 150, 151, 154; African American religion, 24, 26; critique of Biblical studies, 33; *In White Men's Magic,* 30, 42n22
*Women in the Church of God in Christ* (Butler), 65, 77n27
women's "third bodies," 32
working-class: African Americans, 72, 89 (citizenship, 16, 55); Black, 16–17, 46, 51, 53, 54, 60, 71, 72, 133, 156; Black women, 61, 71, 92; movement, 57, 67; Pentecostals, 58; populations, 58; scripture, Father, Divine and, 89–90
world-mapping, 29, 41n15

Young, Robert., 152
Yvette Flounder, 2

# About the Author

**Joseph L. Tucker Edmonds** is assistant professor of religious studies and Africana studies at Indiana University's School of Liberal Arts (IUPUI) and Associate Director for the Center for the Study of Religion and American Culture. He earned his Bachelor of Arts in religious studies and economics from Brown University, his Master of Divinity from Union Theological Seminary in New York City, and his PhD in religious studies from Duke University. Tucker Edmonds's research interests are Black and womanist theologies, alternative Christianities in the Black Atlantic, the role of scripture in African and African American religious traditions, and the relationship between Africana religious identity, citizenship, and globalization. He is sought after in the Midwest as a facilitator of community-based conversations on race, religion, and citizenship and as a consultant to local public and charter schools on transforming the curriculum and classroom culture in light of the racial and religious diversity of their communities.

www.ingramcontent.com/pod-product-compliance
Lightning Source LLC
Chambersburg PA
CBHW050907300426
44111CB00010B/1418